The Best American Short Plays

2015–2016

edited by
William W. Demastes
and John Patrick Bray

APPLAUSE THEATRE & CINEMA BOOKS
An Imprint of Hal Leonard LLC

The Best American Short Plays 2015–2016
Edited by William W. Demastes and John Patrick Bray

Published in 2017 by Applause Theatre & Cinema Books
An Imprint of Hal Leonard LLC
7777 West Bluemound Road
Milwaukee, WI 53213

Trade Book Division Editorial Offices
33 Plymouth St., Montclair, NJ 07042

Printed in the United States of America

Book interior by UB Communications

ISBN 978-1-4950-6540-8
ISSN 0067 6284

www.applausebooks.com

contents

introduction

Starting Over

John Patrick Bray

As I sit to write this, we have just come out of one of the most divisive presidential elections in recent memory. Those who threw their support behind President Donald Trump did so with the hope that we can "Make America Great Again." For those who did not, there is a sense that the next four years will be a period of regrouping after a very unexpected seismic event. It's the kind of event that leaves us all wondering exactly what has happened to a nation that once thought itself to be exceptional for all the right reasons. Citizens on both sides of this great divide wonder as one—though with different conclusions—about how to return our nation to its once solid moral foundation. Who are we? What are our moral obligations? What are our legal rights and expectations? How do we get back what was lost? To be sure, these questions have been haunting many of us for far more than this presidential season. No matter how long we've been thinking about it, a clear path to that longed-for better world seems to be difficult to envision.

Looking for that new day, that new beginning. In many ways, it seems that we are all constantly performing the act of *starting over*, the theme for this anthology. Starting over may include concepts as large as national—and international—realignment. But it can also include matters as small as day-to-day choices of even the most inconsequential sort. This collection of short plays runs the gamut. Some of the works speak to rifts that have ended relationships; some works deal with the death of a person or the death of a dream; something has fallen and now something new must grow. In the process, through reading these works, just maybe we can all learn a thing or two about starting over. In turn, maybe we can discover that small beginnings can find their way to larger ones, teaching us ways to find new beginnings even for our troubling national—and international—distresses.

The Best American Short Plays 2015–2016 begins with *Turtles and Bulldogs* by Scott C. Sickles. In this play, two men from high school reconnect in a graveyard, where one is visiting the headstone of his wife, while the other visits what will be his own resting place in a family plot. Together, they may have the opportunity to start their lives over if only they can both come out of their shells. In *Makin' IndiXns*, William S. Yellow Robe, Jr., is able to highlight how white society has sculpted Native Americans into tropes in popular media, their individual identities altered and blurred in order to fix a master narrative. *Four of Hearts* by Richard Chaney is a series of four short scenes about love and obsession. Set at a park bench with overlapping characters, these scenes are both about starting over and trying to continue when life deals the harshest blows.

E. M. Lewis's *The Gun Show* is the first solo show in this anthology. Lewis foregrounds how the gun-control issue in the United States has become all or nothing, with very little room left for conversation. The play serves as a reminder that both our media and our bullet-point social media memes have lost the nuance of the conversation, which can only be held in middle America, where "safety" means more than drawing a gun on the imagined Other. *Bobo, Booboo, Bibi & Bourbon or, The Clown Play* by Terry M. Sandler might be a familiar story: Have you ever been in love with a friend? Have you poured your heart out only to be rejected? This is what happens to Bobo the Clown, who sulks behind a circus tent, not wanting to continue the show. Sandler asks an important question with this play: After our hopes are dashed, how can we start over as if nothing had ever happened?

Untitled Radio Play by Keelay Gipson is part of an important current conversation about racism in the gay community. The most poignant moment of the play is found in this passage, delivered by a radio host, Benji, who laments:

> And in these harrowing times, we often lose sight of one another. As human beings. We often lose sight of those things which we have in common with one another. We lose our humanity. [. . .] We see this faction or that faction as, inherently, against I, we, us. "Them" has become the currency of the day. And in talking with Papi again, it is clear that this has permeated even our online personas. How can we do better? Or can we? Is it hopeless? Or have we reached a turning point?

For Darcy Parker Bruce, times are equally as harrowing. In *East of the Sun*, she writes, "In the dark, a story casts light upon the shadows." In her powerfully poetic tale, a young woman remembers her father, her abuser. Coaxed by a storyteller who desperately wants to listen, she tries to remember how she has escaped her father (possibly with the help of a polar bear?) in the search for a new life. Parenthood plays prominently in Arthur M. Jolly's *Childish Things*: How do we reconnect with a child who cuts us out of her life? How do we reveal the gravest of news when our loved ones have started their loves over without us? The answer may lie in sharing an old childhood toy in the hope that the memories will do the talking for us.

Before by Penny Jackson is our second solo play, also about guns. We meet an eighteen-year-old boy in a suburban neighborhood. His girlfriend has cheated on him. His friend has given him a pistol. Whether or not he murders his ex, he knows he will never be the same—he has lost a sense of self by taking power away from someone he once loved. Power is a central idea in Angela C. Hall's comedic (and very relevant) *Magnolia Blossoms: A Civil War Melodrama, Episode 1: "If Tomorrow Never Comes . . . Until Today."* A wounded Confederate soldier, Massa Davison, returns home to his wife, Miss Eula, and his slaves (a mother, Selma; daughter, Jesse Jane; and son, Jasper). Miss Eula, who has had an affair with Jasper, tries to convince Massa Davison that he is the father of their son. Miss Eula hopes to escape and start over; Massa Davison has returned to start over (though he is now confined in a wheelchair and must forever wear bandages), while Selma spends each day trying to find new ways for her and her family to stay together (mostly by playing on white superstitions). As a result, the play is hilarious while also making a powerful commentary on how we perform ourselves in order to stay ahead of oppressive forces.

Cody Daigle-Orians's *Certain Unexplainable Events* features four characters who are forever changed by an event that is, well, unexplainable. We hear accounts from three of the characters, and watch Michael, the fourth character, do the unimaginable. But can we believe what we actually see? In John Minigan's *Easter at the Entrée Gold*, a private high school teacher also finds himself in a state of disbelief when he journeys to Montreal to track down a colleague who is attempting to start a new life and a new identity. Both men have a desire to escape, but how far can they actually go given the reality of their day-to-day lives?

Strays is an abstract multimedia piece about Terry, a woman who has changed professions from stripper, to suicide hotline worker, to detective/cat finder. As she tells her papa (after he has bailed her out on a murder charge): "Life is a process. I'm a work in progress, and I'm progressing." While the play is surreal and violent, at its heart it serves as a metaphor for someone trying to leave the shadow of an oppressive family in order to become herself fully.

Lisa Soland's *The Ladder in the Room* gives an optimistic view of intergenerational camaraderie, as a woman living in a nursing home forms a friendship with her caregiver. Full of wit and warmth (with a just a light touch of the fantastic), the play serves as a reminder that the purpose of life is to "try to leave things better than we find them." Liz Amadio's *The Hoodie Play* (written after the death of Trayvon Martin) also deals with intergenerational conflict. Amadio's piece asks us to consider why we as a nation are afraid of our children—particularly those children who are ethnically diverse or who may be on the spectrum. *Big Easy Death Party* by Mariah MacCarthy tells the story of a married couple who take a vacation as a way to deal with the feeling of loss after Louise has a miscarriage. However, in New Orleans, the residents may teach them how to honor the dead and all they have left behind.

If *The Hoodie Play* exposes who we are as a nation, *Rations* by Mark Bowen demonstrates who we could be—morally complex but genuinely *good* people. Set at a gas station in 1944, we meet Mr. Lowenstein, who has just sent a young man away for trying to use black market coupons for gas; however, he *may* be willing to bend the rules for two sailors shipping out. *Rations* is an example of the kind of citizens we wish we were—those who help people in need when they're ready to make the ultimate sacrifice for our country.

While *The Hoodie Play* and *Rations* demonstrate who we are and what we could achieve, Don X. Nguyen shows us who we may have been since the beginning—lazy, reefer smoking, and generally unaffected. In the comedic *Man. Kind.*, we meet the aforementioned hip caveman, Credo, and a prophetic woman in danger, Dalfede, who negotiate safety at a deadly and uncertain time. Israel Horovitz's *Security* is set in our own uncertain time. Two Iranian citizens hope to catch a flight to Buffalo for the holidays. A security guard's fear-based prejudice and inability to communicate leads to harrowing and heartbreaking results. In our last play, *Doughnut Hole* by Donna Hoke, a senior citizen in a bowling league notices there is one doughnut left and is trying to find the nerve to bring it to the only widower in the club. Despite being in their declining years, these senior citizens are still very active and have hopes for a sweeter future.

These plays are all one side of a conversation. You who are reading these plays supply the other. The questions asked in these pieces are not easy to answer: How can *we*, as individuals and as a group, shape a better future for ourselves in a constantly changing world? The very thought of "having to begin again" is enough to stop us dead in our tracks, and yet we continue to struggle, survive, and adapt. Each day, we are presented with a new chance to start over.

Turtles and Bulldogs

Scott C. Sickles

Scott C. Sickles

Scott C. Sickles received the 2016 New York Innovative Theatre Award for *Composure* and won the 2016 Dayton Playhouse FutureFest for *Shepherd's Bush*. His plays have been performed across the U.S. and internationally. He is a two-time Writers Guild of America Award winner for *General Hospital* and a four-time Emmy nominee.

...production history...

Turtles and Bulldogs originally received a developmental production at WorkShop Theater Company (Timothy Scott Harris, artistic director) in New York City in June 2008, as part of the festival Crazy Little Thing Called Love. It was directed by Katie Braden with the following cast:

BARNEY ATWATER David Wirth

COLLIN WEATHERBY Michael Gnat

In 2016, it received the following three productions:

Barrington Stage Company (Julianne Boyd, artistic director) in Pittsfield, Massachusetts, in February, as part of its 10 x 10 New Play Festival. It was directed by John Miller-Stephany with the following cast:

BARNEY ATWATER Andrew May

COLLIN WEATHERBY Matt Neely

Parish Players (Leah Ramano, festival producer) in Thetford, Vermont, also in February, as part of the 10th-Annual Ten-Minute Play Festival. It was directed by Rebecca Bailey with the following cast:

BARNEY ATWATER Mark Cookson

COLLIN WEATHERBY Alex Arcone

Strange Cargo Theatre Project (William C. Kovacsik, producer) and The Three Leaches (Melissa Leach, artistic director), in June, as part of the festival Night of the Offstage Dead. It was directed by Mr. Kovacsik with the following cast:

BARNEY ATWATER Danny Mann

COLLIN WEATHERBY Michael Kennedy

characters

BARNEY ATWATER Early 50s, former high school athlete who acted as a protector to Collin when they were classmates. Rough around the edges, but still handsome. Visiting his wife's grave. Barney has harbored romantic feelings for Collin since their school days. This moment is the first time in his life he is opening the door to his closet and peeking out.

COLLIN WEATHERBY Late 40s, former high school outcast and victim to bullies until Barney stood up for him. Smart and affable, his life has been romantically barren. Visiting his own grave, where he has just buried his beloved cat.

NOTE: It's pronounced *Ath-uh-NAY-shus KUR-kur*.

scene

A graveyard.

time

An overcast autumn day that's threatening to rain.

setting

The stage can be bare except for a small tombstone downstage [optional].

[*At rise:* COLLIN, *a diminutive man in his late 40s wearing a windbreaker, stands mournfully over a grave. After a moment,* BARNEY, *a taller, weathered but still handsome man in his early 50s, wearing a long fall coat, enters and walks past* COLLIN. *They make eye contact and briefly nod in acknowledgment.* BARNEY *stops before exiting and looks back at* COLLIN. *After a moment:*]

BARNEY Collin?

[*No response. Steps closer.*]

Excuse me. I'm sorry to bother you, but . . . I don't know if you remember me.

COLLIN I can't see you, actually. Just a second.

[*Dries his eyes.*]

BARNEY We went to high school together.

COLLIN [*Loses interest.*] Oh.

BARNEY Barney Atwater.

[COLLIN *brightens significantly at the name.*]

COLLIN Oh. Oh, wow. It's good to see you.

BARNEY It's been awhile.

COLLIN Yeah, it has; since high school. So, are you . . .

BARNEY I'm visiting. My wife.

COLLIN Katie? I'm so sorry; I hadn't . . . I didn't know.

BARNEY A few years ago. I come here every now and then, you know, to . . . How about you? Who are you visiting?

[*Reads the tombstone.*]

Oh. So, this is . . .

COLLIN Yeah. It's mine.

BARNEY I guess it never hurts to plan ahead.

COLLIN It's a family plot. My parents are buried right behind it.

BARNEY So they are. I've got one right next to Katie's. I don't have a headstone on it yet. I figured I'll let my daughters pick it out. They're both artistic. One does sculptures. The other one's a decorator.

COLLIN So between the two of them, they'll probably pick out something nice for you.

BARNEY Here's hoping.

COLLIN It's good that you have people who'll be able to take care of that.

BARNEY So, you don't . . . You never . . .

COLLIN Found the right girl?

BARNEY I didn't mean —

COLLIN Although if I ever do, there's a place for her right here, next to me. My parents were great optimists.

BARNEY I didn't mean a wife necessarily. I thought you might . . . you know . . . there'd be someone.

COLLIN I see you're a great optimist yourself. No, there's . . . not.

BARNEY So, why are you here? You're not planning on, you know, taking residence any time soon, are you?

COLLIN No, I'm fine. I'm just . . . Look, if I tell you, do you promise not to laugh?

BARNEY Have I ever laughed at you?

COLLIN No. You never did.

BARNEY I won't start now. I promise.

COLLIN Okay. I . . . I just . . . I just buried my . . .

BARNEY [*Fearing the worst.*] Your . . . ?

COLLIN My cat. I know it sounds . . . but we were together for so many years and . . . I mean, there wasn't a day we spent apart and now . . . You're laughing.

BARNEY No . . .

COLLIN You promised you wouldn't.

BARNEY It's not at you.

COLLIN Okay, then . . .

BARNEY I just . . . I laugh when I get nervous.

COLLIN I make you nervous?

BARNEY Or when I don't know what to say. Anyway . . . I'm sorry about your cat.

COLLIN Thank you.

BARNEY But, um . . . You're . . .

[*Burying it. . . . Gestures toward the grave.*]

. . . here?

COLLIN A lot of people have their pets buried in their plots with them.

BARNEY Is that even legal?

COLLIN Maybe. I think it's okay if the pet has been cremated. But just in case it's not . . .

BARNEY I won't say a word. So . . . What was his name?

COLLIN [*Braced for ridicule.*] Parsifal.

BARNEY You're kidding.

COLLIN No, I'm not, and Parsifal is a perfectly good —

BARNEY My God, how old was that cat? That wasn't the same Parsifal you had when we were kids, was it?

COLLIN No, this one was actually Parsifal Junior. You remembered my cat's name?

BARNEY How could I forget? You spent an hour one afternoon explaining how Sir Percival was your favorite Knight of the Round Table, but you didn't want to name your cat Percy, so you named him after the corresponding character in the opera, even though you don't like opera. It was the longest conversation we ever had.

COLLIN I think it was our only conversation.

BARNEY You talked a lot for a kid with a bloody nose.

COLLIN Did I ever thank you for smacking around the jerk who gave it to me?

BARNEY Not in so many words, but . . .

COLLIN Well, thank you.

BARNEY He shouldn't have been picking on someone smaller than he was.

COLLIN Actually, he was smaller than I was. That's what made the experience so special.

BARNEY Still. He shouldn't have messed with you.

COLLIN I had a huge crush on you after that.

BARNEY I know.

[*Pause.*]

Can I ask you something personal?

COLLIN I don't know. My cat asked me something personal and now look at him.

BARNEY Besides your cat, wasn't there ever anyone . . .

COLLIN Any humans, you mean? No, not really. I mean, there have been dates . . . and flirtations . . . lots of unrequited crushes on unavailable straight men who were nice to me . . . one or two available gay men who stopped being nice to me when they found out I was interested and they weren't. But no. Why do you ask?

BARNEY You were always such a loner. I guess I was hoping you'd turn out to be a late bloomer.

COLLIN Yeah, well . . . Not everybody blooms.

BARNEY Tell me about it.

COLLIN But still . . . You know, I was standing here thinking, I've never had anyone special in my life other than cats named Parsifal. Did I have those cats because there was no one else in my life or did I have no one else because I was so focused on the cats? What if some great opportunity came and went, and I missed it? Did I miss it on purpose because I was afraid to face it? Or did I arrange my life so there'd be nothing to miss in the first place? That's what was running through my mind when you walked by. God, I'm maudlin!

BARNEY We're in a graveyard. You're allowed. Look, I don't know much about people and I really can't criticize anybody else's life . . .

COLLIN But?

BARNEY I think it's probably a little bit of all that.

COLLIN You're probably right.

BARNEY I mean, I know that there are things I wanted that I . . . I don't know—I just didn't get around to because . . . And I know I'm blessed, in some ways. Katie was a great woman and my girls . . . They're my girls, you know. But there are things I . . .

[*Beat.*]

Anyway, I'm sure you and Parsifal had a really good life together. I'm sure you loved each other very much.

COLLIN Yeah, we did.

BARNEY And that is great.

COLLIN It was.

[*Beat.*]

But it's not the same, is it?

BARNEY No, it is not. No, it is not.

[*Beat.*]

COLLIN So do you have pets?

BARNEY Uh, yeah. I have a bulldog. You're going to be so proud of me. His name is Athanasius.

COLLIN Not after . . .

BARNEY Athanasius Kircher! You were right: he was just about the coolest guy ever.

COLLIN Did we talk about him?

BARNEY You had to do a speech on him for your English class.

COLLIN But you were three years ahead of me. You couldn't have possibly seen it.

BARNEY Don't you remember? You were on your way to class to give the speech, when some assholes knocked your books on the floor. After we picked up your stuff, you showed me that picture he did of the Tower of Babel. That totally blew my mind. It didn't even matter there was a shoeprint on it.

COLLIN Did I talk your ear off about Kircher?

BARNEY Yeah, but the bell was about to ring and you didn't want to be late, so you told me everything really fast. It was awesome.

COLLIN [*Beat.*] So, how long have you had Athanasius?

BARNEY I got him right after Katie passed. We both loved dogs, but she was allergic to them. Here, I've got a picture of him on my phone. I'll show you.

[*He does.*]

COLLIN Aw. What a mug.

BARNEY And this one . . . is my turtle.

COLLIN I love turtles. What's this one called?

BARNEY Promise you won't laugh.

COLLIN Have I ever laughed at you?

BARNEY [*Beat.*] I named him Collins.

COLLIN Oh?

BARNEY After you.

[*Pause.*]

Because, you know, you're both slow coming out of your shells, but once you do, you're, uh . . . it's a cheesy comparison, I know, but—

COLLIN [*Genuine: befuddled, not snarky.*] It's very, uh, flattering, I guess.

BARNEY I hope I didn't embarrass you.

COLLIN No, you . . . Of course not. I just . . . I think I'm just stunned that you'd remember me . . . or even think of me at all. I mean, I was this geeky little freshman and you were this . . . this popular senior jock who'd rescue me from bullies every now and then.

BARNEY Like I said, they shouldn't have been messing with you.

COLLIN But nobody else cared. My teachers didn't. The hall monitors looked the other way. Even my parents told me being picked on would help build my character. But you cared. And it's not that I don't appreciate it; believe me, I do. But . . .

BARNEY Because you didn't do anything to deserve it. Sure, you were a little weird and a little light in the loafers, but it's not like you were asking for trouble. And no matter how much shit people gave you, you just . . .

COLLIN Took it?

BARNEY You had this . . . dignity. Like there was nothing they could do that could break you. I thought, "God, I wish those people could be as unimportant to me as they were to (you)."

COLLIN I guess I made it look easier than it was—

BARNEY And you had the saddest eyes I had ever seen.

[*Beat.*]

You still do.

[*Speechless, they look into each other's eyes for a moment. SFX: Thunder softly rumbles.*]

COLLIN It's going to rain soon.

BARNEY Yeah. I should probably go. It was good seeing you.

COLLIN You too.

BARNEY [*Idea!*] Of course, if you're not busy.

COLLIN [*All at once.*] No—What?—I'm not—Why?

BARNEY I was thinking maybe we could . . . Are you hungry?

COLLIN Not just this second, but I will be after I leave the cemetery.

BARNEY Do you want to . . .

COLLIN Yeah, sure. We can catch up some more.

BARNEY Make up for lost time.

COLLIN Exactly.

BARNEY Great. I'll wait over here, so you can . . . Yeah.

[BARNEY *smiles and exits.* COLLIN *looks to the grave again and bows his head. There's a moment of silence before SFX: thunder softly rumbles again and it begins to rain.* COLLIN *shudders a bit when the rain hits him, but continues his prayer.* BARNEY *re-enters and sees* COLLIN *still occupied.* BARNEY *sighs, takes off his coat, goes to* COLLIN, *and holds his coat over them to protect them from the rain.*]

COLLIN Always coming to my rescue, aren't you?

BARNEY Well, someone has to.

[*Fade to black.*]

• • •

Makin' IndiXns

William S. Yellow Robe, Jr.

William S. Yellow Robe, Jr.

William S. Yellow Robe, Jr., is an Assiniboine playwright, director, poet, actor, writer, and educator from the Fort Peck Indian Reservation located in northeastern Montana. A few of his books include *Grandchildren of the Buffalo Soldiers: And Other Untold Stories*, a collection of his full-length plays, and *Where the Pavement Ends*, a collection of one-act plays published in 2001. He is a member of the Penumbra Theater Company of St. Paul, Minnesota, Ensemble Studio Theater in New York, and a member of the board of advisors for Red Eagle Soaring Theater Company (a Native youth theater company) in Seattle, Washington. He is a recipient of the First Nations Book Award for Drama, the first playwright to receive a Princess Grace Foundation Theater Fellowship, a Jerome Fellowship, from the Minneapolis Playwright's Center, and a New England Theater Foundation Award for Excellence.

...production history...

Makin' IndiXns was produced as part of New Native Theatre's inaugural National Native American Ten Minute Play Festival, St. Paul, Minnesota, April 6–9, 2016. Directed by Rhianna Yazzie, and featuring Anthony Gurneau (Red Lake Ojibwe), Brian Joyce (White Earth Ojibwe), and Donavan Mountain (Red Lake Ojibwe).

characters

MAN ON PEDESTAL

COREY Young man, mid-twenties.

TOMMY Young man, mid-twenties.

[*A pedestal with a man standing is onstage. Part of the stage looks like a very cluttered one-bedroom apartment. A desk and metal folding chair are on one part of the stage.* COREY *sits in the chair in front of laptop. He is writing but struggling.* TOMMY *lies on a small cluttered bed looking at a comic book.*]

COREY Damn! I can't get this to work! I have, like, yesterday to create this character for the series. It just doesn't work!

TOMMY Okay, my son, let me hear what you have.

COREY [*As he reads, the* MAN ON PEDESTAL *moves.*] "Horse Power, the ultimate warrior, stands near his war pony as he gazes over the valley."

[MAN ON PEDESTAL *picks up a stick pony and holds it.*]

TOMMY He's not going to cry if he sees some litter, is he? Please tell me he's not going to shed a tear?

COREY Doesn't work, right?

[MAN ON PEDESTAL *drops the pony and goes back to a neutral position.*]

TOMMY Is this supposed to be a contemporary Indian character?

COREY Yes, but when you see the character you are supposed to get a sense of the noble and traditional past his people represent.

TOMMY Says who?

COREY The director. He wants something new, fresh. Ever since that series on Arts and Visions took off, they want something more upbeat and fresh.

TOMMY If he's supposed to be contemporary, what's up with the horse?

COREY Yeah, strike horse, make it a . . .

TOMMY Dirt bike.

[MAN ON PEDESTAL *picks up a small dirt bike cutout.*]

COREY No. A Harley . . .

TOMMY An old-school Harley.

[MAN ON PEDESTAL *picks up a cutout of a Harley from the floor and mounts it.*]

COREY His name is . . . Horse Power?

TOMMY Sounds like a friggin' car commercial.

COREY How about Wild Red Horse.

TOMMY Wow! That sounds nearly like a real Indian name. Keep it.

COREY So. Burt, Red?

TOMMY Red Wild Red Horse? That sucks.

COREY Thomas Wild Red Horse.

TOMMY Better! What tribe is he?

COREY What?

TOMMY What tribe is he?

COREY He's an Indian.

TOMMY From India or here, dude?

COREY We'll just say he's Indian for now and worry about a tribe later.

TOMMY Okay, but I think you would make this a stronger character if you said he was from some tribe.

COREY I'll make one up?

TOMMY What's your profession again?

COREY How about Appalachian Apache?

TOMMY Sounds real to me. So, what makes him so "fresh"?

COREY He's, uh, he's a breed?

TOMMY What the hell is that?

COREY I watched, heard a NPR show and heard a real Indian mention it. It means "mixed blood."

TOMMY Mixed with what?

COREY Black.

TOMMY Thomas Wild Red Pony, the black red man.

COREY To show his blackness, we'll cast a black guy with long curly hair.

TOMMY I don't know. Do you think you could sell that?

COREY What? The black and Indian?

TOMMY I mean, I've heard of them, but I don't think a lot of people have. It might not work.

[MAN ON PEDESTAL *has placed an afro wig on his head and is now taking it off.*]

COREY Wait, wait, we'll say he's, uh, disabled. A disabled Indian vet.

TOMMY Dude, I don't know. That is going to be one hell of a hard image to sell. What are you going to do? Put him in a wheelchair?

[*A wheelchair rolls to the* MAN ON PEDESTAL *and he sits in it.*]

COREY Yeah, sure. He can do all those cool tricks like those guys did in that movie about playing basketball.

TOMMY Let's come back to that.

[MAN ON PEDESTAL *stands and wheels chair offstage. Returns to his neutral position.*]

What's this Indian look like? Johnny Depp–ish or a real Indian?

[MAN ON PEDESTAL*'s face is seen on a screen.*]

COREY Well, he has that "nose," you know? That Indian nose?

TOMMY What? He's Jewish? "He has a nose"? What does that even mean?

COREY All right, but when he talks—

TOMMY Yeah, what does he sound like?

COREY Like those guys in that movie, *Smoke Circles*. They have that wilt; "Good mornin', Thomas."

[MAN ON PEDESTAL *does a few clog steps.*]

TOMMY Wait, dude, they have Jewish-type noses and sound like Irishmen?

COREY No, our Indian is educated. He went to college and . . .

TOMMY Didn't finish but took some hard-ass courses, so he has a hand in a lot of things.

COREY Yeah. Like a wise man.

TOMMY Shaman, dude, he's a freakin' shaman—cool! He talks to the wind, like that song, listens to animals of the forest—very, very freakin' cool!

[MAN ON PEDESTAL *holds up cutout of little animals and a fan blows his hair.*]

COREY And his role in the series is to bring balance in this world of crime! Oh! Man, that's good!

TOMMY Yeah, just him, his Harley, and the little animals.

[MAN ON PEDESTAL *mounts cardboard cutout of the Harley, holding the cutouts of the animals.*]

COREY When we first see him, he is sitting on his Harley outside of the local diner. . . .

TOMMY Eating a cheeseburger?

COREY Does it really matter what he's eating, even if he's eating?

TOMMY How about he's working his iPhone?

COREY Yeah, he's called the council to tell them that he's going to solve the recent rash of murders in the city—

[MAN ON PEDESTAL *is doing this.*]

TOMMY No. The res.

COREY What?

TOMMY The Indian reservation. Dude, what if you get this and you're asked about the authenticity of this character?

COREY We'll do what my friend Geoff does in theater?

TOMMY Yeah, but he sucks.

COREY We just tell everybody we wrote this character with a lot of respect.

TOMMY Does it work?

COREY They're "artists" in theater, of course it works! Done! Now I'll send the file to the office and I am done.

TOMMY This is mad! You can make some damn good Indians!

COREY Just following the program, man!

[*They high-five. Blackout.*]

• • •

Four of Hearts

Richard Chaney

Richard Chaney

Actor-director Richard Chaney's first play, *Idiot-Savant* (1983), was produced in New Orleans at Theatre Marigny on a bill with three Tennessee Williams one-acts. His subsequent plays have been produced throughout the United States. Chaney has lived in New Orleans, San Francisco, Washington, D.C., Seattle, and Tuscon, where he was a member of Old Pueblo Playwrights for ten years. He currently resides in Athens, Georgia.

...production history...

Four of Hearts was developed at Old Pueblo Playwrights in Tuscon, where it received several staged readings and was a finalist in the Southwestern Playwriting Competition. It premiered at Town & Gown Players in Athens, Georgia, in February 2016 under the direction of Kat Marie Mitchell as part of Chaney's one-act collection, *Counting on Love*. The cast included:

JO-ANN Sarah Anne Owens
KATIE Katie Lapka
ROBIN Gillianne Gentzel
HARRY Isaac Callahan
STEVE Seth Jordan
JILL Lauren Wallman
SAUL LOWENSTEIN David Swisher

scenes

scene one (*Heartburn.)*: February 13
scene two (*Heartless.*): February 14
scene three (*Heartache.*): February 15
scene four (*Heartfelt.*): A year later

characters (in order of appearance)

JO-ANN
KATIE
ROBIN
HARRY
STEVE
JILL
SAUL LOWENSTEIN

place

A bench at Balboa Park.

scene one
(February 13)

[*Lights up to reveal* KATIE *and* JO-ANN *sitting on a bench, surrounded by the remains of lunch. A gift-wrapped box, a card attached, sits between them.*]

JO-ANN I thought you'd be pleased.

KATIE I am, Jo-Ann. I am. I'm very pleased that you and I have been together for three years. I just didn't know *you* had decided to celebrate on February 13th. Without telling me.

JO-ANN Surprise! Open it.

KATIE We didn't celebrate our anniversary on February 13th *last* year, did we?

JO-ANN Don't be silly! Open it.

KATIE Because I remember very clearly. It was June. We were white-water rafting on the Snake River in Idaho as part of our second weekend with the International Women's Green Project. I had just finished putting the tent back up, after you had kicked out one of the stakes for the third time. It was late at night. And you lit a match and whispered to me from the opposite side of the woman-made latrine: HAPPY ANNIVERSARY! You literally scared the crap out of me!

JO-ANN June?

KATIE June.

JO-ANN Did you take the time difference into consideration?

KATIE I have an idea. Why don't you just keep this gift until tomorrow and give it to me as your Valentine's Day present.

JO-ANN But, Katie, I didn't buy you anything for Valentine's Day.

KATIE Well, now you have.

JO-ANN But then what will I get you for our anniversary? You told me *never* to buy you anything for Valentine's Day. You said it reminded you too much of Nancy and how you always bought her something expensive and romantic and she always bought you toothpicks.

KATIE Toothpicks?

JO-ANN Something cheap and useful. Toothpicks or white socks or a pocket comb.

KATIE I like pocket combs.

JO-ANN Then I'm sure your relationship with Nancy must have been perfect!

KATIE Don't pout! It's unbecoming. When you stick out your lower lip it looks like your top teeth are missing.

JO-ANN I'm not pouting. I'm pondering.

KATIE Ruminating. Chewing the cud like an old cow.

JO-ANN Isn't that a lovely comparison!

[KATIE *waves offstage.* JO-ANN *squints.*]

KATIE [*Explaining.*] It's the Lowensteins. Around the park every day twice a day just like clockwork. They must be very much in love. I wonder what the Lowensteins give each other on Valentine's Day?

JO-ANN [*Matter-of-fact.*] Jews don't celebrate Valentine's Day.

[*Pause.*]

At least not in Canada.

KATIE What!? That makes no sense. *And* we're in San Diego!

JO-ANN I know. But Canadians are the least romantic of all the peoples in the world. I used to think it was those cannibals in Borneo? But the Internet says no. Canadians are ranked number one. Not a cannibal nation on the top-50 list. Unless you count the Romanians.

KATIE Of course.

JO-ANN If only I had known. I was at the Hallmark store yesterday.

[*Pause.*]

Oh, and Harry was there!

KATIE [*With some distaste.*] Oooo.

JO-ANN And *not* smelling like formaldehyde. I'm not sure who Harry was buying a card for, but he was looking less disheveled, almost clean-cut. And Jill was there, selecting a card for her husband. She had little Dao Ling with her, who is probably the cutest Vietnamese baby I have ever seen, except he needed his diaper changed.

KATIE How many have you seen?

JO-ANN I have seen many a poopy diaper! You forget I have six younger brothers and sisters.

KATIE No, I meant—

[*Pause.*]

Oh, never mind.

[*Pause.*]

I love you.

[JO-ANN *nudges the box closer to* KATIE.]

JO-ANN Me too. Surprise!

KATIE Exactly how are you marking the date of our anniversary? From what event?

JO-ANN From when we fell in love.

KATIE Oh.

JO-ANN I figured that was the most important marker. Not when we met. Not when we had our first date. Not when we first kissed. Not when we were first intimate. Not even when we moved in together and bought the gallery. But the very first time when we looked at each other and I thought, I love you, and you thought, I love her. When all the bells went off. Do you remember?

KATIE How loud were those bells exactly?

JO-ANN Loud. Because it was midnight mass on Christmas Eve.

[KATIE *looks at* JO-ANN, *stunned.*]

KATIE Christmas Eve?

JO-ANN Yes. I know. Today is *not* Christmas Eve, but I hate it when two special occasions occur on the same date, because one of them always gets the short end of the stick. My birthday is July fourth, for example, but I never celebrate it then. Because of the fireworks.

KATIE You weren't born in August?

JO-ANN The choices are better in August because there are no holidays. I'm thinking you might want to move your birthday to August, as well. Because I think the *only* person who should be born on Martin Luther King's Birthday is Martin Luther King. Don't you agree? Unless you're black.

KATIE Which I'm not.

JO-ANN Exactly!

[KATIE *takes her fist and gently rubs her sternum.*]

JO-ANN Indigestion?

KATIE Maybe.

JO-ANN Neither Lincoln nor Washington's birthdays are actually on Presidents' Day.

KATIE And last June? When you lunged out of the darkness to wish me happy anniversary!?

JO-ANN Well, it was midnight. And Flag Day had already passed. And it was beautiful. And I was particularly happy. And you'd been particularly tolerant, given how many times you had to fix the tent that night. Plus, February just seemed so far away! And the only reason I'd chosen February for our anniversary, in the first place, was because you said you didn't want to celebrate Valentine's Day. So I chose the 13th rather than the 14th just in case, because I never know what to expect from you, and that's part of the magic, of course, but here it is, February 13th, and now you're telling me that it's not really our anniversary and it's *not* Valentine's Day and I'm just not sure what to think right now, because I am *completely confused*!

[JO-ANN *sighs.* KATIE *takes the box and reads the front of the card attached to the box.*]

KATIE I "heart" you. Me too.

[*Pause.*]

Happy—

[*Pause.*]

Happy!

[JO-ANN *smiles. Blackout.*]

scene two
(February 14)

[*Lights up to reveal* ROBIN *sitting on a bench expectantly. Her cell phone rings. She quickly answers it, jumps up, and moves downstage.*]

ROBIN Alex?!

[*Pause.*]

Oh, Kelly Sue. I thought you were Alex. You'll never guess where I am?! On a bench at Balboa Park.

[*Pause.*]

Yes! I'm supposed to meet Alex. Can you believe it? He sent me a text early this morning to meet him here. Ultimatums *do* work! I told him he had to choose: Valentine's Day with me or with that wife of his. He disappeared for two days and I wondered if I had made a mistake. But then this morning, February 14th: BINGO!

[HARRY *enters and sits on the bench without* ROBIN *noticing. He carries a small, gift-wrapped box with a removable lid and a card attached.*]

Yes. I know.

[*Pause.*]

Yes. I know. I predict an afternoon on his sailboat. A romantic dinner. A suite at the Del Coronado. An expensive gift, maybe a *very* expensive gift, for keeping me in suspense for two days! Did they find someone to cover my shift at the hospital?

[*Pause.*]

No? Tell them you talked to me and I'm flat on my back. Or soon will be!

[ROBIN *suddenly notices* HARRY.]

Oh.

[*Pause.*]

Kelly Sue, I've got to go.

[*Pause.*]

No, he's not here yet. He's late—and you can be sure I'll make him pay for that big time! Love you. Kiss kiss.

[ROBIN *hangs up the cell phone.*]

What are *you* doing here?

HARRY Just sitting. It's a beautiful morning, don't you think?

ROBIN Are you stalking me, Harry? Did you follow me here?

HARRY My. My. My. We *are* full of ourselves, aren't we? It's not always about you, Robin.

ROBIN I can remember when you thought it was.

[ROBIN *returns to the bench and sits as far away from* HARRY *as possible.*]

What are you doing here?

[*Long silence.*]

Go away!

HARRY Wednesdays and Thursdays are my days off from the pathology lab. I come here every Wednesday. I sit on this bench. On Wednesdays I feed the seagulls. On Thursdays I go to the zoo. On Thursdays I feed the monkeys.

ROBIN There's a sign at the zoo: Don't Feed the Monkeys.

HARRY Yes. I've seen it.

ROBIN You sit on this bench every Wednesday? At 11 a.m.?

HARRY I was late today. I had to wrap my gift. But, yes, every Wednesday.

[*Pause.*]

I take priority here. You don't.

ROBIN Is that gift for me?

HARRY You? No, of course not. It's for the seagulls.

ROBIN Really? What does the card say?

[HARRY *hesitates, then extends the box to her; the card dangling.* ROBIN *leans over and reads the front of the card.*]

I "heart" you.

[*Pause.*]

What's in the box?

HARRY Meat scraps.

ROBIN Meat scraps?! Gift-wrapped for seagulls? You are totally crazy!

HARRY Seagulls are scavengers. It's Valentine's Day. Didn't you know?

ROBIN Yes.

[ROBIN *takes out her cell phone to check the time.*]

ROBIN 11:15.

HARRY Is he late?

[*Silence.*]

Dr. Goldsmith? Is that who you're waiting for?

ROBIN I thought you got fired, Harry. I heard you weren't working at the hospital any longer.

HARRY Oh. Yes. You're right. Nowadays I come here more often. Not *just* on Wednesdays. But I always sit on this bench. And I always feed the seagulls.

[*Pause.*]

I was ill for a long time. Afterwards, I was very sad. I had to go back at night and get my things on the quiet. It was dark. I accidentally cut my hand on a dissection knife. I still have the scar. We can't all be famous and wealthy heart surgeons like Dr. Alex Goldsmith. Some of us are just worker bees, and if we don't go to work, we lose our jobs. You should be careful.

ROBIN Be careful?

HARRY Just a word of warning.

ROBIN Are you threatening me? *You* should be careful. You're lucky I didn't take out a restraining order!

[*Pause.*]

You know I carry a gun.

HARRY I never tried to hurt you.

ROBIN [*Sudden thought, alarmed.*] Was it you who sent me that text this morning?

[*She takes out her cell phone and scrolls down to find the text message. Relieved.*]

No. Alex's number. Not yours.

HARRY I don't know your number. You changed it, remember?

ROBIN Yes.

[*Pause.*]

That couple is waving at you.

[HARRY *returns a friendly wave.*]

HARRY The Lowensteins. The husband puts her in that wheelchair and takes her for a spin twice a day.

[*Pointing.*]

And that woman with the beret and the baby stroller? That's Jill. The baby's name is Dao Ling. Jill and Steve picked him up in Cambodia about three months ago. I've never met Steve. He works all the time. But Jill is very sweet. And if you're still here at lunchtime, you'll meet Jo-Ann and Katie. They close up their gallery every day and bring over sandwiches from the deli. They just celebrated their anniversary. Love is in the air.

ROBIN I won't be here at lunchtime.

HARRY Oh.

[*Long pause.*]

ROBIN Don't let me stop you.

HARRY What?

ROBIN Don't let me stop you from doing whatever it is you do.

HARRY Do you mean feeding the seagulls?

ROBIN Right.

[*Long pause.*]

HARRY Why did you kill Sarah?

[*No response.*]

I know you said it was an accident. But Mrs. Lowenstein says it's physically impossible for a cat to fall out a window. They're too sure-footed. I wanted to believe you. But after you left, I began to question a lot of things you told me. Mrs. Lowenstein says you must have *thrown* Sarah from the window in order for her to have landed so far out in the street and to have been run over by the express bus. Sarah was old and annoying, I know . . . but still, except for you, she was all I had. I don't understand. I bought you an inhaler for your asthma.

[*Pause.*]

Did Sarah leave scars where she scratched you?

[*Pause.*]

I forgive you.

ROBIN You're delusional! I am not going to talk about that damn cat.

HARRY Oh.

[*Long pause.*]

Did you know Dr. Goldsmith's wife has cancer?

ROBIN Alex's wife?! I don't believe you. How can you know that?

HARRY I still have my contacts in pathology. Have you ever met her? I understand she's very nice. They couldn't have any children.

ROBIN Go away!

HARRY I *am* going away, Robin. I'm disappearing. Out of your life.

ROBIN Good.

HARRY I'm leaving San Diego today. Today is the day. Valentine's Day.

ROBIN Good.

[HARRY *extends the box.*]

HARRY I guess you should have this.

ROBIN What would I want with that!? You said it was for the seagulls.

HARRY I've changed my mind.

[ROBIN *stands up, agitated.*]

ROBIN You are crazy, Harry! You *should* leave San Diego. Yes. You *should* start your life over again. At least, what *little* there is of it. I feel sorry for you. I felt sorry for you. Don't you get it? A grown man with a cat?! Like some old maid schoolteacher. Did you really think we were going to have some kind of relationship? That I would make some kind of commitment to a lab technician?!

HARRY I understand. You were waiting for something better. Someone like Dr. Alex Goldsmith.

[*He stands and puts the box on the bench.*]

Goodbye, Robin.

[*As a parting motion,* HARRY *rubs his fist over his heart, then points to* ROBIN. *He walks to the edge of the stage, stops, and turns back to* ROBIN.]

[HARRY *Near tears.*]

I'm sorry for your grief.

[HARRY *exits.* ROBIN, *thoughtful, watches him leave. She crosses to the box. She picks it up. She shakes it: the sound repulses her. She looks up into the sky: no seagulls. She puts the box back on the bench. She crosses away. She looks at the people in the park: no Alex.*]

ROBIN Where is he?

[*She takes out her cell phone. She punches in a number.*]

Come on. Come on, Alex. No voice mail! Please. No voice mail!

[*The ring of a cell phone begins. The sound comes from the box.* ROBIN *hears it and turns. She hesitates, crosses back to the bench, and picks up the box. She removes the lid and looks inside. She carefully removes the ringing cell phone, avoiding the meat scraps.*]

[ROBIN *to herself.*]

Alex's phone. But what . . . ?

[ROBIN *looks back in the box and shakes it cautiously, finally realizing what the box contains. . . .*]

That's . . . Oh my God! Oh my God!

[ROBIN *carefully, and with great disgust, puts the box back on the bench and stumbles away in terror. She looks off in the direction in which* HARRY *exited . . . and then out front, in a panic.*]

Oh my God! Help me! Someone, help me! Please, help me . . .

[*Quick blackout.*]

scene three
(February 15)

[*Lights up to reveal* STEVE *stretched out on a bench.* JILL *enters with a stroller, which contains a baby, unable to be seen, and a gift-wrapped box with an attached card. She wears a beret.*]

JILL Steve. Steve!

[STEVE *stirs.* JILL *shakes his foot.*]

Steve! Wake up!

STEVE I'm not asleep.

[JILL *moves* STEVE*'s legs. She "parks" the stroller. She removes the gift box from the stroller. She sits. She places the gift on* STEVE*'s chest.*]

JILL I bought you a gift. I've kept it hidden in the stroller underneath the diaper bag.

[STEVE *raises his head. He reads the card attached to the gift.*]

STEVE I "heart" you.

JILL Happy Valentine's Day!

[STEVE *places the gift on the ground.*]

STEVE [*Plaintive.*] Valentine's Day was yesterday!

JILL Why aren't you at work?

[STEVE *places his hands over his face.*]

[JILL *Nervously.*]

I came downstairs to take Baby Ling for his walk. We always stop at this bench in the park, after I pick up the mail.

[*Quick thought.*]

Oh! And we have an invitation to a party at Jo-Ann and Katie's, but I'm not sure to commemorate what. All it says is "Help Us Celebrate" and the date's been crossed out twice. I stopped to talk to the Lowensteins and I looked up and here you were!

[*Pause.*]

Were you trying to surprise me?

[STEVE *sits up. He reaches over and takes* JILL*'s hand.*]

JILL What's wrong?

[*Pause.*]

Did you hear about Harry?

STEVE Who's Harry?

JILL [*Quickly.*] Oh. Just someone from the neighborhood.

STEVE Jill, are you sure the park is safe? There was police tape here this morning.

JILL How long have you been on this bench? Since you left the house to go to work? You came home late last night and you left early. Why didn't you wake me up to talk?

[STEVE *stretches out again on the bench.*]

JILL Steve?

[STEVE *begins to cry quietly. He pats the middle of his chest.*]

STEVE I "heart" you too, baby.

JILL Did you lose your job? I don't understand. Have I done something wrong? Is it about Ling? We went all the way to Mongolia for our little Tibetan boy. Was it too much? Is being a father not what you wanted?

STEVE [*Still crying.*] I thought Ling was Chinese.

JILL The last time you cried like this was just before our wedding.

[STEVE *sits up.*]

STEVE I'll be okay. Just give me a moment.

JILL Are you sure (it's not something I did)?

STEVE [*Insistent and interrupting.*] Please! Just a moment.

[*Long pause.*]

JILL How long is a moment exactly?

STEVE Forty-five seconds.

[*Pause, sigh, confession:*]

I'm scared.

JILL Scared? Because of the police tape? You *know* this is a safe neighborhood. The Lowensteins have lived here for fifty years.

STEVE [*Crying harder.*] Fifty years!

JILL Are those the same clothes you wore to work yesterday?

[STEVE *examines what he is wearing.*]

STEVE Maybe.

[*Pause.* STEVE *picks up the box and places it between them.*]

Thank you for the new chain for my watch. It's beautiful. This would be just like O. Henry's *Gift of the Magi* IF it was Christmas and IF I'd sold my watch and IF you'd cut your lovely hair and IF I had bought you combs to hold your hair back. Except.

JILL Yes?

STEVE [*Tearful again.*] Except I didn't buy you *anything*, because I *forgot* it was Valentine's Day!

JILL How did you know I bought you a chain for your watch?

STEVE When I came home last night, you were in bed. I didn't want to wake you. So I gave you a kiss, while you were sleeping, and Baby Ling a kiss, and when I bent over Baby, I knew he needed his diaper changed. I found the diaper bag in the stroller and the I-"heart"-you card and the gift-wrapped box and the new watch chain inside and I looked at the calendar and I saw that it was Valentine's Day. My heart—ached!

JILL Oh. Where did you kiss me?

STEVE In the bed.

[*Pause.*]

I thumped myself on the side of my head, hard: How could I have forgotten?!—do you see a bruise? But I knew why. Because the days have all become a blur. I work and I work. And I come home and we feed Baby and change his diapers. And I look at you and you are so beautiful and trusting and I look at Baby Ling, who is just about the sweetest little—

[*Hesitates.*]

Asian baby that anybody could want. And my heart pounds so hard I can feel it pulsating against the roof of my mouth. I can't sleep. After you fall asleep, I get up and I go look at Baby. And I think what if I *did* lose my job?! What would happen to you and Baby Ling? What if we had to use his college savings just to survive?! What would I tell him? "I'm sorry your father is a failure and that you'll have to work at Starbuck's for the rest of your life—as an assistant manager!" I'm scared and I want to run away, but I can't run away, so I volunteer for all the extra work at work to make extra money. And what do I do with the money? What do I do with the extra money, Jill?! I'll tell you what I do, I DON'T BUY YOU A VALENTINE'S DAY GIFT! That's what I do.

[STEVE *bursts into tears.*]

JILL But you don't *need* to worry, Steve. Baby Ling is going to get scholarship offers from the best schools and he's going to study some obscure techno-science specialty that doesn't even have a name yet. He's going to marry the Lowensteins' great-granddaughter Sophie, who is almost as cute as Baby. He's going to be so happy and he's going to make so much money and he's going to be so generous that you will be able to retire early.

STEVE What?

JILL Mrs. Lowenstein and I have already discussed it.

STEVE Baby Ling is amazing!

JILL I know!

STEVE But what about the Valentine's Day gift I didn't get you?!

JILL Steve, we're so lucky, and I love you so much!

[*Thinking of* HARRY.]

Sometimes love makes people crazy. Sometimes love makes people do awful things. Because not everyone has someone to love them back. Not like Mr. and Mrs. Lowenstein. Not like Katie and Jo-Ann. Not like you and me. Do you remember what I told you? About what I wanted for our anniversary?

STEVE [*Stunned.*] I *forgot* our anniversary?!

JILL No. *Last* year before you gave me that very expensive gift—jewelry or something—you asked me what I wanted for our anniversary and I said: "kisses, just lots and lots of kisses, please."

STEVE Oh.

JILL Well?

STEVE [*Realizing.*] Oh! Thank you, baby! I want to kiss you and kiss you and kiss you for the next fifty years!

[STEVE *grabs* JILL *and tickles her with kisses, until they are both laughing and happily breathless, as the lights dim. Blackout.*]

scene four
(a year later)

[*Lights up to reveal* KATIE *sitting on a bench, finishing her lunch. She waves offstage to* SAUL LOWENSTEIN, *who then joins her. He is pushing an empty wheelchair. He carries his cane. A shawl is draped on the back of the wheelchair. On the inside back of the wheelchair is a sign that reads* IDA'S CHAIR.]

KATIE Let me help you.

[KATIE *positions the wheelchair next to the bench and sets its brakes.* MR. LOWENSTEIN *gingerly sits on the bench next to the empty wheelchair.* KATIE *sits next to him.*]

MR. LOWENSTEIN Thank you, Katie.

[*Confidentially.*]

That hill isn't getting any flatter. Don't tell Ida, but I think she's gained a few pounds. Too many blintzes.

KATIE She looks the same to me. Mrs. Lowenstein never changes.

MR. LOWENSTEIN True. But I think her color is a little off today. Don't you?

[MR. LOWENSTEIN *adjusts the shawl.*]

KATIE I've never seen her look better.

MR. LOWENSTEIN [*To the wheelchair.*] Did you hear that, Ida? Didn't I tell you those doctors were full of baloney!

[*To* KATIE.]

All alone today?

KATIE Yes, I'm afraid so. Jo-Ann is on holiday. But don't ask me which one. She's visiting her nephew in Santa Barbara. I couldn't close the gallery because of the new show.

MR. LOWENSTEIN But isn't today your anniversary?

KATIE Maybe.

[*Hesitates.*]

Four years. I think. Last year, we celebrated on February 13th.

MR. LOWENSTEIN I hope you're not too lonely with Jo-Ann gone? It's the worst thing in the world, you know, to be alone. I hate being separated from Ida. I almost went crazy when she was in the hospital in November.

[*Pause.*]

We received another letter from Harry today. He's still working in the infirmary at the prison. He sounded remarkably cheerful.

KATIE Good for him.

MR. LOWENSTEIN All his recent letters are full of details about one of his fellow prisoners: Tomcat. Which I assume is a nickname. Tomcat this and Tomcat that. I didn't think much about it at first, but Ida believes Harry is beginning to sound a little obsessive again. I hope that he—

[*Stops.*]

Well, I don't want to judge.

KATIE Of course not.

MR. LOWENSTEIN Everyone has their eccentricities.

KATIE Yes.

MR. LOWENSTEIN Live and let live.

KATIE Absolutely.

MR. LOWENSTEIN Even Ida has been known to pull a few pranks. She hides from me sometimes. Last week I woke up in the middle of the night and she wasn't in bed. It took me hours to find her.

KATIE Oh dear!

MR. LOWENSTEIN [*To the wheelchair.*] Hide-and-seek at your age. What can you be thinking!

[*To* KATIE.]

After the stroke, the doctors said she would never walk or talk again. But then medicine is not a science. The human spirit defies all. Especially when you're determined not to let go. Believe and it will be. That's my motto.

KATIE And a very good one it is.

[*She rises.*]

I need to return to the gallery, Mr. Lowenstein. You'll be okay?

MR. LOWENSTEIN Why wouldn't we be? Around the park, twice a day.

KATIE Tomorrow then.

[KATIE *hesitates. She looks for a moment at the empty wheelchair, then exits.* MR. LOWENSTEIN *pats the arm of the wheelchair.*]

MR. LOWENSTEIN [*To the wheelchair.*] Not too cold? Yes, Katie's the sane one. You remember. It's Jo-Ann who keeps sending us Hanukkah cards on Halloween. But they are *both* very nice girls. And they've been very good to me. Just like family. Sometimes an old man needs to be humored. But you know the truth in that, don't you? Better than most.

[MR. LOWENSTEIN *waves offstage.*]

Look at Baby Ling, will you?! Why isn't our little Sophie walking like Baby Ling?

[*Pause.*]

Oh. Maybe she is. It's been a long time since we saw the children and the grandchildren and Sophie, not since—

[*Quick stop, then quietly to himself:*]

Not since.

[*Looking confused.*]

Not since . . .

[STEVE *enters. He is carrying a diaper bag.*]

STEVE Good morning, Saul. Or maybe good afternoon? This stay-at-home-dad stuff keeps me confused. I never know what time it is anymore. I nap whenever Baby Ling naps.

MR. LOWENSTEIN What?

[*Still confused, but then:*]

Oh yes. Baby Ling. He's walking like a pro.

STEVE I know. Isn't he amazing!

MR. LOWENSTEIN He struts like a tin soldier. It must be the Japanese influence. He's going to outgrow that baby fence soon. He'll take it down with one quick karate chop.

STEVE [*Whispers.*] Is Ida asleep?

MR. LOWENSTEIN [*Looking at the wheelchair.*] I think so. She nods off so easily nowadays.

[*Softly.*]

Ida? Ida?

[*To* STEVE.]

Isn't she beautiful?

STEVE She looks very peaceful.

[*He sits. He opens the diaper bag and pulls out a gift-wrapped box with a card attached.*]

I hope this will be okay. I'm not very good at buying gifts.

[MR. LOWENSTEIN *removes the lid from the box and looks inside.*]

MR. LOWENSTEIN It's perfect! Thank you. The crosstown bus doesn't agree with my arthritis any longer and, of course, I don't like leaving Ida alone. Did you find something for Jill?

STEVE [*Panicked.*] Jill?! Oh! Oh no! Well, I'll have to go back. I got so busy choosing something special for Ida, like what you requested, I guess I—forgot! Well, gift or not, I hope Jill's not working late again tonight.

[*He fishes in his pocket and extends his hand to* MR. LOWENSTEIN.]

Here's your change and your receipt.

[MR. LOWENSTEIN *accepts the money and receipt from* STEVE, *then peels off a bill and extends it to* STEVE.]

MR. LOWENSTEIN And here's something for your trouble.

[*Noticing* STEVE*'s hesitation:*]

For Baby Ling. For the college fund.

[*He looks off at Baby Ling.*]

Oops! Facedown in the sand.

STEVE And not a peep in protest! He's just amazing!

[*He stands and picks up the diaper bag as he exits—*]

I'm coming, Baby!

MR. LOWENSTEIN [*Taking a moment to watch.*] Is he okay?

STEVE [*Offstage.*] He'll be fine. Just a poopy pull-up. It probably threw him off balance. I'll see you tomorrow!

MR. LOWENSTEIN My best to Jill!

STEVE [*Offstage.*] And to Ida!

[MR. LOWENSTEIN *shakes his head and chuckles. He puts the money and receipt away. He adjusts the shawl on the wheelchair.*]

MR. LOWENSTEIN These young folks! Harry and Katie and Steve. They're full of dreams, Ida. Do you remember? Work and children and the pain of love and all the sorrow and frustrations of life. The racing of the clock. Tick. Tick. Tick. They don't understand, do they? Because one day the clock will slow down. One day the clock will stop. And you won't even notice it. The newspaper subscription will lapse. The faces on the television will belong to strangers. Their importance will vanish. And one day it will just be the ocean and the waves. The breeze and the sun, warm against your face. The music of life, gentle. The rhythm, the rhythm of your breathing. One day, if you're lucky, you'll simply sit on a bench and hold the hand of someone you love and be content. One day.

[MR. LOWENSTEIN *reaches over to the wheelchair and adjusts the shawl. He rests his hand on the arm of the wheelchair. Lights fade to blackout.*]

• • •

The Gun Show

E. M. Lewis

E. M. Lewis

E. M. Lewis is a playwright and opera librettist. Her work has been produced around the world, and published by Samuel French. Winner of Steinberg Award and Primus Prize from the American Theater Critics Association, Hodder Fellowship from Princeton University, and a 2016 Oregon Literary Fellowship in Drama. She is a member of the Dramatists Guild. Visit www.emlewisplaywright.com.

••• production history •••

The Gun Show was developed in Emerging Artists Theater's One Man Talking Series in New York. After readings at the Dramatists Guild Conference in Chicago and Cornelia Street Cafe in New York City, the play received its world premiere at 16th Street Theater in Chicago, Illinois, in 2014, directed by Kevin Christopher Fox and starring Juan Francisco Villa (Ann Filmer, artistic director). The play had subsequent productions at the following theaters and festivals:

Moving Arts in Los Angeles, CA (2014)
Impact Theater in Berkeley, CA (2015)
Passage Theater in Trenton, NJ (2015)
PlayFest Santa Barbara in Santa Barbara, CA (2015)
The Solo Theater Festival in Tucson, AZ (2015)
Tampa Rep in Tampa, FL (2016)
Project Y's Women in Theater Festival in New York City, NY (2016)
Minnesota Fringe Festival in Minneapolis, MN (2016)
Bellingham Theater Works in Bellingham, WA (2016)
Theater Conspiracy in Fort Myers, FL (2016)
CoHo Theater in Portland, OR (2016)

setting

A bare stage, except for a ghost light, a wooden table, and a sturdy wooden chair.

characters

The playwright is the only character. She should be played by a man somewhere between thirty and fifty. He should be the kind of guy you could cast in a Sam Shepard play. A little bit rough, a little bit soulful, capable of violence.

time

Now.

props

A copy of the script, or some portion of it.

A box of photos and other remembrances. Various items will be taken out and shared during the course of the play.

A photo of Ellen's house for the Growing Up with Guns in Oregon story.

A photo of Irwin and guns for the Learning to Shoot story.

A photo of Ellen and Lauri, alive and well, for the Jackson's Bookstore story.

A New York City subway map and a New Jersey Transit train brochure for the Penn Station story.

A framed photograph of the playwright and her husband at their wedding for the last story.

A picture of the playwright.

A man's shirt.

[*Walk out onstage. The box of photographs and memories is already there. Bring the script in with you and set it down on the table.*]

Something happened ten years ago, something . . .

. . . and I don't know how it can be ten years, because in my head, it's . . . right here, loud and bright, like a movie that's always playing, like I live inside the goddamn movie theater, like the movie theater lives inside my head, and there's only one show, there's only ever one show.

But I don't want to talk about that.

[*Push away from that story like a swimmer pushing away from the side of the pool.*]

Remember that great scene in *Reservoir Dogs*, toward the end of *Reservoir Dogs*? Mr. Blonde has already done the ear thing with the hostage cop, "Stuck in the Middle with You," and doused him with gasoline. Mr. Orange is laying there bleeding to death, and he shoots Mr. Blonde before Mr. Blonde can set the hostage cop on fire. Then the other guys get there with the diamonds, and Mr. Orange tries to tell them Mr. Blonde was going to kill them all and take the diamonds for himself, but Eddie—you remember Eddie? He isn't buying it. He shoots the hostage cop. And then Joe gets there and says Mr. Orange is the informant, and Mr. White says no, but Joe points his gun at Mr. Orange, and Mr. White points his gun at Joe, and Eddie points his gun at Mr. White, and BOOM, BOOM, BOOM—everybody fucking shoots each other—and it's so surprising, it's hilarious, seriously—and Mr. Pink takes off with the diamonds, and Mr. White crawls over to Mr. Orange and takes him in his arms because everything has gone to shit and he got Mr. Orange into it, but then Mr. Orange says surprise! I totally am the undercover cop, and Mr. White points his gun at Mr. Orange's head, and then the cops are there, finally, but they're not in time, because BOOM.

God, I like that movie. I liked it when I first saw it, and I still like it. But then I look at the goddamn motherfucking news. And I'm starting to not be able to tell the difference between real life and a Tarantino movie.

Everyone has guns in rural Oregon. That's where I grew up.

[*Take out a picture of the playwright's childhood home. Smile. Remember.*]

Three shotguns leaned against the wall near our back door. Our neighbors hunted deer up in the mountains every year, and ate what they shot. Most of the men in my family did four years or more in the military, sometimes when there was a war on. The boys at my high school drove pick-ups, and the pick-ups had gun racks in the windows, and the gun racks had guns in them. I've shot guns, out in the woods, drinking beer and using the empties as targets.

We had guns, we used guns, they were part of the fabric of our lives in such a way that I didn't think about them. I didn't think about them any differently than I did about having a toaster or a bicycle. They were useful. They were fun.

But somewhere between there and here and then and now, my feelings about guns have grown more complicated. Almost everybody I've heard talking about this issue so far is preaching to the converted. If you call something a "Gun Control Theater Action," you are preaching to the choir. If you call your event "Guns Across America," you are preaching to the other choir. I somehow really doubt you're going to have a lot of crossover in audience. I am not putting these events down. I'm just saying, that's not what I'm trying to do here.

What am I trying to do here?

[*Take out a photo of the playwright and look at it.*]

I am here to tell a public story and a private story. A story about guns in America and a story about my own experiences with guns in America.

Maybe I could have written it as a magazine article or a personal essay, but I don't write magazine articles or personal essays, I write plays.

[*Beat; smile ruefully; then share the playwright's photograph with the audience, like sharing a secret.*]

I decided not to play myself.

I didn't want to do this myself because I'm a coward. No. Maybe.

I didn't want to do this myself because I'm not an actor. I . . . didn't want to do this myself. Don't read too much into the fact that I asked a guy to play me. Distance. Just a little distance, that's all it's about. Sometimes you have to take one step back in order to get closer to something.

I usually call everything I write fiction. But I'm calling this one truth. Works the same, though, right? I'm here to tell a story, then leave you to figure out what you think on your own.

Maybe a few stories. With a little talking in between. Five stories. And you already heard the first one, about how I grew up with guns. And then there's the "Learning to Shoot" story, and the "Jackson's Books" story, and the "Penn Station" story, and the . . . and one last story to end on.

Five stories.

One down, four to go. Go.

[*A moment. Then push forward, right into the thick of it.*]

This show is about GUNS. Did I mention that?

Right now, the whole conversation seems to be between the granola-eating, Whole Foods–shopping, Rachel Maddow–watching, liberal pinko lefties . . . and the gun-toting, Palin-voting, red-white-and-booyah conservative, card-carrying NRA members, as if there is nobody in between who has mixed feelings about the whole thing.

It's a reflection of the greater problem of this whole two-party system of government, which ends up giving us no real choices, only yes or no, this or that, red or blue, freedom or control. But we don't have time to untangle the problems of the entire U.S. system of government, because I'm talking about GUNS today, and I'm trying to focus.

In 2011, eleven thousand, one hundred, and one people were murdered with guns in America. Thirty two thousand, one hundred, and sixty three people were killed with guns, total.

The guns didn't kill the people, though, the people killed the people.

[*Pause.*]

Here! You'll like this. Top Ten Gun Safety Tips. This is funny. I found it on the Internet. I'll just read the first four.

- No matter how excited you are about buying your first gun, do not run around yelling, "I have a gun! I have a gun!"
- Dumb children may get a hold of your guns and shoot each other. If your children are dumb, put them up for adoption to protect your guns.
- If guns make you nervous, drink a bottle of whiskey before heading out to the range.
- Always keep your gun pointed in a safe direction, such as at a hippy or a communist.

Maybe my uncle sent it to me. He was ten years in the navy and thirty on the highway patrol, and he loves that stuff. "A little bit right of Attila the Hun" is how he describes himself, which I think shows that he has both a little bit of self-awareness and a sense of humor.

He sends me stuff like that—he sends me all kinds of stuff like that—who the hell let our parents' generation onto the Internet? But he spent thirty years in public service.

Navy. Police. Protecting and defending. And despite the tone of a lot of the jokes he e-mails me, I have never, ever seen him act stupidly with guns, and he has never made me feel anything but safe.

Here's something I found from the other side. A political cartoon by Clay Bennett, working for the *Chattanooga Free Press*. It's a picture of the grim reaper, holding a newspaper with the front page headline "Gun Sales Soar." He's tossing aside his scythe and walking toward a John Deere combine.

Milt Priggee did a cartoon about that Seattle police gun buyback event where they collected 716 weapons, including assault rifles and a missile launcher. It shows the cops accepting custody of this guy's missile launcher and saying, "You realize—it's against the law for the public to own a missile launcher . . ." and the guy replies, "Yeah, but if you outlaw missile launchers, only the outlaws will have missile launchers."

I found another one that was pretty good. It said, "I'm going to tell the Republicans that the government is trying to take away their math and science textbooks, then maybe they'll start to hoard those." Ha!

The political cartoon that made the biggest impact on me when I saw it isn't even trying to be funny, though. The title at the top said, "Protect Your Home from a Killer." Then it was just a picture of a handgun, surrounded by some statistics.

- A gun in the home is responsible for the vast majority of children killed by firearms.
- A gun in the home triples the risk of a homicide.
- A gun in the home increases the likelihood of suicide fivefold.
- A gun in the home increases the chance of being killed by a firearm 72%.

What went through my head immediately after I read it was, "That can't be right." It doesn't sound right. How can that be right?

But it was exactly what I'd been wanting—less commentary, more facts. Because the commentary is killing the conversation. It feels impossible to even have a conversation about this—I mean a conversation between the two sides, not just more cheerleading and rabble-rousing amongst ourselves.

Did you hear that Piers Morgan–Alex Jones thing? Jesus. Morgan is this British CNN talk show host guy, and Jones is an American radio talk show host guy, and after a young man murdered twenty children and six adults at Sandy Hook Elementary School in Connecticut, they got together to talk about gun control. It went something like this:

[*During the following, taken from a transcript of the interview, mimic the voice and escalating intensity of Alex Jones. During this exchange, Morgan keeps trying to interrupt Jones, which prompts Jones to talk over him, pushing louder and harder, until by the end he is practically spitting.*]

> Piers Morgan: Alex, I think the main point you're missing—
>
> Alex Jones: "The Second Amendment isn't there for duck hunting. It's there to protect us from tyrannical government and street thugs. Take the woman in India, your piece earlier on CNN, I was watching during Anderson Cooper's show, didn't tell you the women of India have signed giant petitions to get firearms because the police can't and won't protect them.
>
> "The answer is—wait a minute, I have FBI crime statistics that come out a year late, 2011, 20-plus percent crime drop in the last nine years, real violent crime, because more guns means less crime. Britain took the guns 15, 16 years ago. Tripling of your overall violent crime. True, we have a higher gun violence level, but overall, muggings, stabbing, deaths—those men raped that woman in India to death with an iron rod four feet long. You can't ban the iron rods.
>
> "The guns, the iron rods, Piers, didn't do it, the tyrants did it. Hitler took the guns, Stalin took the guns, Mao took the guns, Fidel Castro took the guns, Hugo Chavez took the guns, and I'm here to tell you, 1776 will commence again if you try to take our firearms! It doesn't matter how many lemmings you get out there in the street begging for them to have their guns taken. We will not relinquish them. Do you understand?"

This? This is not helping. Because some people listen to this and start stockpiling firearms in their bunkers to protect themselves from the tyrants, and some people listen to this and say if a guy like this can legally buy guns, we're fucked, because he's a nut job, and where do I sign up for the Take All the Guns Away Rally? And there is zero conversation, and zero room for a solution that is somewhere in between.

Some people actually do want to take all the guns away. All the swords into fucking ploughshares, Kumbayah. Just because that guy is a nut doesn't mean he's one hundred percent wrong.

I don't want all the guns taken away.

[*Look at someone out in the audience.*]

Don't look at me like that. You people . . .

Ha! My father-in-law always says that. "You people."

[*Shake finger in the air.*]

But seriously. You people who live five seconds away from the police station don't understand the whole situation here. You city people. It's easy for you to say take all the guns away.

When I was growing up . . . you know how parents teach their kids to call 911? Well, we were supposed to call 911 like everybody else, in case of someone breaking in and trying to rape and kill us all, but then we were supposed to lie and say the house was on fire, because our fire department was local volunteer neighbors who would come in ten or fifteen minutes. The County Sheriff was an hour away in Oregon City.

An hour away.

You know what can happen to you in an hour?

What I don't think you people, you good city people, understand is that part of this whole gun control conversation is about people being able to take care of themselves. No. That's wrong. People not having a fucking choice, because nobody's coming to help you. Help is a million fucking miles away, and you have to choose if you're going to be the kind of person who just lays there and takes it while someone rapes and murders your children right in front of you, or are you going to do something about it?

For those of you who live in close quarters like . . . you know . . . Los Angeles . . .

. . . it's a very different thing when you fire a gun than it is for those of us who are out in the country, because there's another person five feet away from you, and another person five feet away from them, and you have zero control of the bullet once it's out of the chamber. But cities aren't everything. You don't get to own the American story because you live in the city. We count too. And we understand that it is our own responsibility to defend ourselves.

I own a gun. Did I tell you that? I didn't buy it for myself. Where I come from, it's the kind of present guys give their womenfolk, after they've been together awhile. Paper, cotton, leather, linen, automatic weapons.

Just kidding! That was a joke. It's just a handgun. The kind that fits in your purse. I have it in my purse right now.

Not really.

Inappropriate, I thought, even if this is a gun show.

What I'm saying is, this is a really big country. How often have you lived fifty miles away from law enforcement? Think about it. Have you ever? Then what the fuck do you know about it, and why are you trying to take my fucking guns away?

"You can have my gun when you pry it out of my cold dead hands." John Milius. *Red Dawn*.

That's another good movie. Remember? Commies invade rural America. A bunch of high school kids are forced to take up arms against them. Wolverines!! Patrick Swayze, C. Thomas Howell, Jennifer Grey, Charlie Sheen . . .

Can you believe Patrick Swayze is dead? God. Sometimes I feel old, just thinking of all the people who seemed like they could never die who are dead now. And if you're sitting there judging me because I put Patrick Swayze on that list, fuck you. He was fucking hot in *Dirty Dancing*.

[*A moment; shift gears.*]

Where was I?

Me learning to shoot, that's the second story.

[*Take a picture of Irwin with guns back in Oregon out of the box. Remember.*]

I went shooting with Irwin out in the woods this one time. Back in Oregon. He wasn't my husband then. Not yet. But we'd been going out awhile.

[*Pause.*]

It was this perfect Oregon day. You know? Like it was never going to rain again, it was that bright. But everything smelled green, and clean, because it had rained the night before. I was wearing a bikini top and short shorts and ear protection, and we had laid about twenty guns out on a blanket on the grass.

[*Through the following, you might reenact the shooting lesson—holding the gun, aiming, having stance corrected, everything.*]

We were down by the lake, on Irwin's folks' place. An old gravel pit, really, but if you dig a hole in Oregon, it's going to fill up with water. Sun glimmered on the water. They'd built a little shooting range down there years before, against the hillside. Bullet casings were scattered around. Old, ragged paper targets.

Sound of crickets.

We were the only two people in the universe.

Clean, heady smell of his sweat.

I'd never smelled that smell from that close up before.

Irwin was teaching me how to shoot, the real deal, never point your gun at something you don't want dead, telling me where the safety was. We were only drinking a little bit. Only beer.

He put his arms around me and showed me how to focus on the front sight, breathe out, and squeeze the trigger gently. Handguns. Rifles. His grandfather's gun. Guns he'd bought while he was in the marines. Did I tell you he was a marine? Oorah, baby. Semper fi.

I remember that day so clearly. It was so goddamn fun. He knew what he was doing, and what he was doing was strong and masculine and dangerous, and he was letting me in on it, he was giving that to me.

Focus on the front sight. Breathe out.

Squeeze the trigger gently.

It was louder than anything I'd ever heard before. You nestle the butt of the rifle right up against your shoulder, right here, because it kicks when it fires.

We must have gone through two or three hundred rounds of ammunition that day, and a six pack or two, in no particular hurry. That day is bright and perfect in my memory. Nobody ever made me feel safe like he made me feel safe.

That's the second story.

[*Take the man's shirt out of the box.*]

Raise your hand right now if you've ever held a gun in your hands. If you've ever gone shooting. If you haven't, you don't know how much fun it can be.

[*Put the man's shirt to your face and breathe in. Take a moment. This is a memory you don't want to leave. But everyone is waiting. Put the shirt back in the box.*]

Here's the third story.

I was working at Jackson's Books. Small, independent bookstore in Salem, Oregon.

This is how it goes. It's night. It's quiet.

Me and Lauri look in cookbooks for good lasagna recipes.

Some lady calls up. This lady, she's in some contest. A treasure hunt. The question is, "Who wrote *Pachelbel's Canon*?" So I say it's probably like "Who's buried in Grant's tomb?" but she's not easy about it. "Call me back," I say. "I'll look."

Lauri starts talking some blue-hair into Dostoevsky, I'm sitting on the floor in the music section, and this older guy comes in. And I say, "May I help you?" He shakes his head and rubs his hands together.

Lauri wraps Fyodor up in blue paper behind the counter.

My guy looks a little lost over in Lit. Crit., so I say, "Is there anything I can help you find?"

"Is there anything you got in horr . . . ," he says. "Excuse me?" I say. "Horrerrrr," he says a little louder. "Horror." "Oh, sure," I say.
He's not telling any names, so I say, "How about Stephen King?" I pull down *It*, and hand him *Misery*.

He thumbs through them kind of fast, like he's forgot his glasses. Blue-hair's gathering her stuff.

"You got . . . um . . . *Flowers in the Attic*, something like that?" he says.
"V. C. Andrews," I say. "Right down here."
The door clangs shut.
"I'll take them," he says, handing me all three of the paperbacks.

I go around the side of the counter. Lauri's still standing over at the other register. I scan each of the books, then look up at my register. It says $14.97. "Fourteen ninety-seven," I say, and look up.

And there is a really big black gun pointed at me.

Well, I really can't say how big it was. It looked like a bizzillion-caliber gun with its opening pointed right toward me. The cops told me later, laughing, any gun that's pointed at you looks big.

I just stood there. One hand poised over the register, the other hovering over the books on the counter.

And suddenly, my mind slips me out from the body that sees that gun pointed at me to someplace hovering up above and watching. And the expression that girl (who is me) has on her face is just like that big-eyed look that deer have when they're caught, for that one horrible moment, in your headlights.

". . . down on the floor," you hear him say. He's looking at Lauri.

"Down on the floor. Get down on the floor." By the third time he says this, he's shouting.

Lauri is just standing there, with those same deer eyes you have. Come to find out later, she couldn't even see the gun, with all the stuff on the counter. She did know, though. She didn't understand what was going on, but she knew.

Lauri tells you later that you told her "It's okay" at this point, and that it was only when you said that to her that she crouched down behind the counter. She curled her arms around herself, like a kid under a desk when the bomb siren goes off.

"Get the money out of the register," he says to you. "Get The Money Out Of The Register! GET THE MONEY OUT OF THE REGISTER!"

He pulls a crumpled brown paper bag out of his jacket and throws it on the counter. It slides across and falls lightly to the floor.

"Get the bag—Get The Bag—GET THE BAG," he says, and his eyes are wide and fierce and the gun is pointed at you still.

You feel yourself moving, looking down at Lauri, picking up the bag. The drawers at Jackson's won't come open again if you shut them, so they are always left ajar. We are woefully unprepared for this. You pull out the drawer in front of you.

Your fingernails slip on the bills in the cash register and you can't get hold of them.

"hurryupHurryUpHURRYUP!" the man shouts.

You get your fingers around the corners of the bills, somehow, your fingernails making scraping sounds on the paper, and you think, "My God, I'm going to be killed because I didn't cut my fingernails."

You put the money in the bag and you put the bag on the counter and he shoves the bag back toward you.

"Gettheotherregister! GetTheOther . . ."

You step around Lauri, careful not to step on her hands, which she has set on the ground in front of her to keep her balance.

The man's hands are shaking, as he holds the gun, and as you empty the second register, you understand that if he doesn't shoot you on purpose, he may just shoot you accidently. There is a tightness in your throat. Your own hands begin to shake, almost uncontrollably.

You push the bag of cash toward him, and he shoves it in his jacket. He gestures at you with the gun.

You back away from the counter.
"Down on the floor. Down On The Floor. Get DOWN ON THE FLOOR!" You get down on the floor, on your knees, on the dirty gray carpet.
The man's voice comes from the other side. "You count to a hundred," he says. After a pause, you hear the door fall shut.

You will never know who moved first, but then you and Lauri are grasping each other's hands. You have never felt so close to anyone in your life as in that moment.

You don't count, but a little after the door sounds like it closes, you and Lauri look at each other, then cautiously get up, peering over the counter. There is a man there, but it is just some guy with brown hair and loafers, paging through a book from the "New Non-Fiction" display by the door. He doesn't notice the two of you, rising up from behind the counter like ghosts.

Things get kind of fuzzy there for a while. You sit down on the stool behind the counter.

Lauri asks the man in the loafers if he saw the guy that just went out. The guy had no clue what had just happened. He was shocked. He'd passed right by the man, not even knowing it.

Lauri does all the right things. Locking the front door and calling the police. She had been a bank teller and had had training.

You just sit there, kind of breathless.

The police come. Neither of the owners were home when Lauri called, but the manager and her husband come. Her husband is a retired English professor, and he keeps asking you questions like Columbo or Poirot, "Did he give off any peculiar smells? Did he have a tattoo?" even after the police stop.

The policeman is standing beside you, though, when you see your husband, framed in the glass doorway. He has a rose in rumpled green paper in one hand, and a box from the lingerie place in the other. Because it is your birthday. You are twenty-five.

There is a blank look in his eyes, as he pauses there in the doorway, waiting for Lauri to unlock it with her jingling ring of keys, knowing that something has gone wrong. You look over the shoulder of the policeman at him apologetically.

You finally get to sleep that night after the sun comes up. After getting drinks at Thompson's with Lauri, just till you quit shaking so bad. Your husband says it's the adrenaline—it's natural.

cold out, and I'm exhausted, and it's late, and I'm in Pennsylvania Station, which smells like urine and is constantly, constantly under construction. I'm looking for New Jersey Transit, because I know that's what I need to get home.

There are these two cops standing there in the station, and so I go over and ask them which way to the New Jersey Transit trains, and the big, broad-shouldered, white cop, whose hand rests firmly and comfortably on his sidearm, says, "I'm gonna pistol-whip the next asshole from New Jersey who fuckin' asks me that, read the fuckin' signs." And the big, broad-shouldered, younger Latino cop standing beside him doesn't say anything.

The cop's hand doesn't move from his sidearm. His hand doesn't move. But I am suddenly aware of his hand, resting firmly and comfortably on the butt of his gun, the silver snap on the black leather holster that can be flicked open with his thumb as he draws the gun out of the holster, and he doesn't do that, he doesn't, but I'm very aware of his large, calloused hand.

He never would have said that to me if I was . . . if I was with Irwin. Funny thing, how if you have a gun, your tendency is to use it.

[*Beat; tilt head. No, that's not right.*]

He didn't use it. He didn't draw. He didn't fire. He just . . .

They always say that thing, though. And I think there's something to it. If you ask a pharmacist what to do, they'll prescribe a pill. If you ask a surgeon, the only thing to do is cut it out. If you have a gun . . .

[*Beat.*]

It wasn't really even a threat. Not really. He didn't move when he said it. But I guess it's another one of my gun stories.

I found New Jersey on my own.

I like cops. My uncle is a cop. Cops make me feel . . .

[*Pause.*]

One more story. Do I tell it?

Do I tell it?

Something happened ten years ago, something . . .

. . . and I don't know how it can be ten years, because in my head, it's . . .

The trouble is that the closer I come to telling this story, saying the absolute truth, unvarnished, unadorned, the closer I come to having a panic attack. I mean the head between my knees, gasping like a fish in the fucking cereal aisle kind.

Maybe I'll just tell you four stories today. Leave it at that.

[*Look at the picture of the playwright.*]

If not now, when?

Something happened ten years ago. April 27, 2003.

This is the first story, this is the last story, this is the only story.

Irwin and I were the only married couple in our grad school writing program. You remember Irwin from the learning-to-shoot story, right? Met him when I was nineteen and he was twenty-nine, and everything was shining ahead of us. Met him and married him back in Oregon, then went off to grad school together to be Writers, capital W. And everybody in our program would come over to our place, and I'd cook, and we'd drink, and we'd share our writing and talk long into the night, like grad school is supposed to go. Then grad school was done with, and we went out into the real world. And he got a crazy job in the Internet boom just in time to ride it all the way up, then all the way back down to the Internet bust. And I found a job just as we were getting to absolute zero, but he didn't. And he didn't. And he didn't. And he kind of stopped looking after a while, and he kind of got anxious and depressed.

[*Beat.*]

Irwin's the toughest guy I ever met, Marine Corp, oorah, put himself through college working as a correctional officer, ran a marathon, tough, and he's always the funniest guy in any room he's in. He's the fucking sun, and most of the time I was happy to be a planet, because of the brightness and the warmth. He's the toughest guy I ever met. So it took about two years of shrinks and pills and VA counselors and sometimes walking all night together through the Los Angeles dark, where there are no stars, only airplanes, because he was feeling nervous, all of which we didn't really tell anybody about, because he didn't want anybody to know—

—shh! don't tell anybody, don't tell anybody, don't tell anybody, don't leave me, don't let them take me away someplace, don't you fucking tell anybody, please don't leave, baby, shh!

—before he took a beautiful shiny black Glock and put it in his mouth and pulled the trigger. And when I found him, he was . . . And when I found him, he was . . .

There's not really any doubt when someone uses a gun. Because you can see that he's . . . Blood on the . . . concrete floor of the . . . not—blood on the . . . red and gray. Red and gray. Red and gray. But I put my hand on his chest. Then I put my ear to his chest to . . . because . . . I, uh . . . couldn't . . . I still can't, really . . . believe that . . .

[*Pause.*]

He was really funny. You would have liked him.

Nineteen thousand, one hundred, and thirty four people killed themselves with guns in 2003. Plus one. Nineteen thousand, one hundred, and thirty five.

I'm the kind of widow you don't talk about, because there's a shame in suicide. There's a god-awful guilt, because if you love someone, you're not supposed to let them down, and if they're dead . . . you failed.

But if we don't talk about this, if we don't talk about suicide, we're skipping a huge part of the story. The guns-make-you-safe story.

I don't want to take everybody's guns away. But I sure wish I'd manned up and taken his guns away.

"We have met the enemy, and he is us."

All the people I know who have died from guns killed themselves.

- Mr. Stone, my high school biology teacher
- Kid I went to CCD with, who also happened to be my seventh grade teacher's son

- Ron, a friend of my aunt and uncle
- Richard's dad
- Irwin
- Hunter S. Thompson
- Ernest Hemingway

And don't you try to tell me I can't have those last couple guys because I didn't know them, I fucking love those guys.

Is my list shorter or longer than yours?

I don't know anybody who has ever drawn a gun to protect themselves. Maybe my father-in-law did, in Korea. I don't know. He doesn't talk about it.

Guns don't equal safety.

"No guns" doesn't equal safety. There is no fucking safety.

You can call me an asshole or an idiot, because after all that I don't want to take everybody's guns away. I'm still the Oregon farm girl who grew up with a .22 leaning in the corner by the back door, who doesn't see anything wrong with that, who understands that there are people who should have a few guns and places where they are practical and useful tools.

You can call me an asshole or an idiot, because one particular incident made me think we need to talk about guns, and bring the facts about them out into the open. The main fact I'm talking about being that if there's a gun in your house, you're more likely to shoot yourself with it than protect yourself with it.

You can say "that wouldn't be me" all you'd like. I never thought it would be Irwin. I never thought it would be, right up until it was. And I know I'm not alone.

[*Beat.*]

I never tell this story.

I shoved both of us in a box and put us away. And now it's ten years later—no, Jesus Christ, eleven now—and here we are. Still in the same box I put us in. I can put us back in. I can do it. I'm good at this. But that doesn't get us anywhere, does it?

Irwin killed himself. He certainly could have killed me. I have wondered if he thought about it. I kept the gun he gave me. Just in case I ever wanted to . . . write a play about guns.

[*A moment.*]

Irwin and I are locked together forever. Death didn't part us. For ten years, I've held him tight and close, right here.

[*Clench fist and press it against side, against the lowest and most vulnerable ribs.*]

The tighter my hold, the more caught I am.

It's like how you catch a monkey. I read about this somewhere. It's easy. Apparently. I've never been to anyplace with wild monkeys to try it out. But they say that all you have to do is drill a small hole in a gourd and tie it to a tree. Put a piece of fruit inside. Then come back later to see if you've caught one. What happens is they smell the sweet fruit and stick their hand through the hole and grab it. Their little fists won't fit back through the hole, but they won't let go. You can go back anytime you want. They'll still be there, clutching tight. You can just scoop them up in a bag, and there you go.

We have guns, and the guns have us. We're scooping ourselves up in shiny black body bags.

You're just as stuck as I am, America. In love with something that's hurting us and not sure how to separate it from our identity. Not sure if we can survive without them. What are we without them?

Me and Irwin's story—is just one story, one gun story in a country full of gun stories and a lot of them are a lot more . . . but this one is mine. And I don't want to be silent about it anymore. I failed before. I don't want to fail again. So I'm not going to put us back in the box.

I haven't given you a plan here tonight. Actions to be taken. Congressmen to be called. Protests to carry signs at. All I have to give you is the story I never tell.

[*Hand pages from the script—from the five stories that make up the gun show—to the audience.*]

If I give our story out to enough people, maybe I'll never be able to put us back in. Here. Here.

Take this. Here. Take it.

[*A moment . . . and then look across at the box of memories. Walk over and put your hand on the wedding photo. Pat it twice. Maybe now, you can finally let your story go. And have it back. And go on. Go to the door of the theater. Open the door of the theater. Step out into the world. A moment. Then the lights go out.*]

• • •

Bobo, Booboo, Bibi & Bourbon or, The Clown Play

Terry M. Sandler

Terry M. Sandler

Terry M. Sandler is an actor, director, playwright, award-winning filmmaker, and educator. His anthology, *The Mommy & Me Fishing Trip and Other Plays*, is available through JAC Publishing & Promotions. Sandler earned his BA in theatre from SUNY New Paltz and an MA in educational theatre from New York University. Sandler holds a NYS certification in drama, teaches at Peekskill City Schools, and resides in the Hudson Valley with his family.

...production history...

Bobo, Booboo, Bibi & Bourbon debuted at the Depot Theatre in Garrison, New York, as part of the 2011 Aery New Play Festival on September 9 and 11 under the direction of Terry M. Sandler. Costumes and makeup by Fay Gerbes-Pacht.

BOBO Jason Michalek

BOOBOO Rick Santacroce

BIBI Fay Gerbes-Pacht

BAMBAM Nick Maltes

TUTU Kevin Kenny

CIRCUS CHILDREN Madeline & Margo Sandler, Mark & Colin Crook

Bobo, Booboo, Bibi & Bourbon was performed in part with the Manhattan Repertory Theatre's 2012 Winter Play Festival on January 10, 12, and 14 under the direction of Terry M. Sandler. Lighting by Artistic Director, Ken Wolf.

BOBO Jason Michalek

BOOBOO Rick Santacroce

BIBI Fay Gerbes-Pacht

BAMBAM Nick Maltes

TUTU Kevin Kenny

Bobo, Booboo, Bibi & Bourbon was performed by the NFA Drama Company at the Newburgh Free Academy's Black Box Theatre on February 28–March 2, 2013. Under the direction of Terry M. Sandler. Lighting design by Ben Underhill.

BOBO Axcell J. Sabillon

BOOBOO Joseph Alberts

BIBI Kimberly Rios

BAMBAM Stephen Conti

TUTU Frank Pacella

Bobo, Booboo, Bibi & Bourbon was produced by Hatmaker's Attic Productions, Newburgh, New York, on Saturday, June 20, 2015.

BOBO Matthew Rowe

BOOBOO Darick Newby

BIBI Fay Gerbes-Pacht

BAMBAM Brian Cureton

TUTU Terry M. Sandler

characters

BOBO A depressed and melancholic clown.

BOOBOO Bobo's best friend and biggest fan.

BIBI Sweet and attractive; vulnerable and wounded.

BAMBAM Handsome and strong; arrogant and cocky.

TUTU A stupid clown.

setting

Present day. Behind a circus tent.

[BOBO *is sitting in the back of a circus tent nursing a flask. Over a loudspeaker the ringmaster calls: "Twenty minutes to places! Twenty minutes!"* BOBO*'s best friend,* BOOBOO, *enters in a panic.*]

BOOBOO There you are! I've been looking all over for you. Come on, man! Pull yourself together. Places in a half hour!

BOBO I won't be performing today.

BOOBOO And why not?

BOBO I have a headache, I'm depressed, and overall feel like I've been run over by a Mac Truck.

BOOBOO Oh, hogwash! We need you! The big show can't happen without you!

BOBO That's very nice of you to say and I'm flattered, but—

BOOBOO But nothing! Who's gonna assist me with the "explosive, juggling, dynamite" routine? Who's gonna take the catapult to the crotch? AND WHO'S GONNA DO THE WORLD-FAMOUS DOUBLE-FLIP-TWIST-INTO-THE-SHALLOW-POOL TRICK? There's not a single clown in this joint that could pull 'em off like you!

BOBO Let him do it.

[*Enter* TUTU *the clown, otherwise known as the world's dumbest clown in existence.* TUTU *honks his honker as if to say "hello!" He smiles a stupid smile. He stupidly bows to no one in particular. He then exits the stage like a prima ballerina.*]

BOOBOO Tutu! Are you joking! You're going to let some failed "birthday party" clown do your job? You, my friend, are "Bobo the Bobominator!" There are people, both young and old, who've come from all over the valley to see you. You're a celebrity . . . a star! Now, mister, sober up, put on a smile, and get out to the tent before you get us both in trouble.

BOBO Okay . . . you got me. Just give me five minutes to cry away my sorrows to Mr. Bourbon, and then I'll see you at places.

[BIBI *enters following* BAMBAM, *who rides around on a brand-new child-sized scooter.*]

BIBI Weeeeeeee! These new wheels are wild, Bambam.

BAMBAM Don't I know it! I picked it out myself! Smooth, huh?

BIBI Go faster.

BAMBAM You got it, babe!

BIBI Weeeeeee!

[*They exit. Silence.*]

BOOBOO Alright, Bobo! Wallowing time is up. Let's get you to places, shall we?

BOBO [*Breaking down in sobs.*] SHE SAID, "NOOOOOOOOOOO!"

BOOBOO No? Who said no?

BOBO Bibi. She said no.

BOOBOO Sorry, but I don't understand.

BOBO Here's what happened. I invited her over to my trailer for dinner last night. A nice, romantic, candlelit dinner.

BOOBOO What did you serve?

BOBO Homemade corn dogs with a side of deep-fried pickles and waffle fries.

BOOBOO And for dessert?

BOBO Fried dough . . . with the powdered sugar on the side . . . just the way she likes it.

BOOBOO And so what happened?

BOBO I poured my heart out to her. I told her how much I was in love with her. Ever since the moment I laid eyes on her. Ever since the first time we met . . . on a dark, starry night when she first arrived to us . . . I just had this feeling, you know? Like she was the one . . . so I finally got up the courage to ask her out and she . . . and she said . . .

[*Hysterically crying.*]

BOOBOO I am so sorry, man. No wonder you're not in the mood today.

BOBO I just don't understand it. She and I have so much in common. And we've been friends for so long.

BOOBOO Maybe that's the problem. You're friends. And once you take that friendship further, there's no turning back.

BOBO But if she only gave me a chance. An opportunity to prove to her that I'd make a faithful companion.

BOOBOO Much better than that pompous ass, Bambam! He looked like a chimp on wheels!

BOBO I know, right? God! A complete imbecile! What does she see in him?

BOOBOO Well, from the looks of what he was riding . . . I guess size doesn't matter.

BOBO What am I supposed to do? I'm crushed . . . heartbroken! And so in love with her, it hurts . . . THAT'S IT! I'M GONNA DO MYSELF IN! GONNA THRUST MYSELF OFF THE ELEPHANT AND LET HER TRAMPLE ME TO DEATH IN THE MIDDLE OF THE SHOW!

BOOBOO No, you're not. Be quiet.

BOBO Then . . . in that case . . . I'LL JUMP OFF THE ELEPHANT AND MAKE SURE TO LAND IN THE TIGER'S CAGE!

BOOBOO Are you forgetting that our tigers were raised vegetarian? The only way they'd eat you is if you turned into a carrot.

BOBO Alright! Fine! Then there's one thing left to do.

BOOBOO What?

BOBO Leave. Pack my bags and run away for good.

BOOBOO Just like that? Ten years in the circus and you're just gonna walk away?

BOBO I guess so.

BOOBOO You guess so? You remember how hard it was to get here! Our near death experience? We almost broke our necks hopping aboard that freight train. Looking back, we must've been nuts!

BOBO Yeah . . . and I saved your life, remember that?

BOOBOO Wait a minute now! It was the other way around. I saved your life.

BOBO How quickly you forget, Booboo! You tripped on a rock and I grabbed your hand to hoist you up!

BOOBOO No, Bobo! I'm indeed certain you leaped prematurely and I used the rock to catapult into the boxcar. It was my hand you grabbed.

BOBO You know what? We could fight about this all day! Whoever grabbed whose hand is beside the point. Maybe it was a sign that we shouldn't have been here to begin with.

BOOBOO Well, we're here now. Like it or not! And you're going on today! Like it or not!

[BOBO *sits back down and sobs.*]

Look, I understand you're upset with Bibi. But maybe if you're patient, fate will open her eyes and she'll see that a true prince is standing at her door. Until then—

[*Offstsage from the* RINGMASTER: *"Places in fifteen minutes! Places in fifteen minutes!"*]

Come on! Let's get moving.

BOBO Before we go, I have to tell you about this dream I had the other night. It was really strange!

BOOBOO Save it for later. She's riding up again with Bambi! Look cool and for Christ's sake . . . will you put the bottle away. You don't want her to see that!

BOBO Geez, you're right. You think she could smell it on my breath?

BOOBOO I dunno! Act cool!

[*They ride in once again, making figure eights around* BOBO *and* BOOBOO.]

BIBI WEEEEEEEEEEEEEEEEEEEEE!

BAMBAM [*Making sounds of a car.*] VROOOOM! VROOOOOM! NRRRRRRRRRR! AAAAAARRRRRR! SCREAAAAAACH!

[*Parking.*]

How'da like dat for a ride?

BIBI Bambam, you really know how to excite a woman.

BAMBAM Hell yeah! Dat's what dey tell me. Dey also tell me I can pitch a pretty good tent!

[*He laughs uncontrollably.*]

Well, if it isn't "Bozo da Clown" and "Ronald McDonald!" You guys get a load of my wheels? Dey're for my new bit in da show.

BOOBOO Oh yeah? That's nice. What's your new bit . . . if you don't mind me asking?

BAMBAM It's called da shot-out-of-da-canon-and-swing-off-the-trapeze-and-land-on-the-scooter trick. It's gonna be like Cirque Du Soleil . . . only minus the weird artsy-fartsy, faggity French crap!

BIBI Bambam's been working on this stunt for over a week. And he's asked me to assist him.

BOBO [*To himself.*] How romantic!

BOOBOO So, what's your part in this whole elaborate act?

BIBI Well, after he gets shot from the canon and I catch him from my trapeze, he's going to let go, do five flips in the air, and land on this here scooter, which, by the way, will be balanced on the tightrope. Then I'm going to let go . . . flip three times in the air . . . and if everything goes according to plan—

BAMBAM She'll land on my shoulders, we'll slide off the tightrope, land on the ground, and ride around the ring till da crowd claps so hard dey're hands fall off dey're arms.

BOBO Sounds pretty intense. Does Ringmaster know about this?

BAMBAM Have no fear. I told Ringmaster all about it and he said it was da most brilliant idear since sliced toast. As a matter of fact . . . I wasn't gonna say nuttin . . . but, uh . . . Dah Big Apple Circus sent a couple of scouts out to da show just to see me.

BIBI Oh my goodness! Are you serious? Oh, Bambam! I'm so proud of you!

BAMBAM And if dey want to sign me, I will only sign dat contract under one condition.

[*Beat.*]

Dey gotta sign you, too.

BIBI Oh, Bambam! I don't know what to say—!

[BAMBAM *and* BIBI *share a romantic moment. They lean in for a kiss.*]

BOOBOO [*Pretending he's the voice of the loudspeaker.*] "WILL BAMBAM THE CLOWN PLEASE REPORT TO THE TENT! BAMBAM TO THE TENT!" Hey, I think I just heard your name being called over the loudspeaker.

BAMBAM Oh yeah? What'de say?

BOOBOO They want you to report to the tent right away.

BAMBAM Oh really? Maybe it's Ringmaster and he wants to introduce me to dem scouts!

BOOBOO Yeah, and while you're going, I should get over to the tent and . . . um . . . fix my makeup.

BAMBAM Oh boy! Maybe dem scouts wanna sign me on da spot! Let me get over der—I'll be a few minutes, babe . . . and then I'll be back to pick you up.

BOOBOO Hey, Bambino . . . wait up! Do you mind giving me a lift over. These shoes are so hard to walk in.

[*They exit. An awkward silence.*]

BOBO You . . . your makeup looks really pretty today.

BIBI Thanks. I did it myself for a change. And you look rather . . . colorful.

[*Another awkward pause.*]

BOBO Wow! That sure is quite a stunt you're doing with him.

BIBI Yeah, I know. It was all his idea . . . he's so inventive.

BOBO Yeah . . . he sure is . . . can I ask you something? What the hell do you see in him?

BIBI Bobo, don't start in.

BOBO No, I'm serious. That guy is such a pompous, arrogant—

BIBI That's just a facade. But underneath . . . he's really just a sensitive, loving teddy bear.

BOBO He's a moron!

BIBI Actually, he's quite smart. Did you know he graduated with big-top honors from BBU?

BOBO That guy studied at Barnum & Bailey University?

BIBI And then went on to get his master's from Ringling Brothers. Did his thesis, I believe, on the history of entertainment during the Roman Empire.

BOBO Well . . . I did a prestigious internship touring around with Cole Brothers . . . for a year. . . .

BIBI Oh my! That's impressive . . . who're the Cole Brothers?

BOBO You never heard of Cole Brothers? "Circus of the Stars!" They're only the world's "LARGEST CIRCUS UNDER THE BIG TOP!"

BIBI Okay . . . what'd you study?

BOBO Um . . . you know . . . the usual. How to properly hose down the elephants. What not to feed the lions. Learned how to yell, "PEANUTS—GET YOUR PEANUTS!" There's a real art to selling peanuts . . . not as easy as it looks.

BIBI I imagine not.

[*Pause.*]

BOBO	**BIBI**
Bibi. there's something I want to say. About last night—I just couldn't keep my feelings to myself any longer. I'm such a fool. Of course you'd never go out with me. I mean, we're friends, right? From the moment I laid eyes on you. That starry night you arrived . . . I helped you carry your bags to your trailer.	Listen . . . you don't have to say anything. You made a nice dinner. You put the powdered sugar on the side. Just how I like it. You're not a fool. You have such a good heart. A kind soul. I hope you never change. You remind me of my father . . . so gentle and kind. That was a special time for me, too.

BOBO THEN WHY'RE WE NOT TOGETHER?

BIBI Bobo, it's complicated.

BOBO Let's cut the charades.

BIBI I know your feelings are hurt right now. How do you think I feel?

BOBO Hurt? I'm dying inside. For five years, I've held myself back from saying something!

BIBI What stopped you? Why didn't you come right out and say to me, "Bibi, I love you!"

BOBO I was afraid you wouldn't understand.

BIBI But wasn't it obvious that I had the same feelings for you? Believe me, there were times when I was about to say something, but I'm an old-fashioned girl when it comes to relationships. I remember my daddy telling me that a man must always make the first move in asking out a lady. In this case, the man was too scared.

BOBO Well . . . I'd like to start over. Hi, I'm Bobo and I love you and would you like to go out with me?

BIBI It's too late for that. What's done is done.

BOBO It's not too late. It's never too late. If you love someone enough . . . if you truly care about a person . . . Oh hell! Run away with me, Bibi!

BIBI I can't.

BOBO Sure you can! What's holding you back?

BIBI This place has become my home . . . and the other folks . . . they're like my family. And Bambam . . . well, he's gonna go to New York and hit the big time and he's promised to take me with him—

BOBO There's no guarantee he's going anywhere! Let's leave together—tonight . . . and find a new family. Hell, we could make our own . . . and create our own circus. We could do it together.

BIBI And where would we go?

BOBO We can hop a train and let fate decide!

BIBI I used to believe in fate, but lost all belief when my mama died. Watching my dad go through it all was a nightmare. . . . So angry, depressed, and lost. But there was one time every year . . . the only time I heard him laugh . . . it was when the circus came to our town. And he would take me. And to save money, 'cause we didn't have much, he bought one ticket. "My daughter'll sit on my lap!" he'd say to the ticket-booth man. So there we were. He held the popcorn in one hand and the drink in the other. My job was to hold the cotton candy and cracker jacks. And then the show began! But because of my big head of hair, he couldn't see the show. He always claimed he could, but I knew he was lying. When I laughed, he laughed. He probably had no idea what I was laughing at, but it didn't matter. On the way home, he asked me what my favorite part was and I'd tell him about the little white dogs that jumped through the hoops of fire. And then I'd ask him the same question and you know what he said? The clowns . . . he loved the clowns. And I'd say, "But, daddy, how could you see the clowns with my hair in the way?" "Because, honey. I saw the whole thing by watching through your eyes." And when he passed, I left an empty town, a vacant home, and found what my heart had been missing since Mama died. And during every performance I could hear him laughing in the stands. And with my dad living through my eyes, I realized that this is where I was destined to be . . . and this is where Bambam and I will be raising our child in six months.

BOBO Your . . . what?

BIBI I've been meaning to tell you, but I—

[BAMBAM *reenters.*]

BAMBAM Places in ten minutes. Shall we hit da road?

BIBI Yeah . . . sure.

[*To* BOBO.]

Listen, you could leave this place if you want to. But just know I'll be losing my best friend in the world . . . if you do.

BOBO As long as you're here . . . I'm not going anywhere.

BIBI Good. And just think . . . the baby's gonna need a dependable uncle. How would you like to be "Uncle Bobo!"

BOBO I'd be honored.

[BIBI *leans in to kiss* BOBO *on the cheek.*]

BAMBAM Let's get this show on da road, huh? Hey, Dumbo! Do me a favor today. Give me a little space in dah ring. I wanna make sure dem scouts get a good look at me.

BOBO You got it, Bambam! The ring's all yours!

[*They ride off.* BOBO *is now alone and continues to take swigs of his bourbon. A moment later,* TUTU *appears.*]

BOBO Hi, Tutu! You lost again? The tent's back that way.

[TUTU *honks three times.*]

Oh, don't worry about me, Tutu. I'll be fine.

[BOBO *bursts into tears.* TUTU *feels sad for him, so decides to help cheer him up.*]

Thanks, Tutu. I'm just not in the laughing mood today.

[TUTU *takes out a handkerchief to wipe* BOBO*'s eyes. It turns out to be the oldest trick in the book: The never-ending-handkerchief-in-the-pocket trick.*]

I don't want to burden you with my problems. Even so, I don't think you'd understand.

[*Offering his flask.*]

Here . . . swig?

[TUTU *honks.*]

You're welcome. But it's just that I can't get this dream out of my head. I've been trying to make sense of it. It starts out at the top of the show and we're about to perform the fifty-clowns-in-the-tiny-car trick. So I'm in the car and it's finally my turn to jump out and I can't get past the door frame. I'm stuck . . . wedged in . . . and can't move. There are thirty clowns behind me trying to move forward and I feel them pushing on me. Shouting and screaming profanities. I'm panicking! And they're punching me, beating their fists into my back and kicking me with their big shoes. At this point, the show has come to a halt and I look out into the audience. All the adults are laughing, while the children sob their eyes out. I'm not sure why they're crying, but it's all happening at once. The ringmaster turns into a chimp, the elephants are flinging peanuts, and the tigers are sitting at a table eating a chef salad. The tent starts deflating, it's about to give way and as I looked out the opening of the door, Bambam is standing right above me. I'm begging for his help but he just stands there . . . laughing and chanting, "Bozo the clown is wearing a frown!" And then I see Bibi. She's hanging from the trapeze twenty stories high and she's about to fall and when I try to call for her, I have no voice. I can't make a sound. I'm mute. Mute as a penniless street mime. And then she falls. And I'm stuck, unable to save her. But it doesn't matter at this point 'cause the tent has given out and the world's gone pitch-black. And then I was alone, surrounded by a starry night sky. With two unmarked suitcases at my feet. I wanted to leave, but I couldn't pick up the bags. It's as though they were rooted into the ground. And that's when I realized . . . and should've known all along . . . those weren't my bags to pick up. They belonged to someone else.

[TUTU *finishes the last drop of bourbon.*]

I'm sorry I'm burdening you with my stupid dream. It's not like you would understand anyway.

TUTU [*With a thick British accent, filled with great intellect.*] By Jove! Your dream is brilliant. Rather brilliant, indeed! Back when I attended Oxford, I took a course in psychoanalysis for the fun of it. We learned about Freud and his theories on the condition and interpretation of dreams. Pray tell, I may be a bit rusty, but allow me start off by stating that Freud's theory about the human personality was made up of three aspects known as the Id, the Ego, and the Super Ego. The Id is an important part of our personality because as newborns, it allows us to get our basic needs met. To put it in layman's terms, when a child is hungry, the Id wants food, and therefore the child cries. Now, allow me to tie this in to your dream. The car in your dream represents your mother's womb and the reason why the children in the audience were sobbing was in essence due to the fact that you never fully recovered from your traumatic childbirth. To which we now turn to the ego, which is based on the principal of people's needs and desires. You need to get out of that car and desire a flawless performance. You also described the beating, kicking, and screaming of the other clowns behind you. Could this be your subconscious acting out all the stress, pressure, and expectations you put upon yourself? Perhaps! That explains why the monkey is running the show! In that case, the salad-eating tigers symbolize your inner lost beast . . . to put it more simply, . . . your "lack" of bravery . . . leaving the great big elephant in the room throwing peanuts in order to crack open the hard protective shell in which you hide inside on a daily basis. Your dream also suggests a slight case of inferiority complex, aka, Bambam chanting his silly quips while standing over you. Meanwhile, the metaphorical "tent" is crashing down and you see Bibi in distress. You want to save her from a life-altering decision, but fail at your attempt in doing so when you can't find the words to truly express how you feel. And finally, we enter the Superego, which Freud equates with the conscience dictating beliefs of right and wrong. As you stand alone beneath a starry night sky, you contemplate leaving everything. Those two suitcases symbolize your deeply rooted, weighty baggage. However, the irony is that those suitcases don't belong to you. Therefore, you have no soul, you can't leave, you're still stuck, while the children cry, and the tigers dine, and the elephants throw nuts, and the chimp cracks his whip and "Bozo the clown keeps wearing his frown," and the children cry on and the tent goes down with a boom and bang and clang and GOOD GOD ALMIGHTY! CAN YOU IMAGINE . . . I was only one point shy of an A+.

[*Picks up the flask and drinks the last drop of bourbon.*]

See you at places. Tutu-loo!

[TUTU *exits as* BOOBOO *returns.*]

BOOBOO We've got one minute till places. You ready to go?

BOBO I won't be going on today.

BOOBOO Right.

BOBO I'm just not in the mood.

BOOBOO Nobody is.

BOBO I'm gonna do myself in!

BOOBOO Sing it, Pagliacci!

BOBO Gonna jump off the ol' elephant!

BOOBOO And land in the tiger's cage? Wouldn't it just be easier to run away?

BOBO Perhaps! Then again, if I left today . . . then you'd have to leave with me.

BOOBOO Why? So I could save your life again hopping a train?

BOBO As a matter of fact . . . yes. Thank you for that, by the way.

BOOBOO You're welcome, my friend!

[*The* RINGMASTER *over the loudspeaker: "Places for the top! Places!"*]

Come on. Let's go out there and make 'em laugh, huh?

BOBO "Make 'em laugh." You know something, Boobs? Here we are, day after day, night after night, weeks on end . . . getting paid the "big" bucks to make people laugh.

BOOBOO So . . . what's your point?

BOBO My point is . . . who's out there making sure that we're laughing, too?

[*The two clowns exit. We here the thunderous applause as the* RINGMASTER *shouts, "And now, ladies and gentleman, boys and girls, I present to you THE GREATEST SHOW ON EARTH. . . ." Blackout.*]

• • •

Untitled Radio Play

Keelay Gipson

Keelay Gipson

A multidisciplinary artist, activist, and award-winning playwright, Keelay Gipson has been awarded the Van Lier Fellowship, a Public Artist Residency for the City of New York, and the MacDowell Colony Residency. His work has been seen at the Wild Project, HERE Arts Center, the Theater at Alvin Ailey, National Black Theater, Rattlestick Playwrights Theater, New York Theatre Workshop, and Brooklyn Academy of Music.

...production history...

Untitled Radio Play was commissioned and performed as part of the Amoralists' Wright Club Fellowship. Directed by T. J. Weaver. The cast was as follows:

BENJI BENEDICT Josh Adam Ramos

MISS LADY Justin Sams

PAPI CHULO Jonathan Burke

CHILLGUY529/WAYNE Luke Lowrey

Act I

[*A Grindr conversation, night. Two actors on either side of the stage. One is white, masculine, and conventionally handsome. He is shirtless; this is* CHILLGUY529. *The other is in darkness, his back turned to the audience. A blank profile. This is* BENJI.]

BENJI Hey there!

CHILLGUY529 [*Pause; several minutes pass.*] Hi.

BENJI Hey.

CHILLGUY529 Hi.

BENJI Sup?

CHILLGUY529 Nm u?

BENJI Chillin

CHILLGUY529 Nice

BENJI You?

CHILLGUY529 [*Pause; several minutes pass.*] Same here, man.

BENJI Cool. Into?

CHILLGUY529 Vers here. Oral, rimming, JO, more top here.

BENJI Cool.

CHILLGUY529 You?

BENJI Vers, but lookin to bottom tonight. Very oral here. Love giving head.

CHILLGUY529 Cool.

[Pause; several minutes go by.]

Pic?

BENJI Yeah. You?

CHILLGUY529 Yeah lol.

BENJI Trade?

CHILLGUY529 Yeah.

BENJI *[Pause; several minutes go by.]* ?

CHILLGUY529 Sorry, got distracted. You first.

BENJI lol after you.

CHILLGUY529 You can already see me though lol.

BENJI Not your face tho lol.

[*Pause; several minutes go by.* BENJI *turns around reluctantly. The lights fade up on him. He is tall, masculine, black. He smiles; a face pic. No response. He takes off his shirt; a torso pic.*]

Hello?

[Beat.]

You there?

[*Lights fade on* CHILLGUY529. BENJI *has been blocked. Lights fade out on* BENJI.]

Satellite Radio Station, First Hour

[*The broadcast console of The Benji Benedict Show, a queer talk and interview show; a cross between RadioLab, Savage Love, and The Foxxhole (Jamie Foxx's Radio Show on SiriusXM). The show's producer and co-host,* MISS LADY, *enters. She holds a clipboard, going over last-minute paperwork before airtime. She is a fierce, black grand dame. She wrote the definition of fabulous. She is a man.* BENJI *enters, Starbucks in hand. He sits at his desk and immediately puts his head down.*]

MISS LADY *[Without looking up.]* Well, well, well . . . Look who decided to grace us with her presence.

[No response.]

I saw Wayne earlier. He stopped by looking for you. Wanted to talk. But I handled him. Since you wanna be on CP-Time this morning. . . .

[*No response.*]

You're welcome.

[*No response.*]

He looked good on today, too. You know he's not my favorite, but he was wearing that suit.

[*No response.*]

Okay. Am I talking to myself? You know I don't do one-sided conversations.

BENJI [*Shade.*] Stop talking, then.

[*Beat.*]

MISS LADY Oh, so it's going to be one of those days?

BENJI It already is.

MISS LADY Oh no, yeah . . . I can see that.

BENJI I'm tired.

MISS LADY We're all tired. You think everyone in this building got up and came here today for their joy and comfort?

BENJI That's not what I'm saying and you know it.

MISS LADY No, I don't know it, 'cause you ain't talking.

BENJI I just don't feel like talking, okay?!

MISS LADY And I ain't feel like guessing! That's all you had to say!

BENJI Okay, then.

MISS LADY Okay, then.

[*Long pause.* BENJI *lifts his head.*]

BENJI [*Sincerely.*] I'm sorry.

MISS LADY [*"Thank you."*] I thought so.

BENJI I'm in a mood.

MISS LADY You don't say. I was like, "Nigga, it's too early for all this fever—!"

BENJI You're right—

MISS LADY "I thought the Ebola scare was through with!"

BENJI [*Beat.*] Am I attractive?

MISS LADY I'm sorry, what?

BENJI Attractive. Am I—?

MISS LADY No, I heard you. Just needed time to process, I guess.

[*Beat.*]

Sure. You're not my type, but—

BENJI I mean objectively.

[*Feeling self-conscious.*]

Never mind.

MISS LADY [*Beat. Answering him.*] Yes.

BENJI You say that like you're still thinking about it.

MISS LADY Yes, Benji. You are attractive.

BENJI Okay.

MISS LADY [*"You sure?"*] Okay . . . ?

BENJI For my age, you mean, right?

MISS LADY I thought we were talking objectively?

BENJI We were, but now—

MISS LADY Girl, don't even. You're still young.

BENJI [*Taking heed.*] You know what, you're right.

MISS LADY And black don't crack.

BENJI Huh. Right.

MISS LADY [*Beat.*] Girl, who has got you sweating like this?

BENJI Nobody.

MISS LADY Don't play. Bad night?

[*Beat.*]

What happened? He shit on your dick? Or did you . . . on his?

BENJI Your eloquence never ceases to amaze.

MISS LADY I do what I can.

[*Beat.*]

No, really. What's going on?

BENJI It's nothing. It's stupid. It's just— Have you ever doubted your ability to turn heads and, like, needed some type of—I don't know—confirmation that you do, in fact, got that thing that floats boats.

MISS LADY Okay, Helen . . .

BENJI Not even fleets of ships. Just. Somebody's boat.

MISS LADY [*Beat.*] Yeah.

BENJI Yeah?

MISS LADY I know that. Feeling you're talking about. I know that.

[*With perfect timing.*]

But that's what Instagram is for.

[*Looking at her watch.*]

Shall we?

BENJI We shall.

MISS LADY [*Looking over the schedule.*] Today's rundown: In the first block you've got "Ask a Pornstar."

BENJI [*Whining.*] You mean it's—?

MISS LADY Wednesday already.

BENJI Who came up with such a stupid idea for a—?

MISS LADY You did.

BENJI [*Shade.*] Remind me to find the definition of "rhetorical" for you later.

MISS LADY It boosts ratings.

BENJI Fuck ratings.

MISS LADY Do you like drinking overpriced coffee during your morning Uber rides from ten blocks down the way.

BENJI Yes.

MISS LADY Then we can't "fuck ratings." Especially since we're the highest-rated show on the station. Second block—it's your lucky day—is last week's segment on PrEP.

[*Off* BENJI*'s look.*]

The station got big hits with it online and they want to re-broadcast—

BENJI Amazing! Maybe I can get a massage or something.

MISS LADY Wouldn't count on it. Wayne is looking for you, remember?

BENJI Shit! He say why?

MISS LADY No . . . that's your friend.

BENJI Why don't you like him?

MISS LADY We haven't the time, baby.

[*Beat.*]

I have a sneaking suspicion, though . . .

BENJI What?

MISS LADY Ten bucks says he's meeting with corporate.

[MISS LADY *holds out her hand.* BENJI *does the same. They shake on it; the bet is made.*]

Third block, as always, Dr. Phil Realness. Shall we?

BENJI Do I have a choice?

MISS LADY Do you wanna get paid?

[*No response.*]

Great! You're on in sixty seconds.

[MISS LADY *moves to another part of the stage, the control room, as* BENJI *slowly lifts his head, puts on his headphones, and adjusts his microphone.* MISS LADY *does the same in the control room.* BENJI *starts to vocalize as* MISS LADY *gets the various sound equipment fired up. They do this with routine staleness.* MISS LADY *holds up a hand. She counts down silently from 5 . . . 4 . . . As she does, a Latino beefcake enters and sits at the mike across from* BENJI *. . . 3 . . . 2 . . . This is* PAPI CHULO, *the retired sex worker; he's dumb as rocks but earnest as fuck. He puts on a pair of headphones. The lights shift . . . 1 . . .*]

BENJI [*The most jovial we've seen him so far.*] Ladies and gentlemen and those who don't identify as either or! It's 7 a.m. and you know what that means! You're listening to *The Benji Benedict Show* on SiriusXM satellite radio. If you're joining us for the first time, allow me to re-introduce myself! I'm your host, Benji Benedict—

MISS LADY Sounds oddly similar to something else, darling!

BENJI Here with my trusty side-chick . . . Miss Laaaaaaa-daaaaaaaay!

[*The sound of thunderous applause.*]

MISS LADY Hey, y'all!

BENJI Miss Lady?

MISS LADY Yeah, baby?

BENJI Was that a dick joke just now?

MISS LADY [*Beat; feigning modesty.*] Whatever do you mean?

BENJI I'm quite sure you don't know. Miss Lady?

MISS LADY Yeah, baby.

BENJI How's today shaping up?

MISS LADY Baaaaaaaby. It's shaping up to be a lovely day. Clouds in the sky a little later in the day. With a high of eighty-five and a low of seventy-two. Showers may be coming your way after 5 p.m., so you friends of Dorothy may wanna bring an umbrella, just in case. We don't want you bitches melting on us.

BENJI Traffic?

MISS LADY Who cares? I take cabs.

BENJI Current events?

MISS LADY Well, now that you mention it. My baby daddy—

BENJI Drake, for those who don't know—

MISS LADY DRIZZY DRAKE!

[*A snippet of "Hotline Bling" plays under the following.*]

His fine ass.

BENJI He's so thick now!

MISS LADY Honey, that's just how I like 'em! Drake! Is at the top of the charts again for the fourteenth—I think it is —

BENJI Fourteenth week at number one! Wow!

MISS LADY I didn't think he had it in him.

BENJI Shall I make that joke or do you wanna—?

MISS LADY BIIIIIIIIIIIIITCH!

BENJI [*Laughing.*] Drake, if you're listening . . . Miss Lady has a flooded basement in need of pumping!

[*The sound of frenzied monkeys.*]

If you'd like to help her out, call us here at 1-888-K-W-E-E-N-Z. That's 1-888-593369.

MISS LADY What are those last two digits?

BENJI Six. Nine. Why?

MISS LADY [*Beat.*] Just making sure.

BENJI And if you're not Drake and wanna throw your hat in the ring . . .

MISS LADY I'm picky.

BENJI [*Laughing.*] She's really not. . . .

[MISS LADY *laughs audibly.*]

You can call us here, as well. Again, that's 1-888-K-W-E-E-N-Z.

[*Beat.*]

Alright. Shall we?

MISS LADY Do I have a choice?

[*"Hotline Bling" out. The sound of a drum roll.*]

BENJI Do you wanna get paid? Speaking of fine-ass men . . . Today in the studio with us we have . . .

[*Looking over his notes.*]

Papi Chulo.

PAPI CHULO Yo.

BENJI A retired gay-for-pay sex worker.

MISS LADY [a la *Will Smith's "Miami."*] Ay, Pa-pi!

BENJI That, of course, isn't his real name, but if you Google him, you'll find plenty of material to keep you busy—Miss Lady—?

MISS LADY Huh?

BENJI [*She's not really Googling.*] Google him after the show.

MISS LADY Got it.

BENJI Papi?

PAPI CHULO Sup?

BENJI May I call you Papi?

MISS LADY Not anymore, apparently. . . .

BENJI We'll get to that. First, how are you, Papi?

PAPI CHULO Chillin', how you?

MISS LADY [*Feeling some kind of way.*] Oooooooooo . . .

BENJI [*To* MISS LADY.] You alright, Miss?

MISS LADY That voice, honey . . .

BENJI Don't mind her.

PAPI CHULO She's fine. What up, Ma?

[MISS LADY *takes off her headphones and walks it off.*]

BENJI [*Laughing.*] Miss Lady is no more good, y'all!

[PAPI CHULO *starts laughing.* MISS LADY *comes back to her seat. After she puts her headphones back on.*]

MISS LADY Child . . . I just found my new husband.

BENJI [*To* PAPI CHULO.] How much you charge?

[PAPI CHULO *laughs.*]

MISS LADY Huh-uh, girl . . . I'ma turn him . . .

PAPI CHULO [*Beat.*] I'm gay actually.

MISS LADY Word?

PAPI CHULO [*With a smile.*] Yeah . . . Oh, and I'm not retired. I mean, I am in a way. I'm retired from sex work, but not from porn.

BENJI Come again?

[*The sound of boos and jeers.*]

MISS LADY [*To* BENJI, *re: the bad joke.*] They're too easy today.

PAPI CHULO Like, I mean, like, I don't do escorting anymore. Like having sex for money.

BENJI Unless it's on camera.

PAPI CHULO Yeah, unless, like, it's that.

BENJI [*Pause.*] Papi, you single?

PAPI CHULO No comment.

BENJI Alright, alright. I see you, I see you. Keeping it close to the chest.

[*Shade.*]

Don't wanna ruin the intrigue.

PAPI CHULO Something like that.

BENJI [*Shifting into interview mode.*] Was that part of the gig? Playing up the ambiguity of your orientation?

PAPI CHULO Yo . . . I'd be lying if I said no. Gay-for-pay is in.

BENJI Right. Let's talk specifically about the sex work—the escorting. Why did you decide to leave that behind?

PAPI CHULO I guess it's like . . . I don't know—I guess it's just, like, people change, you know?

MISS LADY [*Digging.*] Oh, do they?

BENJI In my experience, people don't change. They just . . . shift the parts around and learn how to deal with them.

PAPI CHULO Oh, word?

BENJI What caused you to shift, Papi?

PAPI CHULO [*Pause.*] Okay. So, I've been, like, reading this, like, what you call it? It's like an article but they, like, update it, like, on the regular, you know?

BENJI A blog?

PAPI CHULO Yeah, like a blog. And they got videos! And, like, columns and stuff. And I've been doing them. Like, going through them, you know?

And I've come to realize, in doing these videos and columns and stuff, that, like . . . I am enough. I am, myself, all that, like, all that I need. Everything I need is right here . . .

[*He points to his head.*]

And right here. . . .

[*He points to his heart.*]

And, like, I should stand in that and know that as, like, a fact.

Shout out to FreeingYourTrueSelf.Tumblr.com—I don't know where I'd be without y'all. I love y'all over there!

BENJI What did this blog make you realize?

PAPI CHULO Well. First off, I realized that me tricking with mostly older men and mostly white men, you know? I realized that that was, like, because and on account of my dad. Like . . . duh, right?

MISS LADY And because they had coins.

PAPI CHULO That too. But. It wasn't until this blog that, like, all this shit started to come to me. Like, this blog . . . it probably saved my life, you know?

BENJI Shit, like . . . ?

PAPI CHULO Well, it's like, when I was escorting, I was being someone else. Completely.

BENJI But aren't you being someone else in porn?

MISS LADY A mailman, a milkman, a teacher, a daddy.

PAPI CHULO [*Serious.*] Yo, that's a trigger.

BENJI [*Beat.*] Why is it different?

PAPI CHULO In porn, I'm acting, feel me? But when I was escorting, it's like . . . I would take that shit home with me.

BENJI 'Cause money was involved.

PAPI CHULO Not even. Because it was intimate. And you can say sex is sex all you want, but sex is intimate. It's supposed to be, anyway. And, sometimes, without thinking . . . I would take that shit home with me.

BENJI And you don't take it home with you now? From set?

PAPI CHULO Yo, porn is a workout. They give you a pill and you're fucking for four hours. It ain't fun. It's hot to y'all but it's work.

BENJI Noted. Do you ever feel the same way about porn as you did about escorting—before you stopped?

PAPI CHULO I mean, check it: Sometimes I wish I could have a blank slate. You know? No porn, no escorting. Nothing.

BENJI [*Taken aback.*] Really?

PAPI CHULO It's hard. Because, and like, in my line of work it's about fantasy. And the real bitch of dealing in fantasy all of the time and for work is, like, that people lose their humanity. They become animals. Fantasy-crazed animals.

BENJI Right, but what I'm wondering is—

MISS LADY Why the disconnect?

BENJI Right! Why are you cool with the fantasy of porn but not with the fantasy of escorting?

PAPI CHULO [*Beat. He thinks.*] Like, for instance, when, say, like, when people are watching me in a film . . . they are only seeing what was put together for them to see. And they know I'm not a milkman or mailman or shit like that. They see me but they chose me. They chose this fantasy.

BENJI But don't they do the same thing when—?

PAPI CHULO Hold up, hold up, hold up, hold up. . . . Let me finish. Requesting me for a night . . . They see me and how I present myself and, like, they see a hard-looking, possibly ghetto-type nigga, right?

And, like, I gotta be honest and tell on myself and say that the flat-brimmed hat with the fresh kicks and jockstrap don't help, but—
They want a ghetto-type nigga to come through and fuck them when they see me. . . .

Right?

BENJI Right.

PAPI CHULO But is that really me, though?

[*Beat.*]

The difference is—let me tell you—when it's in person, they put all their shit on you. The fantasy they want becomes real. And some people got some fucked-up fantasies. I'll never make that mistake again.

BENJI Can you tell us about one or some of them?

PAPI CHULO [*With a sigh.*] So, when I first started out escorting, right? I figure, I look black and I am—black and Dominican—so same thing sorta, so I'm just gonna click black, right?

MISS LADY Right.

PAPI CHULO Wrong. I clicked black and I wasn't getting no messages. Like, none. There would be all these guys looking at my profile—'cause on the site I would use you could see who had visited you and whatnot—

BENJI Sure—

PAPI CHULO All these white niggas would visit me and only a few of them would hit me up. And then when they did? The shit that they'd be saying was mad offensive, feel me?

MISS LADY Shit like what?

PAPI CHULO Shit like—"Oh, fuck me with your big black dick" and "punish me with your big black cock."

BENJI [*Not surprised.*] Really?

PAPI CHULO Shit was gross. It was like, yeah, it's big, but you ain't gotta say all that!

MISS LADY Child . . .

PAPI CHULO So, if I'm being real and honest, I'm gonna say that I, more often than not, would start, you know, start clicking the Latino button. I just didn't wanna deal with all that mess anymore.

And because . . . well . . . I wanna get paid. There's a pecking order of what people find attractive when it comes to sex. Asians are at the bottom. Then blacks. Then Latinos. Then whites at the top.

MISS LADY They want "sugar" and "spice"—no "darkies" no "rice."

PAPI CHULO In the real world, no one would ever say to your face, but online ain't real life. And like it or not, it's true: On those sites, being black don't get you paid.

BENJI And when it did . . . ?

PAPI CHULO I paid for it. Took it home. All the objectification bullshit.

BENJI It's just funny that you seem have a problem with someone else objectifying you, but you objectify yourself on the—

PAPI CHULO [*Fierce.*] What I choose to put myself through is my business! And I have every right to do what I gotta do to make it in this life, in this world. I choose to get paid for dicking down, that's me. But that don't give someone permission to act out their fucked-up racist bullshit with me 'cause they don't quite love themselves enough yet to be decent and because they got a check. You can be decent and still have a check.

[*Beat, as they take that in.*]

No disrespect. But. Yeah. Remember when I said people become animals?

[*Pause.* BENJI *and* MISS LADY *look at one another.* MISS LADY *moves her mike away and picks up a nearby telephone.*]

Did I say too much?

BENJI No. No, Papi.

[MISS LADY *gives a wave.*]

We gotta take a few calls. But before we do, I have a little something to say. . . . In talking to Papi, I couldn't help but be reminded that there is so much work to be done. And I mean that in the much broader sense. Yes, sure, porn could be better. How many times must we revisit the teacher-student storyline? Anyway. This world is . . . fragile, to say the least. And in these harrowing times, we often lose sight of one another. As human beings. We often lose sight of those things which we have in common with one another.

MISS LADY Amen.

BENJI We lose our humanity. We see this faction or that faction as, inherently, against I, we, us. "Them" has become the currency of the day. And in talking with Papi, again, it is clear that this has permeated, even, our online personas. How can we do better? Or can we? Is it hopeless? Or have we reached a turning point?

MISS LADY I hope so.

BENJI Well, then, Miss Lady . . . Let's pray that your hope is enough. Thank you for indulging me.

[*Shifting gears.*]

Alright. Let's take a couple of calls! Caller Number One, you are on with Benji Benedict!

[BENJI *hits a nearby button on his console. As he does, blackout; the following is heard in darkness:*]

CALLER #1 Uh, hi . . . I've been listening to your conversation with Papi and I just wanted to say that . . . I love your work . . . and are you single?

[*The sound of a tape fast-forwarding.*]

CALLER #2 This whole conversation is bullshit. Like, why even have this dipshit on the show? "You're just mad 'cause you're black and ugly and nobody wants to fuck you!"

[*The sound of a tape fast-forwarding.*]

CALLER #3 Racism is unfair anywhere and it should not be tolerated. However, you cannot stretch this into the world of sex and dating. Refusing somebody a job on the grounds of their skin color is illegal and so it should be, but if people are now suggesting that you can't refuse somebody a date or sex on the grounds of their skin color, we are getting into very ridiculous territory.

Satellite Radio Station, Second Hour

[*Lights up.* PAPI CHULO *is gone.* BENJI *and* MISS LADY *sit across from one another at the main console. Audio from the pre-taped segment on PrEP plays faintly in the background. Standing before them, in a very nice suit, is* WAYNE, *the station manager. He is white and has a very mercurial way about him; a lovable asshole.*]

WAYNE . . . And another thing: if we're going to have porn stars on, why didn't we get an Ivy League, "just so happens I do porn but can form actual cohesive thoughts" kind of porn star? You know? I mean, I can't be the only one who expects the show we do to live somewhere between entertainment and quality, am I?

MISS LADY I thought his thoughts were pretty cohesive.

BENJI Me too.

WAYNE But it was off topic.

BENJI The topic changed. It's allowed to do that.

WAYNE No shit, it changed. When you pitched this segment it was as a way to make the men you guys watch during your private time relatable?

MISS LADY To be fair, they're probably the men you watch too.

[*Off* WAYNE*'s look.*]

Gay-for-pay is in.

WAYNE "Where did you grow up?" "How did you get into porn?" "What's your favorite story from on-set?"

MISS LADY The topic changed.

WAYNE The topic became inflammatory. And the calls that followed . . . Jesus!

BENJI To be fair, we can't control what people are going to say.

WAYNE No, but you can help guide them toward not saying what they're going to say.

[*Beat.*]

Benji? What was that wrap-up about?

BENJI What?

WAYNE All that "what the world needs now" bullshit?

BENJI It wasn't bullshit, Wayne.

WAYNE It was . . . bait-y.

MISS LADY That's not fair.

BENJI Well, it wasn't what you normally do. Is that a fair statement? Today's whole first segment was loaded. And that wrap-up was . . . it was something else. What am I supposed to say when Corporate comes breathing down my neck, huh?

MISS LADY You say that it was a conversation and that shit happens when grown folks is talking.

BENJI And they'll say, "Did he pre-interview?" And I'll say . . .

[*No response.*]

Did you?

[*No response; speaks volumes.*]

Come the fuck on, guys!

[MISS LADY *clears her throat.*]

. . . You all!

[*Charming his way out of it.*]

So don't let it happen again is what you're saying?

WAYNE You know I hate dropping the hammer on you guys. It's not my style.

[MISS LADY *gives him a look.*]

You all . . . get away with a lot. Please help me help you keep it that way.

BENJI [*Patronizing.*] As always, Wayne, thank you for your dedication and understanding.

MISS LADY [*More of the same.*] What would we do without you?

WAYNE Fuck off.

BENJI Calm down, Wayne. Jesus.

[*Beat.*]

It's been awhile since I've seen you this tense.

[WAYNE *sighs. Pause.*]

WAYNE Benji, I'm not gonna bullshit you. We need to talk.

BENJI [*To lighten the mood.*] Well, I figured that much, Wayne. We never go out anymore and now you come in here dressed like we're going to the prom . . . I hope you asked for my father's blessing.

WAYNE I met with Corporate today.

[BENJI *reaches into his pocket and pulls out a ten. He hands it to* MISS LADY *without missing a beat.*]

BENJI Oh yeah?

WAYNE Yeah. . . . Did I mention how much I hate this part of my job?

BENJI Am I . . . Are you about to fire me, Wayne?

WAYNE No, no. God, no. Well . . . not . . . Look, as station manager, I've been given the daunting task of talking to you about a potential shift.

BENJI Shift, Wayne?

WAYNE For you and your show. And, on the one hand, it's stupid 'cause you're, like, one of the highest rated shows on our station—

MISS LADY The highest rated . . .

WAYNE Not lately.

MISS LADY Bullshit.

WAYNE [*Removing a folded piece of paper from his coat pocket.*] Numbers.

[WAYNE *hands it to* MISS LADY, *who begins glancing over it;* BENJI *doesn't look at his ratings, never has.*]

Which brings me to the other hand. . . . Numbers don't lie. And the markets we usually hit are dropping like flies.

MISS LADY And why is that?

WAYNE [*Beat.*] Let's focus less on the problem and more on the solution. What I've proposed is a potential move. Just a measly few yards down the hall. Same team. Same show—a few minor tweaks—but same spirit.

BENJI Wayne—

WAYNE I know, I know, Benji. I know where your mind is going, right now. And I can assure you—

BENJI You have no idea where my mind is going right now. Where would I be moving to?

MISS LADY Psh. You already know.

[*Long pause.*]

WAYNE You'd be moving from LGBTQ Talk to Urban Talk.

MISS LADY Big surprise!

WAYNE I just felt—Corporate just feels, it would be advantageous for everyone involved if you—

MISS LADY So, we're supposed to talk about "bottom shame" and "pup play" on the Black Station—?

WAYNE Urban—

MISS LADY That ain't gonna fly, baby. And you know it.

WAYNE We'll cross that bridge when we come to it. I'll be there in the beginning stages to help the transition go as smoothly as possible.

BENJI And then when the time comes, you'll hand us off to Marcus—?

WAYNE He already knows about the move—

MISS LADY That moralistic, house-nigger motherfucker—

WAYNE [*Fierce.*] Hey, hey, hey! I'm all about a relaxed fucking managerial style, but I will not have you talk about a co-worker—your new supervisor—like that in my fucking presence, okay? That's cause for a write-up, you understand, Matthew?

MISS LADY [*Very measured.*] That's not my name.

WAYNE [*Beat.*] Miss Lady. Do you understand?

MISS LADY If there's one thing I understand, it's transitions. And they ain't easy . . .

WAYNE [*Pause; trying to laugh it off.*] God, you guys. I thought you weren't gonna make me be that guy today, right?

[*No response.*]

Right?

[*Beat.*]

Right, okay, Benji! Come on, buddy. We've been making moves since '08 together. We've had a good run, huh? And I'll still see you. Just a few yards down the hall.

[*No response.*]

Oh, come on, what? You're not gonna talk to me now? Just 'cause I got all HR on Ma—Miss Lady, over here? She's okay. I'm okay. We've had bigger bouts before.

[*No response; in a whisper.*]

Look, I know it doesn't feel it right now, but all the particulars are negotiable. If, at any point during this shift, something feels off—anything—we can work it out until it doesn't. Corporate has promised me that much.

BENJI But what did you promise them?

WAYNE [*Beat.*] Look, I went up there and threw myself on the chopping block for you, Benji. I bragged and I begged and I cut myself open for you. So they'd do right by you.

And then I come back down here and you make my bragging look like lying. And I know that today was a fluke, or whatever, but you got off topic. You were inflammatory on air. You. The shit on today's show shouldn't have been on today's show. Plain and simple.

And if me telling you that makes me the bad guy, then—

[BENJI *stands and puts his hands in his pockets.*]

BENJI As always, Wayne, thank you for your dedication and understanding. We appreciate it.

MISS LADY We do?!

BENJI [*Beat; offering his hand.*] We do.

[MISS LADY *scoffs and returns to the control room; the third segment is about to begin.* WAYNE *cautiously shakes* BENJI*'s hand.*]

WAYNE Well . . . thanks. For hearing me out, I mean.

[*After awhile, the two find themselves still shaking hands. The up-and-down motion comes to an end and now they're holding hands, staring at one another; a standoff.*]

MISS LADY Benji. Sixty seconds.

[*They continue staring for a bit longer. When they break contact, it is* WAYNE *who initiates it. Then he moves next to* MISS LADY *and crosses his arms.* BENJI *moves to his desk and prepares for broadcast. He does so with contemplative stillness.*]

WAYNE [*To* MISS LADY.] You understand what I'm saying, right?

MISS LADY [*Shade.*] I have a show to produce.

[MISS LADY *holds up a hand and silently counts down from . . .*

5 . . .

4 . . .

3 . . .

2 . . .

1 . . .]

Satellite Radio Station, Third Hour

BENJI We're back! And I'm your host—Benji Benedict here and I'm—here to take your—

[*Long pause.*]

You know what . . . Before we take your calls, I have a little something to say . . .

[*Pause.*]

I've been in radio for about fifteen years now. Started out at my college radio station. I was Benjamin then. *Benjamin's Bomb-Ass Beat Hour* was the show. Hip-hop and R & B from the greats: Biggie, 2Pac, Jay-Z, Mary J., Faith Evans . . . you get the idea.

I didn't necessarily like this music, though. Not at all, really. I much preferred show tunes. The greats: Bernstein, Sondheim, Rodgers and Hammerstein . . . you get the idea. But I was the only black DJ at the station, so, of course, I had to play the music people expected the only black guy at the station to play. And I did. In spite of myself, I did.

Fast-forward to my last broadcast of the semester, before break, when instead of "Life After Death" I played the entire cast album of *Phantom*. And not the selections either. No. The full, two-disc set. Needless to say, I wasn't asked back the following semester. I guess that was the first time I noticed something about myself. Maybe some of you have noticed it too.

There seemed to be space for me to be either black or gay . . . not both. You see, I noticed that day that I reside, unwelcome, in two communities. The black community, which views homosexuality as "The White Man's Disease." And the gay community, which views blacks as exotic or unattractive. One or the other, never any more complicated than that.

Earlier in today's show we heard from—Forgive me, I'm blanking at the moment—

MISS LADY Papi Chulo.

BENJI Right. Who said that, though he identifies as mixed race, he has found in his career as a sex worker that promoting his blackness is seen as a potential hindrance to his success. Harsh truths, maybe. Harsh truths . . . harsh truths . . . harsh truths . . .

[*Beginning to unravel.*]

Last night, guess what I was doing? Harsh truths. Well. I found myself online. One of those apps, you know? What's the one—the one—the one with the . . . it's the yellow one. It's—I know, the—I'm blanking at the moment!

[*He laughs; it's a crazy laugh.*]

Ah, which one's not important. But there I was, nonetheless. Online. Trolling for dick—I'm not ashamed to say it.

[A la *Harold Hill.*]

No, I'm mighty proud to say it. I'm always mighty proud to say it. . . .

I keep my profile blank, save for my stats, as to keep some semblance of privacy. And that often results in men chatting me up with—with—with cautious trepidation until their request for my face pic is honored. Pic, question mark. Now, more often than not, I send my photo. And if you've seen me on a poster or at an event, I'm not a bad-looking guy. That said, more often than not, my sending my photo is met with radio silence. . . .

[*That laugh again.*]

What a fucking coincidence, right?!

[WAYNE *rushes in, aghast. He speaks quietly, but his face gives away his true sentiment.*]

WAYNE [*In a whisper.*] Take a call, take a call.

[MISS LADY *shrugs.* WAYNE, *red in the face, puts his hands on his hips; a warning.* BENJI *stands and delivers the following tauntingly.*]

BENJI Last night I was ghosted by a man, not of my race. Not the first time, but there's no crying in baseball and there's no crying over spilt milk and there's no crying over those with milky-white complexions who have no time for the "darkies" or the "spice" or the "rice." The conversation just goes and goes and goes until my face pic is sent and then . . . nothing. Fucking blocked, even!

WAYNE [*To* MISS LADY *in a whisper.*] Take a fucking call.

MISS LADY Nobody is calling!

BENJI That coupled with our guest today and, to be completely frank, your fucked-up and half-cocked phone calls in the first hour have got me thinking: I've tried so long to belong to this group or that. Fit into a binary. I wished away my skin color, then my sexuality, alternating between the two depending on the day, at times. I've worked through my own shit, become an adult, and just when I think I'm seated at the center of myself . . . I come across a profile that says "white dudes only" or get blocked by some idiot who thinks that racism doesn't extend into the realm of social media or hook-up apps. Some dipshit says, "Sorry not a match" or "No hard feelings, just a preference," and I want to scream . . .

[*Losing it.*]

YOU'LL NEVER BE HALF THE MOTHERFUCKING PERSON I AM OR KNOW THE WORTH YOU ARE THROWING AWAY BECAUSE IT RESIDES IN A BODY NOT COLORED THE SAME MOTHERFUCKING SHADE YOU ARE.

[*Beat. To* WAYNE.]

To those motherfuckers who make me feel like I'm that lonely, frightened, and worthless disc jockey and that I'll never find love because I can't quite love myself yet . . . I say to you . . . kiss both sides of my ass. Two times.

[WAYNE *picks up the phone and points to it; a signal for* BENJI. *Pause; to* MISS LADY*:*]

Do we have any calls?

MISS LADY [*Looking at* WAYNE *for confirmation.*] Uh . . .

WAYNE [*Into the mike.*] Uh, yes we do, Benji. Line one.

[WAYNE *shoves the phone into* MISS LADY*'s hand and nudges her; time to fake a call-in (which is common in radio when the lines are dead).*]

MISS LADY [*Still looking to* WAYNE.] Uh . . .

BENJI [*Jovial, as if nothing happened.*] Hello, this is Benji Benedict! Caller, you're on the air!

MISS LADY I, uh, I really . . . I'm sorry . . .

BENJI Don't apologize.

MISS LADY Longtime listener, first-time caller . . . and what you said just now . . . it really, uh, it hit me. . . . You know, 'cause, uh . . . sometimes . . .
Sometimes . . .
Sometimes, in the past
Sometimes I wished I could turn myself inside out
Don blond or brunette hair
And know for one day.
The lily white slate of Them
Those unhindered by norms
Dictated by mostly fear
Ah, to lay down the burden of unhinged masculinity
Rich exotic texture-less
I would move through life
Common-dicked
Thin-lipped and plain
Blended into the crowd
Sometimes, in the past

Sometimes I wished I could accessorize my mother's outfits
As her gay son
An ornament
A pearl earring instead of a curse
Her ancestors, ill-fated, brought upon her generations after they had passed
Sometimes I wished away the swish of my walk
The timbre of my voice, suited for church but known to the church-going folk as tailor-made for the soprano section
Sometimes I wished my skin would start fresh, born anew daily
A ring around the tub I could scrub off or leave on depending on how I felt that day
But none of this could be
Contending with self was the only remedy
Time and the failure of suicide the only additional medicine
So . . .

[MISS LADY *trails off.* BENJI *stands.*]

BENJI Caller? Are you there?

MISS LADY . . . Yeah. I'm here.

BENJI Stay on the line.

MISS LADY Okay . . .

BENJI [*To* MISS LADY.] Let's take a little break.

[*Blackout. End of play.*]

• • •

East of the Sun

Darcy Parker Bruce

Darcy Parker Bruce

Darcy Parker Bruce holds an MFA in playwriting from Smith College. Her work has been produced from New York to Hawaii and she has been in residence with Sewanee Writers' Conference, Great Plains Theatre Conference, and Exquisite Corpse Company in Brooklyn. She is currently teaching playwriting in Connecticut.

... production history ...

Dates: June 10–25, 2016

Location: Actor's Theatre Playhouse, New Hampshire

Director: Michelle Page

ROSEMARIE Brenda Galenus

AARON TELLING TALES Bridget McBride

DANIEL Arthur Pettee

characters

ROSEMARIE A young woman

DANIEL A giant white bear

AARON TELLING TALES A storyteller

place

In the dark by the river, and east of the sun and west of the moon.

"Where are you going, so fast and so far—carried away on the back of a star?"

[*Low light up, the moon and the stars and the shadows of the forest.* ROSEMARIE *is lost, cold. Enter* AARON TELLING TALES.]

AARON TELLING TALES Tell me a story! Doesn't have to be true!

ROSEMARIE When I was a child I was afraid of many things—

AARON TELLING TALES False! You were afraid of only two things, I know what they were!

ROSEMARIE *Go on then.*

AARON TELLING TALES You were afraid of the woods and you were afraid of the dark and the two together nearly killed you once or perhaps—

ROSEMARIE Perhaps?

AARON TELLING TALES Perhaps they saved you?

ROSEMARIE Perhaps I died and wasn't saved at all.

AARON TELLING TALES Perhaps you met someone—
Who led you into the dark or did you forget?

ROSEMARIE I followed him and I followed him because—

AARON TELLING TALES Because you loved him?

ROSEMARIE I NEVER LOVED HIM—

AARON TELLING TALES Because you didn't know any better.

ROSEMARIE Because the lake was still and glassy and because I could see the stars and the moon and cloudless sky stretching out and into the horizon and it was as if there was no difference only everything was like the heavens and it was all around me and so—

AARON TELLING TALES And so?

ROSEMARIE And so I *wasn't* scared because—

AARON TELLING TALES Because?

ROSEMARIE Because we were past darkness, don't you understand? We were past the dark and the unknown and the lake became a river and the sky was everywhere and we were walking on light and—

AARON TELLING TALES I've heard of places in the earth, so deep and dark they swallow up the light—

ROSEMARIE I don't want your stories—

AARON TELLING TALES *Then tell me yours.*

ROSEMARIE Was he real?

AARON TELLING TALES Was he a beggar, a prince, or a thief?

ROSEMARIE None of those—

AARON TELLING TALES Did he carry you away—

ROSEMARIE I walked, my own two feet—

AARON TELLING TALES Did your father run after you—

ROSEMARIE *I went on my own—*

AARON TELLING TALES To the river?

ROSEMARIE On the backs of stars.

AARON TELLING TALES Was he a charmer, your prince the bear?

ROSEMARIE He saved my life.

AARON TELLING TALES Spin it.

ROSEMARIE Saved me from my father's hand, he saved me from—

AARON TELLING TALES Maybe nothing is real—

ROSEMARIE Saved me from my father's touch—

[*A low growl begins and gets louder.*]

AARON TELLING TALES Someone's coming—

ROSEMARIE *Daniel?*

AARON TELLING TALES In the dark, a story casts light upon the shadows—

[*The shadow of a great bear passes and is gone.*]

ROSEMARIE *Daniel? Are you there?*

AARON TELLING TALES In the dark, in the woods, by the lake—

ROSEMARIE *Don't leave me here, Daniel!*

AARON TELLING TALES East of the sun—

[*A comet streaks across the sky.*]

ROSEMARIE *There! Did you see that?*

[ROSEMARIE *chases it as it goes.*]

AARON TELLING TALES And west of the moon.

[*Exit* AARON TELLING TALES.]

ROSEMARIE A comet—

[*Enter* DANIEL.]

ROSEMARIE Daniel! Daniel, there was a comet, did you see it? Did you see it just now the tail was as long as the river and so bright—

DANIEL Slow down—

ROSEMARIE I think I can catch it—

DANIEL Not like that—

ROSEMARIE I can catch it and then we can go—I know of a road, a road going—going somewhere else—a road that's thick with wood and full of fireflies and wet with rain and so there's a place—a place just for us—

DANIEL Light a candle and wait awhile, Rosemarie. Before the sunrise, I'll be back—

ROSEMARIE [*Beat.*] With blood on your chin and on your tongue and your breath stinking and hot with rage—

DANIEL Light the tallow, Rosemarie. Light it now and wait for me—

ROSEMARIE And sit in darkness?

DANIEL And trust that I'll return—

ROSEMARIE I think, maybe we should go, we should just leave and walk that road—we'll just follow the comet until the light burns out and then maybe—

DANIEL I'll take you away from here. Soon. Soon but first—

ROSEMARIE Don't leave me! When you leave me—

DANIEL I won't be gone for long.

[DANIEL *begins to leave but* ROSEMARIE *holds him back.*]

ROSEMARIE When I'm alone, it's as though I keep turning over stones and every time—every time another shadow, and my mind, my mind can't take it. I've let it go, I've put all my thoughts and fears, put them on that comet. The backs of stars will save me, they'll save you! Daniel—the both of us, away on the backs of stars!

This lake becomes a river becomes a road that will take us away from here, and my father's voice—his voice will rest upon the shore and the tide will drag him out to sea.

And I'll be alright, don't you understand? I'll be alright as long as you stay with me. As long as I can dig my fingers into your fur and rest my cheek on your back—Daniel.

Daniel—Daniel, please.

DANIEL I don't need saving, Rosemarie. Your father doesn't worry me.

[*There is a silence. The stars are bright and the wind picks up.*]

ROSEMARIE I know that I'm not beautiful. I'm not quiet, I'm not wise—I'm lonely, I'm so lonely and I need you—I need someone to hold on to, but not just anyone, don't you understand? Not just anyone will do. You were there. That night. In the forest by the lake in the dark and the cold, you were there. Suddenly a shadow, a thought, a whisper of hope, and a dream and then you were real. Hot breath on the back of my neck and that wet fur smell that makes me dizzy. And your heartbeat, oh your heart. Your heart beside me beat itself straight into my chest and I knew, I knew I would be alright.

[*Beat.*]

I think the stars know what's coming and so they've gone silent. But not completely. Like how when you go, you're not really gone. I think that's love. I think I get it. I think I understand.

[*Beat.*]

It's solid. It's soft. It's always there.

DANIEL I will kill him.

ROSEMARIE I wasn't afraid of him—my father. I wasn't afraid because I knew I could run. My own feet, my own breath, and my heart slamming in my throat, *I'm not afraid of him*. But I'm afraid of being alone and I think—I think because of him that maybe, maybe I always will—

DANIEL In the spring the flowers bloom. The days are longer. The ground gets warm. You are like the spring, Rosemarie. And in time, warmth will come to you. Until then you may warm yourself near me.

ROSEMARIE It doesn't suit me. To be kind in this, it doesn't fit. I don't want a calmness, I want a storm—

[*Beat.*]

I know what's coming. I know what you're going to do and I don't want to stop you.

DANIEL And I will not be stopped.

ROSEMARIE You'll tear out his throat.
I'll tear out his throat.
And bring it back to me.
And bring it back to you.
And I'm glad.

DANIEL This is what you asked of me.

ROSEMARIE But what if he kills you?

DANIEL It's a simple love, my love for you. I know I love you. That's enough.

[*Beat.*]

Have you changed your mind?

[*Another silence and the stars flicker.*]

ROSEMARIE I can feel his hands on me—everywhere he touched me, it's like a map that leads me somewhere I don't want to go.

DANIEL Then light the tallow, Rosemarie. Light it now and wait for me.

ROSEMARIE Blood in your fur and his skin under your nails.

[*Exit* DANIEL.]

Here in the dark, in the woods by the lake—east of the sun,
And west of the moon. I'll wait for you.

[*Enter* AARON TELLING TALES.]

AARON TELLING TALES So what did he tell you, your prince the bear?

ROSEMARIE He's not a prince—I told you once—

AARON TELLING TALES Surely, though, more man than bear. Or how does he come to you at night?

[*Beat.*]

Or does he?

ROSEMARIE His name is Daniel. His name is Daniel and if he is a man,

[*Beat.*]

he isn't, though. I would have seen—

AARON TELLING TALES Here in the north country. Here where the wind drives even the sturdiest astray—here perhaps, it's not so hard to believe that man and bear could be one.

ROSEMARIE You leave us alone! Leave me be! You want your stories? Don't take them from me. You go to town and talk to the girls there. The ones with the silken shoes and the dresses that fit. Doe-eyed brides waiting for their tales to begin. Their stories—their stories are better.

AARON TELLING TALES [*With ferocity.*] Your darkness is sweeter. It echoes the tundra and the shadows on the plains.

ROSEMARIE You take pleasure in my misery.

AARON TELLING TALES I take what you owe—and you owe me a story.

ROSEMARIE I don't owe you anything!

AARON TELLING TALES But who was there in the dead of night—telling you tales while the cold winds blew? Who held your hand when you picked yourself up—when you tore at your clothes and refused to grow up?

ROSEMARIE You aren't real, just a voice—a voice too loud inside my head just go—*just go away.*

AARON TELLING TALES Who watched as you left him, smelling of fear, fresh blood freezing in the cold night air?

[*Beat.*]

And said not one word—

ROSEMARIE As I ran to my death? As I fled from my past? His voice on my heels as I ran from his grasp?

AARON TELLING TALES You ran away. From him but not from me, sweet Rosemarie. I always have and always shall be—

[*With a bow.*]

a friend—

[*A silence, the wind is fierce.*]

ROSEMARIE You remind me of him.

AARON TELLING TALES Your father?

ROSEMARIE You remind me of the way he'd chew tobacco—the way his breath stank of it. You remind me of his walk, his limping and his heavy step.

AARON TELLING TALES What else?

ROSEMARIE You remind me of his hands, like iron shackles wrapped around my wrists.

[*Beat.*]

Of how his fingers would rest on my lips. I can't—

AARON TELLING TALES Don't stop.

ROSEMARIE Daniel—

AARON TELLING TALES An ending, Rosemarie—if you please.

ROSEMARIE There's nothing left to say.

[*Beat.*]

He left me there to freeze. It's like you said. I was afraid of the woods and the dark, and the two together almost killed me—until they saved me, until—

AARON TELLING TALES Until the bear.

ROSEMARIE He's coming back for me.
Watch for his shadow in the trees.

AARON TELLING TALES I want to meet your prince.

ROSEMARIE He's not—

AARON TELLING TALES A beggar, a thief—a man. He's a bear. He stinks of river water. Will you ride him over the hills? On the backs of stars, Rosemarie. You'll stink of the river as the two of you flee. Why not go into town?

ROSEMARIE Why not drown myself?

[*Beat.*]

I trust him.

AARON TELLING TALES Learn to trust me.

ROSEMARIE You should have stopped me.

AARON TELLING TALES When?

ROSEMARIE Coming back. That night—I should have stayed in the woods.

AARON TELLING TALES What good am I? Except for telling tales?

ROSEMARIE [*To herself.*] What good are you? When you can't protect yourself? The tallow is almost through.

AARON TELLING TALES That story, Rosemarie. The one that you just told me. Don't forget it. Wrap it around yourself and you will never freeze again. Let the bear become a man and let him lead you—

ROSEMARIE I know of a road.

AARON TELLING TALES Out of the woods.

[*A flash of red, a thunder crack, and the roar of the great bear. Exit* AARON TELLING TALES.]

ROSEMARIE It's almost dawn.

[*Beat.*]

I know of a road going, somewhere—

[*Enter* DANIEL, *all in red.*]

Going home.

DANIEL Going home.

ROSEMARIE Is it over?

[*Beat.*]

Is he dead?

[DANIEL *comes to rest beside* ROSEMARIE. *There is a silence.*]

DANIEL Here there are trees. And they remind me of you. And there is a sweet wind rich with the scent of heather. And that reminds me of you. And there are stars. There are stars on your cheeks when you remember what used to be. So stay with me. And forget.

ROSEMARIE Are you real? Are you really here?

DANIEL It was very cold that night.

ROSEMARIE And is he really gone?

DANIEL You kept the tallow lit.

ROSEMARIE Are you a beggar? A prince, or a thief?

DANIEL Don't be afraid—

ROSEMARIE Are you a man? Or are you a bear?

DANIEL Dig your fingers into my fur—

ROSEMARIE I know of a road—

DANIEL —rest your cheek on my back—

[ROSEMARIE *sighs.* DANIEL *is no longer a bear, but a man.*]

and don't be afraid.

[DANIEL *offers* ROSEMARIE *his hand. After a moment, she takes it. They stand.*]

ROSEMARIE And if the moonlight guides us deep into the brush—

DANIEL And if the starlight mends in you what needs to be fixed.

ROSEMARIE And if we go together—

DANIEL And if you let me in—

ROSEMARIE Then I'll forget—

DANIEL What came before—

ROSEMARIE The woods.

DANIEL The woods.

[*A silence. The wind is dying, the sun is breaking, and the woods are waking.*]

DANIEL You lit the tallow, Rosemarie.

ROSEMARIE And in the darkness, burnt it down.

DANIEL Do you have another? One for the road?

ROSEMARIE We have the stars. The stars and the moon and the river—

DANIEL We have each other.

ROSEMARIE I know of a road, a road thick with wood and full of fireflies and wet with rain.

[*Beat.*]

East of the sun, and west of the moon.

[*Lights down. Music up.*]

• • •

Childish Things

Arthur M. Jolly

Arthur M. Jolly

Arthur M. Jolly is a playwright and screenwriter. He is a Woodward/Newman Drama Award finalist for *A Gulag Mouse*, a two-time Joining Sword and Pen winner. He has been recognized by the Academy with a Nicholl Fellowship in Screenwriting, is a Lifetime Alliance of Los Angeles Playwrights member, and member of the WGAW Caucus and Dramatists Guild. He is represented by Brant Rose Agency.

...production history...

The play premiered in April 2016 at the Mount Hood Community College, Gresham, Oregon. The cast was as follows:

RACHEL Jennifer Kuenzi

JERRY Michael Tippery

BUNNY Ashley Fray

TEDDY Ryan Townsley

Directed by Jade Rabell

It its first professional production at the Short + Sweet Hollywood Festival at the Stella Adler Theatre, September 10, 2016:

RACHEL Kay Capasso

JERRY Frank Collison

BUNNY Mia Fraboni

TEDDY Jeffrey Paul Morgan

Directed by Matthew Singletary

characters

JERRY Old enough to have an adult daughter, infirm.

TEDDY Smart, funny in a goofy way.

BUNNY Caring, a little less aware than Teddy.

RACHEL Estranged bitter. Hurt.

setting

A living room.

time

The present.

[JERRY *rummages through an old cardboard box.* TEDDY *and* BUNNY *enter.*]

TEDDY [*Silly voice.*] Helllooo, Daddy!

JERRY Teddy!

[*To* BUNNY, *kindly.*]

You.

BUNNY Hey, Dad.

JERRY I missed you guys.

BUNNY Well, you know how it is. You were busy, we were—

TEDDY Battling the dinosaur.

JERRY Still with that crazy dinosaur?

[TEDDY *pulls a stuffed dinosaur out of the box.*]

TEDDY I'm this close to getting my PhD. If I could just get him to stop biting my face—

[*He attacks his own face with the toy.*]

Get off me, you crazy xenoceratops!

JERRY One day you'll win.

TEDDY Soon. The research is about done, all that's left is compiling the data, logging some of the more recent dig sites. Paleontology stuff. It's hard to come up for air sometimes.

BUNNY Life . . . got in the way.

JERRY It's been ten years.

BUNNY No.

TEDDY I refuse to believe that.

JERRY Ten years.

TEDDY Well, now I feel like neglectful crap. Silly Bunny?

BUNNY Don't call me that.

TEDDY I—Ten whole . . . I can't speak for you, but I haven't changed a bit. I'm still exactly the same—fabulous. You look a little ragged.

[*To* JERRY.]

You look like hell. Like a bunch of coat hangers in a dry-cleaning bag.

JERRY I've been sick.

BUNNY We heard. So we're here. You're out of the hospital.

TEDDY Home sweet home.

BUNNY That's good.

JERRY Not always.

BUNNY You're back home.

JERRY That I am. They stopped talking about curing, about fighting . . . they started talking about "prolonging." When a doctor says the word "prolonging," it's not good.

TEDDY [*Serious.*] Are you gonna die?

JERRY I told my doctor—whaddaya mean, prolonging? That's what you do, that's all you doctors do—you prolong. It's not like you cure this, you cure that, that's good forever, that'll do ya. It's all prolonging.

BUNNY That's why we're here?

TEDDY [*After a pause.*] You don't . . . You want us to talk to—I should've figured. . . . How is she?

JERRY Still not talking to me.

TEDDY You think she'll talk to us?

BUNNY What? You want us to—like—a go-between?

TEDDY [*To* BUNNY.] And look who just caught up. Yeah, what are we—what were we ever . . .

[*To* JERRY.]

Dad, that time has gone. We can't be your puppets now.

JERRY Puppets?

TEDDY That's what we were. Puppets—mouthpieces. We only told her what you were too cowardly to say.

BUNNY That's why, huh? That's what you got us here for.

TEDDY Not anymore. Once, but—you gotta grow up, Dad. Face her. You want us to tell her that you're—what, that you're . . .

[*Beat.*]

Bunny can't even pronounce the word "prognosis." This is not a good idea. That's the worst idea. In the history of ideas, that one's right up there with invading Russia in winter and giving kids snackables.

JERRY Do you know why you were a scientist?

TEDDY I think logically.

JERRY You were the one with the theories. Always—when something needed an . . . Alice falls down, in the kitchen, on the floor. I'm trying to sit her up, get some coffee in her—guess who hears. Guess who comes tripping down the stairs in her sparkle pajamas. . . . You were the one who could explain.

TEDDY Not explanations . . . theories.

BUNNY The spaceship. Aliens.

TEDDY The aliens came to say—

JERRY To tell her—

TEDDY To tell us . . . what?

JERRY I don't remember. Whatever aliens come to tell people.

TEDDY Mama was so surprised, she jumped up, out of her chair—

JERRY The bottle breaking—

TEDDY She was so surprised, she dropped the bottle—

JERRY Jumped up—

TEDDY So high, she hit her head on the ceiling.

JERRY She's fine. She'll be fine in the morning. Daddy's gonna help Mama to bed.

BUNNY I'll hold you.

JERRY She will hold you.

BUNNY All night.

TEDDY Silly Bunny will hold you.

BUNNY Quit calling me—anyway, the aliens broke the bottle. Mama didn't drop it, it was always the aliens.

TEDDY It was the dinosaur. Breaking things was the dinosaur, acting funny was aliens. The dinosaur would turn around too quick, and oh my goodness—his tail swept all the dishes off the table! You should've seen—knocked a coffee mug through the TV!

JERRY The TV, I'd forgotten that old TV. . . . And then he'd bite your face.

TEDDY Always biting my face. It was funny.

BUNNY She'd laugh. Eventually.

JERRY That's why.

TEDDY She's coming here?

JERRY I need to tell her. About me. About . . . prolonging.

BUNNY And you think she'll listen to us?

JERRY I'm scared, Bunny. It's been ten years.

BUNNY This is crazy. We can't tell her.

JERRY Is it that crazy?

BUNNY Dad—it's ridiculous.

JERRY Maybe . . . you just hold me?

[BUNNY *makes some kind of physical contact—but maybe just puts a hand on his shoulder. Find the moment.*]

TEDDY Jesus, Daddy. I'd love to. You know I would, but . . . but that dinosaur has my face!

[*He makes the dinosaur bite his face.*]

Get off my face! Crazy xenoceratops!

[TEDDY *breaks away, gasps for air.*]

BUNNY Teddy, I swear, you are—

[TEDDY *grabs his face again.*]

TEDDY Get off my face! Off my face!

[BUNNY *and* JERRY *laugh. A doorbell.*]

[*Lighting change. Dark on the three of them, up on* RACHEL *as she enters.*]

RACHEL Dad?

[*Lights revert.* JERRY *sits alone with the box, holding a stuffed teddy bear and bunny rabbit.*]

JERRY Hey, Rach.

RACHEL This place hasn't changed.

JERRY I know. Look what I found. Helloo–oo, Daddy!

[*The teddy "sees"* RACHEL.]

Rachel! You came back!

[*In* BUNNY *voice.*]

Hello, Rachel. Look, Teddy—Rachel's here.

[*As teddy.*]

I can see that, Silly Bunny. I just hope that crazy dinosaur isn't with her!

RACHEL Dad . . . what are you doing?

JERRY [*As* TEDDY.] We've got to tell her.

[*As* BUNNY.]

Yes, but it's bad news, and there's no easy way to tell someone bad news.

[RACHEL *approaches, takes the stuffed toys from* JERRY*'s hands.*]

RACHEL Teddy and Bunny. Where's the crazy—

JERRY Oh, he's in there, too, somewhere.

[RACHEL *picks the stuffed dinosaur out of the box, looks at it, drops it back in.*]

RACHEL Where's Mom?

JERRY Upstairs. Taking a nap.

RACHEL Oh no—

JERRY A nap nap. She's fine. She's been fine for ages.

RACHEL At three in the afternoon. Are you lying to me, or is she lying to you?

[*She looks at the teddy bear.*]

I always hated this friggin' thing.

JERRY He made you laugh.

RACHEL He lied. And he never changed a damned thing.

JERRY You were too young for the truth.

RACHEL I lived the truth, the truth was what happened. What we lived with. What Teddy—what you said . . . who did you think you were fooling?

JERRY I was just trying to—

RACHEL Don't. Like hell you were, you were glossing over—trying to push it all under the rug, sweep it—I'm not gonna . . .

[*Beat.*]

I don't know why I came here. I don't have to be part of this, I don't have to walk back into this. It's a sickness. Not her, not even you—it's me. It's like—okay, adult children of alcoholics, we put ourselves—I read this, we put ourselves in these situations. We walk back into . . .

[*Beat.*]

I feel like I crawled out of a river of shit, a frigging sewer pipe I fell into, and I'm standing there, just—just crap, coating me—steaming, drying in the sun. And it dries, and it cracks off you, like an eggshell, like emerging . . . and eventually, after years, you think you got it off, you got it out of your nostrils, the dust of it, the residue that has seeped into your pores. And you're standing there, and someone, a—a stranger. Practically a stranger. Some guy you stopped talking to ten years ago calls you up and says, hey—wanna jump back in? Wanna go wading around in that cess pit again, you've got hardly any of that on you anymore. And you'd think that, maybe you wouldn't, maybe you'd tell him to go to hell.

And your friends, your boyfriend—they're all like—what are you, crazy? That's shit. That's a river of shit right there, don't go back into that. And you tell them: It's just a quick dip.

I'm just gonna jump in, swim around a little bit—I'll get out so quick, it won't get on me. You, your whole mind is . . . you think like that. That makes sense.

[*Beat.*]

She's taking a nap.

[*She chucks the toys in the box.*]

I don't want to hear what you have to say. I have my own life now. I've got my . . . I'm a grown-up.

JERRY I just need to tell you—

RACHEL Keep it. Tell it to my stuffed animals.

[*She heads to leave.*]

JERRY Wait! Rachel! Please!

[*She pauses. He tosses her the rabbit.*]

Take her. Silly Bunny. She . . . Just to hold on to. You might want to, when—

[RACHEL *exits, with the rabbit.* TEDDY *enters.*]

TEDDY Did Silly Bunny just—

JERRY She left.

TEDDY She didn't say goodbye.

[*Pause.*]

Great, now I get to be alone—stuck in a box with a crazy dinosaur. Easy for you, you just have to deal with an alcoholic wife and myocardial carcinoma. I got a xenoceratops in there with me! And he's crazy! Get off me, you crazy . . .

[*Beat.*]

Dinosaur.

JERRY I can't laugh.

TEDDY . . . And apparently I'm losing my touch.

[JERRY *reaches out, pulls* TEDDY *close to him.*]

No, no . . . no! This is not my job! Bunny! Silly Bunny! Come back here, you crazy rabbit! Get off me! Get off me, you crazy daddy!

[*They embrace.* JERRY *weeps on* TEDDY*'s shoulder.*]

This is not in my job description. It's ridiculous.

JERRY [*In his* TEDDY *voice.*] Get off me, you crazy daddy.

[JERRY *holds* TEDDY *close. Lights slowly out. End of play,*]

• • •

Before

Penny Jackson

Penny Jackson

Penny Jackson's plays include *Safe*, *I Know What Boys Want*, *Going Up*, and *Louise in Charlestown*. She is a recipient of a MacDowell Colony Fellowship, and her short story "L.A. Child" received a Pushcart Prize. Proud Member of the Dramatist Guild and the League of Professional Theatre Women.

... production history ...

Before was produced at the Atlantic Theater in New York City for Playwrights for a Cause on July 24, 2016. The cast included Peter Collier and was directed by Lori Kee. The evening of one-act plays was produced by Planet Connections Theatre.

characters

SCOTTIE a high school senior. An ordinary good-looking boy.

time

The present.

place

An American suburb.

act one

scene 1

[*Music: blur. There's no other way.* SCOTTIE, *an ordinary eighteen-year-old boy in a T-shirt and jeans, enters, carrying a bag. He adjusts a camera on a tripod.*]

SCOTTIE Josh, you freaked me out today and I need to record what the hell is happening because the facts are still messed up in my mind. My mom's always checking my computer, but I can hide this camera. So it's just you and me, dude.

When you texted me, "Hey bro, I have the answer to your problem," I thought you were coming over to help me with my college essay. But when you slammed the door and said, "We need to go down to the basement, like *now*," I thought what the fuck? I mean, you're the cool one, Josh, the one who never breaks a sweat, and here you were, acting all CIA with me.

[*Pause as* SCOTT *checks camera.*]

So where were we? Right. Down in my basement. You're checking it all out, as if you need to be sure no one is down there, like someone's really going to be hiding in the washing machine. "What's up?" I asked. You just shook your head and grinned.

"I got a present for you, Scottie. A present you'll find really useful."

You were carrying a shopping bag, Josh. A shopping bag from Abercrombie and Fitch and I thought are you going to give me a T-shirt. But you took out a Keds shoe box. Like, what the fuck are you doing with a Keds shoe box? Then you placed it on the Ping-Pong table and opened it and it's a gun.

A gun on the Ping-Pong table. At first I thought it was a toy. Like when we were kids, and my dad bought me this stupid toy gun from Mattel. But when you picked it up I knew it wasn't a toy anymore.

The first thing I thought of was my mom. She hates guns. I mean, she took a bus to D.C. to stand in a crowd for hours in one hundred-degree heat to protest about guns. She was glued to the TV during Newtown, sobbing every time they showed a picture of that school. Then I thought of Robin. The first time we kissed was in my basement, by the Ping-Pong table.

"What the fuck is this?" I asked. I didn't want to touch that gun or go anywhere near it.

"Didn't you tell me you wanted to kill Robin? I'm helping you out, man. That's what friends are for."

That was kind of an exaggeration. I did say at one point that Robin should die for what she did. But I was so messed up after all those shots at Jamie's party that I could have said anything.

"I didn't mean it. Do you really think I want to shoot her?"

I couldn't stop staring at the gun. It was black and shiny. I thought I smelled gunpowder. When you picked it up and placed it in my hand, I thought, Shit, this is the real thing, cold and hard and heavy. I can't remember what you told me. Something about buying it on Craigslist and this was going to help me figure out my "Robin problem." You yawned like you were bored, and started playing with a Ping-Pong paddle. Then my mom called and started walking downstairs, and that's the only reason I grabbed the gun and threw it in my backpack. You charmed my mom like you charm everyone and before I knew it you were gone.

"He's such a nice boy, that Josh Harrison." Jesus, my mom didn't have a fucking clue. I told her I had to study for my SATs and ran to my room and locked the door.

So here I am. Josh. The gun is still in my backpack. I've been thinking. I have some options here.

1. I could drive to the lake and throw it in.
2. I could tell Billy, who would have been scared shitless, which would not have been a bad thing since he's the one who fucked Robin. Too bad Billy is also my younger brother.
3. I could call my dad in New Hampshire, but since his new marriage, he doesn't really want to deal with me because he just inherited three new sons from his new wife, so let' s just say Dad is overwhelmed.
4. I could tell my mom, who would freak out and probably call the cops and throw me in jail and never speak to me again.

And you know what's the shittiest thing—I can't call you, Josh, my best friend, who got me into this whole friggin mess.

[SCOTTIE *unzips the bag and peeks in.*]

It's still there. Fuck. What should I do?

[*Fade out.*]

scene 2

[*Music. Kendrick Lamar's "U."* SCOTTIE *appears with a bottle of Johnny Walker Red. His hair is messed up and he is drunk.*]

SCOTTIE It's now 2 a.m. I'm wasted, dude. No way I can deal with this sober. So here's where we're at. Door's still locked. Bag right here. Took the gun out and just stared at it. Stared at it and stared at it until it became part of me, like another arm or leg. I was the gun and the gun was me. I could hear Billy upstairs with his friends Paul and Mick laughing, and I was pissed. Were they laughing at me? Were they joking about Robin? But again, could I really shoot my brother? He did fuck Robin.

But how can I kill Robin? I loved her. Still love her. When my parents were splitting up, she was there for me the whole time. When I broke my arm, she wouldn't leave the hospital and brought me Ben and Jerry ice cream. Have you ever been in love, Josh? Do you know how it feels when your heart just shatters? And seeing Billy every friggin day doesn't help.

I told my mom I was sick and couldn't eat dinner. I just kept looking at that gun and then I smoked some of the weed that Robin gave me for my birthday. Then I started on this bottle of Johnny Walker that I stole from my dad's house, not because I wanted the booze but because I wanted to take something from him that he loved. And I don't know if you remember, but my dad loves Johnny Walker.

So this is the plan. I'm heading over to Robin's house. This has to be resolved now. I wonder what she'll say when she sees the gun? Stay tuned, dude. You started this mess, and let's see who gets to clean it up.

[*Fade out.*]

scene 3

[*Music: Blur's "Song 2." Three in the morning.* SCOTTIE *is wearing a leather jacket and looks terrified.*]

SCOTTIE Shit!

So I was outside at Robin's house on her front lawn and I called her from my cell phone. She showed up pretty fast.

"Jesus, Scott. Do you want my dad to crucify me? You know I have a curfew."

Robin's dad has loose fists. That's why Robin's mom split to Mexico. She begged Robin to follow but Robin wanted to stay because of me. What a joke.

"Robin, we need to talk." We stood under her porch light, Robin in a blue nightgown, her blond hair blowing in the wind. Her beauty really hurt me. I thought if I shot her in the face, she wouldn't be so beautiful anymore.

The gun was in the left pocket of my leather jacket, the same leather jacket Robin gave me for my birthday last year. It doesn't smell like leather but of her shampoo, since she liked to lean her head against my shoulder.

"I told you, babe, I'm sorry. I was drunk and I shouldn't have gone with Billy but I did. I'm bad. I'm screwed up. You're too good for me."

Everything Robin told me is true. Her parents are really head cases. Her dad hits her and her mom slept with half the fire department. Maybe her fucking my brother was Robin's way of telling me to stay away. And I should have stayed away. But I didn't.

It was dark, but then a car passed by and I saw Robin's face in the light and I thought she smiled. That made me do it. And she sure as hell wasn't smiling when she saw the gun.

"Oh, Scottie, no, no, no!"

Robin started moaning, and instead of running away, she fell to the ground and started clinging to my legs.

"Don't kill me. Please don't kill me. Please, please, please. Oh God. Oh God!"

That's how I finally understood. I used to be powerless. But the gun is everything. The gun takes over.

I watched Robin rock back and forth, making these weird wailing noises, this is what went through my head:

Do I really want to kill my girlfriend?

What about college and my dreams of working at the Olympics?

As for jail, well who wants to spend the rest of his life in a cell with a bunch of crazy psycho murderers?

But I would be a psycho murderer too.

But, man, that gun, it gave me a jolt. Holding that gun, seeing Robin practically melting, gave me a hard-on.

"Please, Scottie. I'll do anything," she said again and again. "Anything you want."

And I knew she would. She would do anything. That's the power of a gun. A blow job right there. Robin would have probably let me fuck her too. Anything so I wouldn't shoot her. That's why no one should have a gun.

Because I'm basically a good guy, a nice guy who was hurt by his girlfriend. I'm not someone who wants to kill. I'm not like those monsters at Columbine. Josh, you know me. I'm just a normal high school senior who loves soccer and pizza and *Star Wars* and so wishes his girlfriend hadn't fucked his brother. As I watched Robin, who was just crying and crying, I considered my options.

1. I shoot Robin and end up in prison for the rest of my life.
2. I shoot Robin and escape detection and the police think it's a random robbery.
3. I shoot Robin and then I shoot myself and the papers will call it a lovers' suicide pact.
4. I shoot Robin and Billy, and then drive to New Hampshire to shoot my dad, his new wife, and his three new stepsons. A real family massacre.

So which number did I choose?

[*Pause.*]

I told Robin that the gun was fake. A toy. That I just wanted to scare her. I watched her run back into her house.

Me?

I fell down on the lawn.

Then I puked all over my new sneakers.

[*Beat.* SCOTTIE *takes off his leather jacket. Adjusts the camera.*]

Today I wouldn't speak to you at assembly. I didn't speak to Robin either. She stayed far away from me and looked so grateful I didn't kill her. Robin won't tell anyone. She is that fucking terrified. You don't even care. You asked, "What's up, dude," like you had no idea what you gave me yesterday. You probably forgot all about it. But I didn't.

Now I look in the mirror, I think, I could be James Holmes, Aurora, Colorado. If I shoot one person, it's so easy to shoot another.
And another.
A movie theater. A school.
A whole town.

Before you gave me the gun, I was different. Will I ever be me again?

I can't get rid of this fucking thing. Every time I pick it up, I put it right down. I keep the gun in my soccer bag.

[*Picks up soccer bag.*]

Here it is.

Couldn't sleep at all. I woke up in the middle of the night, screaming till my throat's raw.

[SCOTTIE *exits to Nirvana's "Smells Like Teen Spirit."*]

• • •

Magnolia Blossoms: A Civil War Melodrama,

Episode 1: “If Tomorrow Never Comes . . . Until Today”

Angela C. Hall

Angela C. Hall

Angela C. Hall is a playwright/performer/dramaturg/college instructor who currently works at the University of Georgia as a writing coach for the Institute of Women's Studies, and as an instructor with the Writing Intensive Program, a multidisciplinary program that focuses on the critical-thinking skills required for effective academic writing. Her one-act play, *Green-light*, produced by Rising Sun Performance Co., recently ran off-off-Broadway in New York City, and was nominated for a New York Innovative Theatre Award for Best Original Short Play. Her one-act play *Wife Shop* was published August 2013 in *The Best American Short Plays 2011–2012* and has received productions across the country. Hall has received a prestigious grant from the Wilson Center for Arts and Humanities to develop *The Pregnant Tree*, an epic that explores white-face minstrelsy and the traumatic history of lynching in the American South.

... production history ...

Magnolia Blossoms began as a workshop piece at APW (Athens Playwright's Workshop) in February 2014. It received a number of workshops and readings at APW from March to May 2015. *Magnolia Blossoms* received a staged reading at Spotlight on the Arts festival in Athens, Georgia, November 2014. Magnolia Blossoms was produced as part of the New Play Festival at University of Georgia in March–April 2016 as part of its 2015–2016 season.

characters

MISS EULA JASPER

JESSE JANE

MASSA DAVISON

SELMA

STAGEHAND

scene 1

[STAGEHAND *enters with three placards. He raises the first, which reads, "Magnolia Blossoms: An Antebellum (or Civil War.) Soap Opera." Then the second, which reads, "Episode 1: If Tomorrow Ever Comes . . . After Today." Finally, the third, "The Big House, May 1862."* STAGEHAND *exits. Curtains open to soap opera-y music, melodramatic strings.* MISS EULA *rests on a davenport. She is writhing and rubbing her hands over her body.* JASPER, *a slave, stands over her.*]

EULA Oh, Jasper! My insides are on fire. I'm scorching, burning alive! Kiss me, please! Before I die right here where I lay.

JASPER I cannot kiss you.

[JASPER *walks away.*]

I can never kiss you again.

[EULA *rises and grabs* JASPER *from behind, throwing her arms around his chest.*]

EULA Do not so mercilessly tease me.

JASPER I do not tease.

EULA Why do you insist on torturing me so? I will drop dead right here, I swear it.

[JASPER *dramatically turns and grasps her shoulders in his hands.*]

JASPER Did you not hear me? We can no longer be!

[EULA *opens her bodice.*]

EULA Look upon these breasts. They are yours for the taking.

[JASPER *gazes at* EULA*'s breasts.*]

JASPER Put them away.

EULA They are yours!

[JASPER *gazes for a couple of seconds, but then turns his back.*]

JASPER I will not be tempted by your . . . whiteness.

[EULA *runs after him, hugging him from behind.*]

EULA Is it your wish that I die? Do you want to see me dead, Jasper?

[JASPER *suddenly turns around, and holds* EULA *away from him.*]

JASPER Massa Davison is back, Eula.

[EULA *suddenly backs away, stunned by the revelation.*]

EULA What?

JASPER When I went down to pick up the small ration of flour from the Dixons, they said they'd seen him in town. He's hurt, though. Real bad.

EULA It cannot be!

[JESSE JANE, JASPER*'s younger sister, enters.*]

JESSE JANE It is, Misses! Massa Davison long thought dead weren't dead at all! Seen him with my own eyes.

EULA When?

JESSE JANE Just now.

EULA Where?

JESSE JANE In the courtyard.

[EULA *straightens her clothes and buttons her bodice. She goes to window, looks down.* JASPER *and* JESSE JANE *stand behind her.*]

EULA I don't see anybody, just a man—in a wheelchair—with a bandaged-up face.

JESSE JANE Oh, that's him, Misses.

[*They all give a shocked, expressive, stylized look, as if in close-up on a TV soap opera. Their poses freeze, accompanied by dramatic music.*]

scene 2

[STAGEHAND *walks onstage, placard reads, "He's Alive!!!"* JASPER *pushes* MASSA DAVISON*'s wheelchair into the parlor.* DAVISON *has a blanket covering him from waist down. His face is wrapped in heavy gauze-like bandages, only his lips and eyes are visible.*]

DAVISON I'm home, Eula! By God, I made it back to you.

EULA But clearly not in one piece. Your legs, Davison. Where are your legs?

DAVISON They were blown off in the war.

EULA The war? What war?

DAVISON The Civil War.

EULA I've not heard from you going on a year. When you left here you said you was going to get fitted for a new waistcoat. Not to fight in the war.

DAVISON Yes, my dear, and I did secure the waistcoat, a fine burgundy velveteen with satiny lapels. But when I saw the suffering of the men in the infirmaries—

EULA In the infirmaries? What were you doing in the infirm—?

[*Holds up his hand.*]

DAVISON Let me speak, Eula. I could not in good conscience watch them die alone.

EULA That is certainly admirable, but—

DAVISON I have a duty to this land, and to our home.

EULA I suppose.

[*Beat.*]

And what about your . . . your face?

[EULA *comes closer, reaches her hand to touch him, but* DAVISON *whirls his wheelchair around, away from* EULA.]

DAVISON Don't look at me. I am ugly.

EULA You are not ugly. You're a beautiful man . . . with no legs . . . and thin lips that cut like razors when you kiss me . . . and skinny fingers, not like Jasper

[*Looks to* JASPER.]

and his full lips that could swallow a woman's—mouth whole—and thick, sturdy fingers . . . and broad shoulders—

DAVISON Oh, Eula, it was the most horrible, wretched time. And only thoughts of you kept me alive. Getting back to your pure, lily white skin and your supple white breasts, and your innocent perfectly pouty pink lips that speak words that drip with honey and—sweet cream—and sugar—and warm maple syrup poured copiously over a stack of hot buttered biscuits, and—

[JASPER *clears his throat, intentionally interrupting* DAVISON*'s soliloquy.*]

EULA You were always a poet. It is what snared my heart.

DAVISON We shall begin our lives anew, sweetheart.

EULA Yes!

[*Beat.*]

But first, I have a surprise for you, darling.

DAVISON I need nothing more than your lovely face.

EULA Yes, but this is the most marvelous surprise. Jesse! Jesse Jane!

[JESSE JANE *enters with a baby, wrapped in a blanket. She hands the baby to* EULA, *but* DAVISON *is more interested in* JESSE JANE *than the bundle of joy she carries.*]

DAVISON Jesse Jane. My, my, my. Jesse Jane. Are you not a sight for sore eyes. A pure vision for raw and aching eyes.

[JASPER *and* EULA *look from one to another as* JESSE JANE *and* DAVISON *clearly share a moment.*]

EULA That will be all, Jesse.

[JESSE JANE *exits.* DAVISON*'s eyes follow her out of the room.* EULA *grasps* DAVISON*'s bandaged face and literally turns it away from* JESSE JANE. EULA, *turning attention back to* DAVISON.]

Did you not hear me? Allow me to introduce you to our son.

DAVISON I have a son?

EULA Yes, darling. A son. Take him. Gaze upon his face.

[EULA *gently places the baby in* DAVISON*'s arms. He nearly fumbles the child.*]

DAVISON Damn this wretched body! I am no good! I cannot raise a son from this chair.

EULA We will raise him together.

[DAVISON *finally looks down at the baby.*]

DAVISON But you deserve so much more, a man who can satisfy and do so much—

[DAVISON *stops mid-sentence, staring down at the baby. Beat.*]

Well, he is awfully—brown.

[*Looking up at* JASPER.]

As brown as Jasper here.

JASPER [*Nods, looking over* DAVISON*'s shoulder as he too peers at the baby.*] I'd say so.

EULA Jasper had to deliver him for me. Selma was so ill that day, and Jesse had to tend to her, so—

DAVISON Jasper's seen your—private parts?

JASPER Oh yes, I've seen 'em, Massa.

EULA Only to deliver the baby.

JASPER And they are as purely white as you claim.

EULA Jasper!

JASPER White as snow.

DAVISON I will not be mocked. I am the master of this house! I must walk again!

EULA But you have no legs!

DAVISON I will walk, I tell you. I am still a man! A man with a heart and a steely resolve! I will walk.

[DAVISON *hands the baby to* EULA.]

Jasper, wheel me into the courtyard.

[JASPER *and* DAVISON *exit, leaving* EULA *desperately clutching the baby.*]

EULA Oh, my beautiful molasses baby. What ever will we do? We must see Selma straightaway. She will have the answers. She alone predicted this travesty. She will now show us ways to undo it. She is blind, but she sees, molasses baby, she sees. There is hope yet!

[EULA *runs excitedly from the room.*]

scene 3
Slave Quarters

[STAGEHAND *walks onstage with two placards. The first reads, "Slave Quarters." The second reads, "The Ubu."* SELMA *sits in a wooden rocking chair,* JASPER *at her side.*]

JASPER You should've seen her face, Mama. White as a ghost!

SELMA They're always white as ghosts. Now, get me some sticks or rocks or something. She'll be down here soon.

JASPER Well, which?

SELMA It don't matter.

[SELMA *dons a head scarf and a tattered apron as* JASPER *comes back with a stack of twigs.*]

JASPER Didn't see no decent-looking rocks.

SELMA These will do. Put 'em over in that jar. Now, Jasper. You mustn't laugh.

JASPER It is so hard, Mama.

SELMA White folks fear what they don't understand. And that fear has kept us pretty safe here, safer than most others in our lot. We can't mess that up. Or they will separate us. And ship you and sister to God knows where.

[SELMA *rises.*]

Now, give me my blind walking stick.

[SELMA *moves to a table. She leans on the walking stick.*]

Where's Jesse?

JASPER She's up at the house.

[*There's a knock at the door.*]

EULA Selma! Selma?!

[SELMA *takes a moment, to gather herself, preparing for the "performance."*]

Selma, you in there?!

[SELMA *then nods for* JASPER *to open the door.*]

SELMA Yes. I am.

[EULA *enters, distraught and disheveled.*]

I was expecting you, Miss Eula.

EULA You were?

SELMA Yes'm.

[EULA *sits in a chair opposite* SELMA.]

EULA You were right yet again, Selma. That wind you said was gonna blow in, has blown.

[SELMA *stares quizzically.*]

You know what you said to me about the coming hard winds that was gonna shake the ground and unbury the dead.

SELMA Yes, yes. That wind.

EULA Well, it has come. In the form of my long-thought-dead husband.

SELMA I felt it.

EULA You did?

SELMA Yes. Plain as I'm sittin' here.

EULA What am I gonna do? Tell me what you see, Selma. I need your wise, mysterious, magical Negro words.

SELMA Jasper, bring me—

[*Pauses for dramatic effect.*]

the sticks.

JASPER No, not the sticks, Mammy!

EULA [*Frightened.*] The sticks?!

SELMA The Ubu sticks. I only use them in the most desperate time.

EULA The Ubu sticks?

[JASPER *brings over the jar of twigs.*]

SELMA Now sit here, Missy.

[SELMA *spreads the sticks out onto the table, arranging and rearranging them arbitrarily to feign a serious endeavor.*]

Stand at her side in case she—falls.

EULA Oh my God!

JASPER I will catch you.

EULA I know you will, Jasper. You have always—caught me.

[JASPER *stands at* EULA*'s side.* SELMA *waves her hand over the sticks.* SELMA *suddenly draws in a deep breath. She mumbles some nonsensical words and sounds.*]

SELMA Are you looking at these sticks?! Turn your head. Don't look on the sticks 'til I tell ya. Close your eyes, Missy, or they will burn like hell fire.

[EULA *tightly closes her eyes.* SELMA *grins, amused by the ruse.* JASPER *stifles a laugh. Beat.*]

Open your eyes. One at a time. Slowly. And look down on the Ubu.

[*Beat.*]

Now blow! Blow on these sticks, Missy! Hard as you can!

[EULA *blows on the sticks.*]

Blow!

[EULA *blows again.*]

Blow harder, Missy! It's got to come from the depths of your soul. Now, BLOW, Missy!

[EULA *blows until nearly out of breath.* SELMA *rests. She studies the sticks.*]

EULA [*Anxiously.*] What the sticks say?

SELMA [*Shaking her head.*] Oh, it is not good.

EULA What is it, Selma?

SELMA The sticks say you must climb the ladder.

EULA [*Frightened.*] The ladder? What ladder?

[*Beat.*]

SELMA Jacob's Ladder.

EULA Jacob's Ladder?

SELMA Yes.

EULA How do I do that?

SELMA When the cock crows three times toward the east and two times toward the west and the moon sinks beneath the clouds on the tenth day. That is when you must drink from the gourd of death and life.

EULA What? What do you mean, Selma? What does it mean?

SELMA If you do not, the blood is gonna run down the walls of your house like water from a stream. I have seen it. The Ubu has shown it to me.

EULA I do not comprehend your enchantment. You must make it plain. Make it plain, Selma.

[SELMA *speaks in a loud and thunderous voice that shakes* EULA.]

SELMA The Ubu has spoken!!

[SELMA, *seemingly spent, collapses her head onto the table.*]

EULA Selma?! Oh, what has the Ubu done?

JASPER She'll be fine. When she uses the sticks, they drain her energy.

EULA But I must know what she means.

JASPER We may have to leave this place. You, me, and the baby.

EULA I cannot.

JASPER Then you must find Jacob's Ladder before it is too late.

EULA Will you help me, Jasper? Help me find Jacob's Ladder, and I will climb it. I will climb it like I climbed the magnolia trees in my grandmother's backyard when I was just a little girl. We will find it together. Oh, Jasper!

[*The two collapse into each other's arms.*]

scene 4

[STAGEHAND *enters with placard that reads, "MEANWHILE, back at the Big House . . ."* DAVISON *sits in his wheelchair facing* JESSE JANE, *who sits on the davenport.*]

DAVISON You will love me again.

JESSE JANE I would've had to love you before to love you again. I did not love you before. I do not love you now.

DAVISON You are saying this because I am half a man.

JESSE JANE That's as good a reason as any, I suppose.

DAVISON But, Jesse Jane, nothing but thoughts of you kept me alive. Getting back to you and your dark skin

[*Touching her lips with his bandaged hands.*]

and these perfectly plump lips that sing songs of freedom and hum Negro spirituals that drip like dark roast coffee from the mountains of Brazil. And, dear God, the sweet smell of your breath like cocoa from the . . . the . . . cocoa plant.

[*Picking up her hands. He cannot grip them as he'd like.*]

Damn these hands straight to hell!

[*But he finally places her hands between his bandaged hands. He speaks as he kisses each finger.*]

And these hard dark hands and slim fingers that pick cotton from sun up to sun down, these strong legs that wrap around me like a gnarled magnolia tree branch. . . . Oh, my sweet Jesus! Kiss me, Jesse Jane! Kiss me! Make me live again!

[*He tries to lean in to kiss* JESSE JANE. JESSE JANE *holds up her hand.*]

JESSE JANE No. Stop.

[*Beat.*]

You don't have legs. I need a man with legs. And your face is all . . . messed up.

DAVISON Then I will get me some legs. And a new face. No matter the cost! No matter the journey. I will go inside the bowels of this very earth. I will have legs and a face, and you will long to have me near you again.

[DAVISON *rolls toward the door, bumping the doorjamb a few times as he unsuccessfully tries to maneuver it out of the room. Tired of watching the pathetic scene,* JESSE JANE *comes over to push the chair through the door, but—*]

Unhand this rolling chair! Do not take pity on me. I am a man! I do not require your assistance.

[*A few more bumps.*]

Goddamit to hell!

[*He finally gets through the door. Now safely on the other side of the door . . .*]

You will love me again, Jesse Jane!

[*After* DAVISON *exits,* JESSE JANE *doubles over in laughter.*]

scene 5

[STAGEHAND *walks onstage with a placard that reads: "THE NEXT MORNING."*]

[JASPER, JESSE JANE, SELMA, EULA *(who is holding the baby) are all gathered in the parlor.*]

EULA I will find that ladder, Selma. Do not count me out.

SELMA I know you will. You is a fine climber.

EULA [*Sudden confidence.*] I am, aren't I, Selma? Ever since I was a little girl, I climbed . . . chairs and tables and curtains.

[DAVISON *rolls into the parlor.*]

Why have you called us all here, darling?

DAVISON I have gathered you because it is time.

EULA Time for what?

[*Dramatic music.*]

DAVISON To remove the bandages.

EULA Are you sure?

DAVISON Yes. I am. Jasper. Hand me the shears.

[JASPER *gives the scissors to* DAVISON. *They all look intently, anxiously as* DAVISON *awkwardly grips the shears, after a few seconds of struggle . . .*]

Jasper, if you would so kindly oblige me in this endeavor. I would be most appreciative.

JASPER Yes, suh, Massa.

[*In a display of absolute absurdity, the two men together slowly cut away, then unwrap* DAVISON*'s bandages.* JASPER *steps away as* DAVISON *removes the final layer of gauze. His back is to the audience so that the audience does not see the unwrapped face, only the other players see* DAVISON*'s face. They all have equal looks of horror when the face is finally revealed.* EULA *faints.* JASPER *catches the baby. Forgetting that she is supposed to be blind,* SELMA *has the most audible response.*]

SELMA Good Sweet Lord in Heaven! What evil has wrought this ghastly beast?

[*They all look at her. She goes back to a state of "blindness."*]

I mean, what he look like? Somebody tell me what he look like.

[*Melodramatic, cliff-hanger music plays as their faces freeze in repulsion.*]

• • •

Certain Unexplainable Events

Cody Daigle-Orians

Cody Daigle-Orians

Cody Daigle-Orians is a Louisiana-born playwright now living in Hartford, Connecticut. His work has been produced and developed at the Astoria Performing Arts Center, New Jersey Repertory Theatre, the Actors Company Theatre (NYC), the Playhouse Tulsa, the Growing Stage, SNAP! Productions (Omaha), Gadfly Theatre (Minneapolis), StageRIGHT (Seattle), and Prologue Theatre Company (Chicago).

... production history ...

Certain Unexplainable Events was produced as part of the 2016 Third Annual Los Angeles Science Fiction One-Act Play Festival. The play was directed by David Dean Botrell. The cast was as follows:

THE ONE WHO SAW IT Amber Montana

THE ONE WHO DIDN'T GO Conner Scott

THE ONE IN HER CAR Cece Paige

MICHAEL J. T. Neal

The play was produced at the Acme Theatre in Los Angeles, May 5–29, 2016.

characters

THE ONE WHO SAW IT female 17

THE ONE WHO DIDN'T GO male 18

THE ONE IN HER CAR female 18

MICHAEL male 18

time

The present.

place

A suburban city in the Midwest.

[*Four actors. Four areas. The actors are aware of each other, but they do not interact (until the very end). They speak to us.*]

THE ONE WHO SAW IT I don't know if you think about life, like, in any kind of . . . real way. You know, like, really thinking about it. You know, like, how getting up in the morning is, on one hand, this totally nothing sort of thing. But on the other, it's like . . . the most dangerous thing you can do. You know?

[*A silence.*]

The night it happened, my mom and I had this fight. It was completely stupid. You know. She was upset because we'd made this agreement, apparently. (I don't remember this. Like, I seriously don't recall this conversation we supposedly had.) This agreement that Wednesdays were going to be "family nights"—like anyone actually has those anymore, you know?—and we were going to, like, eat dinner together and sit in the living room and watch a movie or something, talk to each other and completely ignore the fact that we all have individual lives, you know? Or whatever.

So this was really important to do on Wednesdays, apparently. And this conversation where she told me this—this conversation I don't remember having. At. All.—this conversation included a mention that we were starting to do this last Wednesday.

And last Wednesday I wasn't home. I was with Michael.

So my mom and I were having this fight. And I was like, "I don't remember talking to you." And she was like, "You willfully ignore things I say." And I was like, "No. I just don't remember us having this conversation." And she was like, "You were wearing your maroon top." As if that is going to somehow make me remember this conversation. And I'm like, "What maroon top?" And she was like, "Now you're just being belligerent." And I feel like I went to bed in this world I understood and woke up in some other place entirely, with this woman who thinks I'd wear maroon.

So I'm trying to explain to my mom that I'm not being belligerent, that I'm really not remembering that we'd talked about family night, and my iPhone lights up, and it makes the little text noise, and I just check it, you know? Like, no big deal. I got a text. I'll check it. And it was Michael. And my mom is, like, offended that I checked my phone in the middle of her yelling at me, as if I'd somehow broken some kind of rule of good manners, and she's like, "Who is it?' And I really don't want to answer, because, you know, she's already mad, and mentioning Michael is just going to get her more mad, and I'd like to not get lectured for another half hour, so I say, "Grace. It was Grace." And she stares at me for a second, and goes, "It was Michael, wasn't it?" And I was like, in my head, "OH MY GOD! If you weren't going to believe me, why did you ask me?" But I say, "No, it was Grace. She had a question about our civics homework." And she goes, "You had civics homework you haven't done yet?" And I'm thinking, "OH MY

GOD. SHOOT ME NOW. PLEASE. JUST PUT ME OUT OF MY MISERY."

THE ONE WHO DIDN'T GO Anything the human mind can imagine must therefore exist somewhere in the universe. Aristotle.

Maybe. Maybe not. I don't know. I think it was a Greek philosopher. Not the exact wording. But that's the idea. I think it was Aristotle.

We always talked a lot about that. You know, we were kinda like obsessed with the thought that anything we could imagine—anything, from, like, the weirdest little mutation at the cellular level to these epic, like, universes that are completely unlike the one we inhabit—anything we could imagine was real someplace.

Like. Okay. Close your eyes. Right now. And imagine the weirdest combination of animals you could. Like, okay, imagine a snake crossed with a buffalo crossed with a pterodactyl. And the whole thing's green. No. Orange.

Okay. You imagined it. So . . .

Somewhere in the universe, that big orange thing you just saw in your head is flying around or doing whatever it does.

I mean. That's the theory. The general idea, maybe not a theory. But, like, that's cool. You know? I tell Michael all the time, it's cool because maybe we're not just imagining things that already exist. Maybe our imagining it conjures it into existence. So, like, somewhere, some creature or God or whatever imagined us, and poof! There we are, and we're sitting here in my bedroom imagining worlds into existence somewhere else. Like, poof! There they are.

It was a cool thought, and he'd bring it up a lot, yeah. But I always thought it was just because it was this cool thing we'd thought about together. You know?

I didn't think he was . . . serious or anything.

So I was watching this documentary on Netflix about these Japanese dolphin killers in this cove or whatever, and it was awesome. Like, sad, but awesome. And I get this text from Michael. And it was like 9:30 and I was thinking, "You know, uh, little late to be wanting to do something." Because my dad had, like, put a moratorium on me being out of the house after 9. There was this, like, serial car tire slasher situation going on. Remember? And he was concerned it would "escalate." Like, how? How does tire slashing "escalate"?

Offtrack. Michael texts me, and he's like, "Tonight. 10:30. I'm doing it."

And I'm like, "Okay then, good for you doing it, whatever it is," and I text him back saying, "Can't. Curfew. What 'it' are you doing?"

And I wait for a couple minutes, and I don't hear anything from him. So I think he's probably drunk or something. Michael's not a teenage alcoholic or anything, but, you know, when his parents are out of town he gets into the whiskey. So I texted Sarah and said, "You should check on Michael. He seems weird."

And I went back to watching my documentary. It was cool. They wanted to get this footage of the dolphin killing going on in this secret cove, so they smuggled these cameras into the area disguised as rocks and they even hired divers to secretly dive in this cove and put microphones in the water and all this. You know it's like, "Yo, I get that you want to make a movie and all that, but, my God, that's like . . . dedication."

THE ONE IN THE CAR He didn't dump me. He didn't.

It was a completely mutual thing. He was just being really weird all the time. And I was trying not to get another disappointing score on the ACT. And he would just come over to my house with all these drawings of things. These, like, totally weird drawings of wormholes or whatever. And he'd say things like," I want to go through one." And he'd shove this drawing in my face of this little stick figure with glasses (Michael wears glasses) getting sucked up into this tornado-looking thing that branches off into this drawing on another page he'd hold up beside it that connected our street to like . . . I don't know . . . Saturn or something. And he'd look at me like I was supposed to agree with him or tell him I thought it was cool. And I was always like, "Michael . . . stop watching Syfy."

I just wanted him to be serious, you know. We were graduating in two months and he'd only taken the ACT once. And he got a 23. Which isn't bad. But it's not good. And I would ask him, "What colleges are you applying to?" And he'd go, "I haven't." Like, yeah. He hadn't applied to anywhere. Not even like the technical college. Nothing. He was just . . . not being serious. And I never thought I'd marry the guy, but, you know, he'd have to come over and have dinner with me and my parents and he'd be kind of embarrassing. My dad's like, you know, serious business, and Michael's all, "Oh you want to see my picture of a tear in the fabric of the universe?" And I'd get this look from my dad, like totally, "WTF?"

So I told him how I was feeling and he said if I wanted to break up he'd understand. And I said, "Do you want to break up?" And he said, "I guess." So . . . it was mutual. Okay? He didn't dump me. We just . . . stopped.

So it's technically not weird that I was sitting in my car across the street from his house. I live on that street, too. And I was taking the ACT the next day, and I was kind of nervous, and I just wanted to . . . I don't know . . . talk to him. Because even thought he was weird and all, he was still, like . . . someone who made me feel better. Less . . . worried.

But I was scared, you know. I didn't want to look like some pathetic ex-girlfriend and I'd heard he'd gone out on a date with Sarah Ollerman last Wednesday, and if he was seeing her, I didn't want to look like I was trying to break them up. I mean, I don't like Sarah or anything, but I'm not a . . . you know, I'm not that.

And then I get this text message from Michael. Like, how freaky is that? "Tonight. 10:30. I'm doing it." And I'm sitting there thinking, "Okay, does he see me sitting out here in my car?" And I'm kind of freaking out, and then I get another text message from him, and it's like, "Hey. Sorry. Last one wasn't meant for you."

And I just sort of sit there for a bit, waiting for another one. You know, like, maybe he's going to ask me how I'm doing. Because we hadn't really spoken or seen each other or even, like, commented on each other's Facebook stuff since we broke up. And I thought . . . I don't know. Maybe he'd want to know how I am.

I waited.

He didn't send another text message.

THE ONE WHO SAW IT So, I finally settled all that crap about family night with my mom and I get to my phone and I see that Eric has texted me, too.

I read Michael's: "Tonight. 10:30. I'm doing it."

I read Eric's: "You should check on Michael. He seems weird."

And it's strange, because I don't really know how I knew, but the second I read Eric's text message I knew exactly what Michael was going to do at 10:30. And honestly, it seems completely crazy that my mind would go there right away, as if that was the only obvious answer to the question, but it did.

And it freaked me out.

So, I texted Eric back and said, "Has he called you?"

THE ONE WHO DIDN'T GO Sarah texts me back and asks if he's called me. I text her back and say, "No. But you should call him."

It's not that I don't like her. I do. But I don't see why they're together. You know, I sort of understood why he was with Becca, because she has her life together and all that. But this girl . . . I don't know. She just seems . . .

Like you know when two people are just enough alike that they make the worst parts of how they're alike worse? Yeah, that's this girl and Michael.

THE ONE WHO SAW IT I texted Michael. "Call me." I waited. Nothing.

I called Michael. He didn't answer. I called him again. He didn't answer. I called Eric.

THE ONE WHO DIDN'T GO I let it ring.

THE ONE WHO SAW IT I called Michael again and this time I left a message. "Hey. It's me. Call me. I . . . you're not doing the thing we talked about on Wednesday, are you?

Nothing for a few minutes. Then a text message from Michael: "Yes."

THE ONE IN THE CAR I guess I just fell asleep. I wasn't really sitting there building up the courage to talk to him anymore. I just . . . didn't want to go home. So I guess I just dozed off or something, and I guess, I don't know, forty-five minutes go by and all of a sudden I wake up—not from anything, just wake up all of a sudden—and there's Michael standing outside my car, looking at me.

I totally freaked out. I mean, like, I screamed and I jumped, and my heart was pounding. (Because, like, you seriously don't want to wake up in your car in the middle of the street in the middle of the evening with some person standing outside your driver's side window.) And he just stands there with this little smirk on his face. And I am horrified. Totally embarrassed. And he motions for me to roll down my window. And I do. And he says, "Can you drive me somewhere?"

He had his backpack, and I was like, "I'm not driving you to Sarah Ollerman's house, if that's where you need to go, because that would be really rude of you to ask." And he says, "No, that's not where I'm going. She's meeting me someplace." And I'm like, "Oh, so you want me to drive you to meet your new girlfriend now? Is that what we're doing?" And he's like, "I'm not going to meet her. She'll just be there, I think. And you're the one sitting outside my house in your car."

Ouch.

So, I ask him, "What are you doing anyway?" And he gets this really weird look on his face. "If I tell you, you won't drive me." And I'm like, "Okay, well, honestly Michael, that makes me not want to drive you wherever you're going either." And he's like, "It's nothing bad. You just won't believe in it."

Believe in it?

THE ONE WHO SAW IT So, it's like 10 o'clock, and I think my parents are in bed, or at least they're in their room upstairs so they won't be a problem. And I sneak out and head toward Michael's house.

On the way, I text Eric: "If he comes to your house, make sure you don't let him leave."

THE ONE WHO DIDN'T GO Sarah texts me this totally weird dramatic text, and I'm like, "Oh God. Now I'm going to be stuck in the middle of some ridiculous crap with Michael and this new girl." I mean, Becca was uptight and whatever, but she wasn't drama, you know?

I didn't text Sarah back.

THE ONE IN THE CAR So I tell Michael, "No, I'm not bringing you wherever you're going. And you know what, you could have, like, asked how I was when you texted me earlier. Like, cared about how I was doing. I have the ACT tomorrow. You know? Like, I'm really nervous and you just want me to drive you someplace? And . . ."

And he walked off. Like. I'm not kidding. Just, in the middle of my sentence, he just . . . walked off. Who does that?

THE ONE WHO SAW IT It was like, 10:15 and I got to Michael's house and Becca is sitting in her car across the street, crying. Which is totally weird because she's his ex-girlfriend and everything. And she looks up and we make eye contact and there's this second or whatever, and then she starts crying harder.

THE ONE IN THE CAR Like, seriously? Okay, so fine, universe. You want to make me feel completely miserable? Fine. You win. This girl shows up and sees me across the street from my ex-boyfriend's house. Crying. Thank you, universe. Thank. You.

THE ONE WHO SAW IT I go over to her.

THE ONE IN THE CAR She comes over to me. Great . . .

THE ONE WHO SAW IT Can you drive me someplace?

THE ONE IN THE CAR YOU'VE GOT TO BE KIDDING ME!

THE ONE WHO SAW IT Michael's in trouble.

THE ONE IN THE CAR This girl is, like . . . the kind of girl you're pretty sure isn't a virgin anymore. And you're pretty sure she hasn't been one in, like . . . a while. And she's always telling people these ridiculous stories about her life, you know, like she supposedly has this awful home life, but her dad's like a pastor and her mom teaches first grade and they live in this beautiful house. I mean . . . beautiful. And she acts like she grew up on the means streets of somewhere, you know.

But, like, when she said to me that Michael was in trouble . . . I've never believed this girl in my whole life and right then, I was like, "Oh man. Michael's in trouble."

THE ONE WHO DIDN'T GO So I don't hear anything for a while. And it's like, 10:20. So I text Michael again: "Yo. Whassup?" And within twenty seconds, he calls me.

MICHAEL You there yet?

THE ONE WHO DIDN'T GO Where?

MICHAEL You know where.

THE ONE WHO DIDN'T GO Uh . . . no, dude, I don't.

MICHAEL "That's too bad. I won't get to say goodbye.

THE ONE WHO DIDN'T GO Oh yeah? Where you going?

MICHAEL In person anyway. I'd rather it in person. Bye, Eric.

THE ONE WHO DIDN'T GO And he just hung up. That was it.

I didn't know what the hell he was talking about.

THE ONE WHO SAW IT The drive was awkward.

THE ONE IN THE CAR Ohmygod. So awkward.

THE ONE WHO SAW IT We didn't talk.

THE ONE IN THE CAR She only said anything when she was giving directions.

THE ONE WHO SAW IT "Left on Blue Dock.

THE ONE IN THE CAR I wanted to ask her.

THE ONE WHO SAW IT Please don't ask. Please don't ask.

THE ONE IN THE CAR I didn't.

THE ONE WHO SAW IT When you get to the gas station on Plymouth take a right.

[MICHAEL *moves downstage center. He takes his backpack off, sets it on the ground. From it he produces a binder overflowing with drawings—the drawings Becca spoke of earlier. He also produces a flashlight. He studies the drawings on the ground.*]

THE ONE WHO DIDN'T GO I feel kind of stupid, because I should have figured it out right then. But you know . . . I didn't. Like, I didn't . . .

Had we talked about it? Yeah. Of course we did. We talked about it. But, like, we also talked about the possibilities of time travel as they related to how we'd make sure that Mr. Porotoli wouldn't decide to be a teacher so he wouldn't be teaching us English so he wouldn't bore us to death. I mean, it was never serious or anything. Never. For me anyway. It's like, we'd watch *Doctor Who* or whatever crap they were playing on Syfy and we'd talk about weird crap and it was just . . . how we were friends.

Like . . .

It was never something we meant for real.

THE ONE IN THE CAR So there's this old parking tower downtown that's about to get torn down. They're going to replace it with an office tower or something because they built a bigger parking tower in another part of downtown. But whatever. That's where she drives me to. This old parking tower. And this is, like . . . not the good section of downtown either. This is the part of town people left to move to other parts.

THE ONE WHO SAW IT I got out of the car and looked up to the top level and saw a flashlight.

THE ONE IN THE CAR I didn't see any light up there.

THE ONE WHO SAW IT So I ran . . .

THE ONE IN THE CAR So she just took off . . .

THE ONE WHO SAW IT Up the stairs . . .

THE ONE IN THE CAR I wasn't running after her. Are you kidding?

THE ONE WHO SAW IT Hurry hurry hurry hurry.

THE ONE IN THE CAR I locked the doors. This was a bad section of town.

THE ONE WHO SAW IT I got to the roof and there he was, across the tower, sitting on the ground with all of his drawings all around him.

He looked up and saw me.

[MICHAEL *looks up and sees* SARAH. *This is the first time two characters in the play actually speak to each other.*]

MICHAEL You came.

THE ONE WHO SAW IT Michael . . .

MICHAEL I'm going through one.

THE ONE WHO SAW IT Let's go home.

MICHAEL I've been working on this for months. Remember I showed you last week.

THE ONE WHO SAW IT Michael . . .

MICHAEL I've done all this math I didn't even think I could do and I read everything I could find on the Internet, and I've found one. I'm going through it. Tonight. It's going to be open soon.

THE ONE IN THE CAR Then, like, all of a sudden there was this like . . . rumble of thunder.

MICHAEL See? It's coming.

THE ONE WHO SAW IT I want you to come home with me.

MICHAEL Not tonight, Sarah. When I get back.

THE ONE IN THE CAR I checked the weather on my phone real fast. There wasn't supposed to be rain or anything.

[*Thunder rumbles.* MICHAEL *stands, goes to* SARAH.]

MICHAEL I won't be gone long. They open all the time. I'll be back.

[*He kisses her. Then he turns and with breakneck speed runs into the darkness at the back of the theater.* SARAH *spins to us and tells us what she sees.*]

THE ONE WHO SAW IT All of a sudden, he's sprinting across the roof of the parking tower, and I'm yelling after him, "Michael! Michael! Stop!" But he doesn't stop. He just keeps going until he reaches the other end of the tower. And it's weird, because I don't ever remember him being so agile like this, he took one big jump up on the railing—the big cement railing that was the edge of the tower—and he stood on it for a second, then with a laugh he just . . . jumped. Off into space.

And I screamed. I just . . . screamed. You know. What else could you do in that moment? But I'm screaming and I'm waiting to see him fall. . . .

But he doesn't.

He doesn't fall. He hangs there in the air, like someone's got him on a string or something. And he dangles there and he starts to turn a little, like someone was spinning the string he's hanging from, and he turns and he catches my eye as his head turns to face me and I hear him yelling from across the tower:

MICHAEL [*In the darkness, we do not see him.*] See? I told you!

THE ONE WHO SAW IT And then, all of a sudden, there was a pop and a flash and he was gone. Just . . . gone.

[*A long silence. The three of them soak this in.*]

THE ONE WHO DIDN'T GO So, like, we never talk about what happened.

THE ONE IN THE CAR Would you want to talk about it?

THE ONE WHO DIDN'T GO We see each other and school and stuff. And even through all the memorials and the funeral and whatever, we didn't talk to each other.

THE ONE IN THE CAR Would you? I don't even want to think about it.

THE ONE WHO DIDN'T GO I don't feel guilty.

THE ONE IN THE CAR Who does that?

THE ONE WHO DIDN'T GO I mean, I couldn't really know what he was planning to do.

THE ONE IN THE CAR Who invites his friends to watch him jump off a parking tower?

THE ONE WHO DIDN'T GO When he told me he wanted to find some way out of this place, I thought it was just . . . you know . . . talk.

[SARAH *moves to the binder and the drawings. She sits with them.*]

THE ONE WHO SAW IT Anything you can imagine must exist somewhere in the universe. So this is what I imagine. I imagine him hanging in the air, suspended by some thread I cannot see. I imagine him spinning to see me. I imagine the pop and the flash of light. I imagine him disappearing into the drawings he left on the ground.

I imagine him somewhere other than where he is. If I imagine it, it must exist, right?

Right?

[*We hear the echo of* MICHAEL*'s laughter, faint.*]

• • •

Easter at the Entrée Gold

John Minigan

John Minigan

John Minigan's plays have been produced throughout the U.S., Canada, Europe, Asia, and Australia. He has developed new work with the Orlando Shakespeare Theater, New Repertory Theatre, the New American Playwrights Project, and Actors' Repertory Theatre of Vermont. He is a member of the Dramatists Guild. Please visit www.johnminigan.com.

...production history...

Easter at the Entrée Gold was first produced on January 28, 2011, as the first-place winner of the New Works Festival at the Firhouse Center for the Arts in Newburyport, Massachusetts, directed by Anne Easter Smith.

LEVERETT SPENCER Alan Huisman

PETER SIMMONS Andrew White

The first professional production of *Easter at the Entrée Gold* was by Hey Jonte! Productions on August 9, 2016, at the Samuel French Off-Off-Broadway Festival at the East 13th Street Theatre/Classic Stage Company, directed by Miranda Jonte, assisted by Chelsea Thaler. The production was stage-managed by Kyrie McCormick.

LEVERETT SPENCER John Moss

PETER SIMMONS Noah Wilke

characters

LEVERETT SPENCER Fifty-ish. An English teacher at St. Xavier's. Soft around the middle and chin with puffy circles under his eyes and once fine features that have sagged prematurely. He still shows hints of the manic intensity he once had in the classroom.

PETER SIMMONS Late twenties. An English teacher at St. Xavier's, a prestigious boys' boarding school. Athletic, with Ivy League good looks.

scene

A well-appointed suite at Le Reine Elizabeth, a posh Montreal hotel.

time

Easter Sunday, mid-morning. The recent past.

NB: A "/" in the speech of one character indicates that the other character's next speech interrupts at that moment.

[*A suite in Le Reine Elizabeth Hotel, Montreal. A well-appointed sitting room with a door to an inner bedroom. The furnishings—couches, chairs, painted tables, lamps, etc.—are regal, impressive, in excellent taste. On the walls, though, are abstract paintings with garish colors and bold, irregular shapes. Enter* PETER.]

PETER Hello? Excuse me, is this Leverett Spencer's suite?

[PETER *speaks haltingly in French.*]

Pardonnez-moi, je cherche Monsieur Spencer. Est-ce que cette chambre est la chambre de Leverett Spencer? Hello?

[*The door opens.* PETER *enters.*]

Spence? Are you here? All right, let's do this.

[*He considers the inner door. Goes to the inner door, turns knob. It's locked. He jiggles the door and knocks.*]

Spence? Are you in there?

[*Knocks again, tries knob.*]

Jesus.

[*He goes to telephone, puts the receiver to his ear. He looks at the directory. Suddenly—*]

Oh, bonjour, hello. I didn't— Is this the front desk? This is Peter Simmons; I spoke with you downstairs. Well, I spoke with someone. He had a mustache, blue eyes, blond— Look, I came to take Mr. Spencer back to the states and I'm in his suite and nobody's here, only there's a locked door— I think, a bedroom? I know, but look, can you get someone up here to open it? I'm afraid Mr. Spencer— Because that inner door is locked. If he's done himself some harm—

[*The inner door unlocks loudly.*]

Hold on, somebody just unlatched the door. Yes, you're right, it's probably him. I'll be certain to call, yes. Asshole. Leverett? Is that you?

[*He hangs up.* PETER *takes a couple of steps toward the door. The door opens. Enter a middle-aged woman in a lime green chiffon dressing gown, house slippers, large and cheaply glamorous tinted glasses. Her blond hair curls almost into a beehive.* PETER *is taken aback.*]

Oh, pardonnez-moi. I was looking for Mister—

[*There's something wrong with the picture. The middle-aged woman needs a shave. Her hair doesn't quite sit comfortably atop her head.*]

Jesus God. Spence?

LEVERETT First of all, Peter, let me tell you: your French is very good. "Est-ce que cette chambre est la chambre de Leverett Spencer?"

PETER All right. Okay. Spence, what/ the hell is—

LEVERETT [*Interrupting at* "/"] Have you had breakfast?

PETER Break— I did. On the plane.

LEVERETT You flew?

PETER Yes.

LEVERETT I thought you'd drive.

PETER I'm going to drive you back in your car./ Why are you—

LEVERETT [*At* "/"] Yes, yes. I see. I had it in my head a certain way. You'd drive yourself— That's wrong; I see that. I thought you'd get here late tonight and we'd drive back overnight, or tomorrow.

PETER We've got classes/ tomorrow.

LEVERETT [*At* "/"] It was in my head a different way. If I had known, I'd have been more prepared.

PETER You would have dressed?

LEVERETT Don't be mordant, Peter. I need you to be my ally.

PETER It's just/ a little sur—

LEVERETT [*At* "/"] So will you be my ally?

PETER I'd certainly like to be, Spence.

LEVERETT But will you be?

PETER I just said I would.

LEVERETT You said you'd like to be. That's not the same.

PETER It's got to be a hundred degrees in here. Why do they keep it so hot?

LEVERETT That's me. I love the heat. I should have gone to the tropics. I should have gone to Crete! Like mighty Theseus! Can you picture me? Sword in hand? Ball of yarn? Spence and the Minotaurs?

PETER Can I turn it down?

LEVERETT It's a dry heat. Very well, do what you like.

PETER It's fine. We'll be leaving as soon as you get out of that circus outfit.

LEVERETT Peter. Oh, you'll miss Easter dinner! We'll be on the road, I'm sorry.

PETER I called my parents and let them know.

LEVERETT But what about your lovely fiancée?

PETER Lauren's going to her parents' house.

LEVERETT And maybe that's not where you want to be anyway.

PETER Why not?

LEVERETT I don't mean to imply you'd rather be here with me. Or on the road. I do thank you for this.

PETER You'd do the same for me.

LEVERETT But this wouldn't happen to you, would it?

PETER What exactly did happen, Spence? Why did you—

LEVERETT It seems so crazy, doesn't it?

PETER This must be costing you a shit-ton of money.

LEVERETT But does it seem crazy? Did Brother Gus say I was crazy?

PETER He didn't say/ any—

LEVERETT [*At "/"*] What did he tell you? "Leverett's lost his mind and holed himself up at Le Reine Elizabeth." Did he describe my situation?

PETER He said you were having some trouble driving.

[LEVERETT *laughs.*]

He said you were ready to come back but you needed a ride.

LEVERETT Mr. Simmons, what do you think? Do you think I'm crazy?

PETER Look, I—

LEVERETT Do you think I've lost my mind?

PETER Spence—

LEVERETT I try to remember: there are people more fucked up than I. I haven't met them.

PETER I didn't say you've lost your mind.

LEVERETT So lime green is my color?

PETER I knew this wasn't about driving. I'm happy to try to help.

LEVERETT That's why I asked Brother to send you.

PETER You asked for me specifically?

LEVERETT He wanted to come himself. I don't think he could have appreciated this, do you?

PETER I'm here to help. Is there anybody you want me to call?

LEVERETT Room service.

PETER How is room service going/ to help?

LEVERETT [*At* "/"] I'm going to need a little strength for this; I don't know about you.

PETER For what? I'm here to get you packed and get/ on the road.

LEVERETT [*At* "/"] If it were just a matter of getting packed and on the road, do you think I'd have come all the way to Montreal in the first place? And booked the Entrée Gold Suite at eighteen hundred dollars a night?

PETER Eighteen hundred? Spence.

LEVERETT It isn't gauche to talk price if you can't afford it.

PETER But why would you/ spend—

LEVERETT [*At* "/"] I said, "Give me the best suite you've got." "The Entrée Gold?" he said. "Absolutely," I said. We'll have to take these pictures down.

PETER Why?

LEVERETT I thought the suite would do more for me, but it just felt cold. So up went the heat, down came the paintings. I bought these on the street.

PETER What did you do/ with—

LEVERETT [*At* "/"] So much passion in those brushstrokes.

PETER Where did you put/the others?

LEVERETT [*At* "/"] I left them outside the door, in the hall. For eighteen hundred dollars a night, someone takes everything away. They'll have to come down.

PETER Will they fit in your car?

LEVERETT We'll leave them by the door. Someone will take them away.

PETER We should get started, then.

[PETER *takes a painting off the wall.* LEVERETT *watches.* PETER *stops.*]

Spence, come on. We've got classes tomorrow.

LEVERETT I'm not going to be teaching any classes tomorrow. You know that as well as I.

PETER I think if we/ get back—

LEVERETT [*At* "/"] Don't patronize me. Brother Augustine will tell the boys of Xavier that Mr. Spencer was called away suddenly, or that I'm on retreat. Yes, that's good: he'll say I'm on retreat. The parents will like that, too. "Mr. Spencer is on retreat." They'll think I'm going to rejoin the order. Can't you hear them? "The Fairy Queen is going to be a monk again."

PETER Don't do that.

LEVERETT I know the names. Captain Pinky. The Fairy Queen.

PETER Is this about the names?

LEVERETT The boys don't mean any harm.

PETER Is this— Spence?

LEVERETT What?

PETER Are you gay?

LEVERETT Why, do I look gay? Did Brother Gus say I was? He doesn't even use the equipment God provided, so he has no right to make judgments about how anybody else does.

PETER Look, Spence, I'm not here/ to talk about—

LEVERETT [*At "/"*] Right you are, Mr. Simmons. I'm just a little thrown. I thought you'd drive and get here later. And yes, I would have dressed. I didn't answer the door because I didn't know if I should reveal myself in my full glory. "But what the hell," I said. "It's Montreal. I'm an American . . . a-broad."

[*Pause.*]

No? This wig is such a story. Friday night, I was going to see a dirty movie. Thought about it all the way up in the car. Montreal is far enough away; I won't be seen by anyone I know. And then I couldn't bring myself to do it, somehow. The look in his face when you buy the ticket. So I went to this little movie house, Cinema du Parc, and the woman selling tickets was wearing this. "I have to have your hair," I said. "I really do!" Well, she got quite serious and told me, "Monsieur, this is a wig." "No," I said, "a wig? It's lovely." "Merci," she said. "One ticket?" "No," I said, "I want your hair. One hundred dollars for your hair." "This wig?" "Oui, ma'am'selle," I said, "one hundred dollars American." And voila! Off it came! And then she said, in joual, I suppose, "My God, a hundred dollars." As I walked away, I guess the thought occurred to her. "Monsieur," she said, "it's for your wife?"

[*Pause.*]

So I shopped. I thought, "Who needs a movie, I've got me." I bought the gown, the slippers, some little things, some jewelry. That's when I bought the paintings—on the street, from a lovely man. It took two taxis to carry it all. The porters downstairs were a bit suspicious, but there we are.

[*Pause.*]

Well?

PETER I think you got taken on the wig.

LEVERETT Not Ru Paul, is it. I thought I'd feel sexy. You have an expectation. With hair like his, I'll look like this. Lose fifteen pounds, I'll look like that. But even when you do those things, you're stuck with who you are. Disappointments. The paintings, the weather, the clothes.

PETER Then why not take them off? I mean—

LEVERETT I know what you mean. I didn't ask you here for sexual relations. I can't take them off, not yet.

PETER I'd rather not go through the lobby with you looking like this.

LEVERETT I know I need to do it. I just need you to help me take them off.

PETER Spence—

LEVERETT Figuratively, Peter. You're a lovely man, but that's not what I'm after. I'm not a sexual person. The boys don't understand, you see. They're teenagers. It's all ballistics to them. To be perfectly honest, I don't use the equipment either. Too many years in clerics, I suppose. The grip of celibacy is even stronger than a firm right hand. I thought the wig would do something. I thought the robe, the hotel, the foreign city might actually make me interested in having sex. Wrong! Just another old man in a dress.

PETER So how do we get you out of the dress, figuratively.

LEVERETT I've always believed that affection could exist without . . . the ballistics. But I need to know what you think, Peter. I need to hear from you.

PETER From me? About what?

LEVERETT The whole issue.

PETER Sex.

LEVERETT In a word.

PETER That'll solve your problem.

LEVERETT It might help.

PETER Uh-huh. Well, it might make life less complicated. To feel affection, without everything else.

LEVERETT You don't think it happens.

PETER You can pretend, but, really, they're all mixed up. Ballistics.

LEVERETT Then teaching will be a dangerous profession for you, Peter.

PETER But I'm teaching in a boys' school and I'm not gay.

LEVERETT Two bridges to cross, then.

PETER Did something happen with one of the boys?

LEVERETT You cut right to the chase, don't you? We were talking about you for a change.

PETER I'm not in trouble.

LEVERETT I'd be your ally if you were.

PETER What does that mean?

LEVERETT I'm stuck at Le Reine Elizabeth. I think you might be stuck someplace, too. I'm willing to help.

PETER Well, thank you, but I'm here/ because Brother—

LEVERETT [*At* "/"] We all get stuck, Peter. We ought to help each other when we do.

PETER It doesn't help to change the subject. Did/ something happen with—

LEVERETT [*At* "/"] You see why I wanted room service? Some nice croissants and a café au lait would make this so much more pleasant.

PETER What we need to do is pack. We can still talk,/ but we'll get—

LEVERETT [*At* "/"] I'm not ready.

PETER Well, get ready, all right? Brother Augustine calls me at four in the morning, Easter Sunday morning, and tells me to fly up here to drive you back. So I did it. I've done everything anybody's asked of me, so now I'd like to get things moving.

[*Pause.*]

I'm not a therapist. I'm sorry. I'm just a driver.

LEVERETT What's it like, Mr. Simmons?

PETER What?

LEVERETT The boys don't feel about me the way they feel about you. I want to know what it's like.

PETER Spence, you are one of the most respected—

LEVERETT Oh, I'm Mr. Chips! Don't patronize me, Peter. I might be a eunuch in a wig, but I'm not an idiot.

PETER I wasn't trying/ to imply—

LEVERETT [*At* "/"] You went through first-year teacher purgatory last year and you survived. You didn't let them crush you and they love you for that; they really do. Not just the boys on your team—all of them. And affection like that— Well, it can make you feel you can do anything.

[*Pause.*]

I'm not accusing you.

PETER I'm going to get a cup of coffee, okay? I'm going to go downstairs and have a cup of coffee, and in twenty minutes, I'll be back. I want you dressed, packed up, and ready to go. Okay?

[PETER *starts to go.*]

LEVERETT I came to Montreal because I wrote a letter.

[*Pause.*]

God, this is so much harder than I thought. It was so nice just chatting at first.

PETER You write letters, Spence. You're famous for it. You wrote to me on Christmas break. You write to students, even while school is in session.

LEVERETT This one had a poem in it.

PETER You sent me a W. H. Auden two years ago, as soon as I got hired.

LEVERETT You sent back Stephen Spender and I knew we'd get along. We do get along, don't we?

PETER We do. Don't worry about your letters.

LEVERETT I'm worried about the poem.

PETER What was it?

LEVERETT An original. Did you know I wrote? I haven't for years, but I was moved to take up pen and ink. Inspired by Erato, the tragic muse.

PETER Erato's not the tragic muse.

LEVERETT When you write to little boys, she is.

PETER I see. And you sent it.

LEVERETT Thursday morning. Popped it into U.S. mail. That's why I drove up here in the wee hours of Friday. I haven't slept a wink, you know?

PETER Who'd you write to?

LEVERETT Steven McGinn. A junior.

PETER I know him.

LEVERETT Yes.

PETER Maybe he won't understand it. Was it subtle?

LEVERETT Like desire in a nudist colony.

PETER Well, maybe he still won't understand/ it compl—

LEVERETT [*At* "/"] His parents will. I mailed it to his home address. He went home for Easter.

[PETER *laughs.*]

PETER I'm sorry, Spence. I shouldn't laugh. That was not a smart thing to do.

LEVERETT For a normal person, no. For a lunatic, it's genius. What does Theseus say? "The lunatic, the lover and the poet, are of imagination all compact." So I dropped it in the mail and promptly panicked. I had to go somewhere and I thought: Canada. What did those ads used to say? "Come to the world next door!"

PETER Does Brother Augustine know about the letter? Why didn't he tell me?

LEVERETT You wouldn't have come. It's true affection, Peter. I would be happy to be his lifelong friend. God, I'm thirty years older than he is—almost forty. Even I think it's immoral. At least if I were your age— It might be wrong, but it wouldn't be quite so evil.

[*Pause.*]

You see why I needed you?

PETER Not really, no.

LEVERETT Come now, Peter. I've told you what I've done. It's your turn.

PETER My turn for what?

LEVERETT You said you'd help.

PETER I don't know what/ you want me—

LEVERETT [*At* "/"] You said you'd be my ally

PETER If you get fired,/ I don't really know—

LEVERETT [*At* "/"] I will be fired. I shall be. This is not about the job. I've told you what I've done. Help me with this.

PETER How? What do you—Jesus, it's hot in here.

LEVERETT I would like you to make me feel less crazy.

PETER All right, okay: I don't think what you felt was crazy. Writing the letter, even. But sending it? And to his parents' house? Acting/ on the feeling—

LEVERETT [*At* "/"] You're making yourself the newest disappointment of the weekend.

PETER I'm doing the best I can.

LEVERETT I didn't ask Brother Gus to send you up because I think you're a good driver. I asked because you understand what I feel.

PETER What is that supposed to mean?

LEVERETT You covered your tracks beautifully.

PETER Look, I didn't come up here to be insulted.

LEVERETT Pay attention, Peter. I'm asking for your help. I know what happened and I know with whom. I have a theory about/ where and when, but—

PETER I'm not going to stand here and listen to this.

LEVERETT Don't leave.

PETER If you made up some fantasy to make you feel/ less crazy—

LEVERETT [*At* "/"] I've seen the looks you give each other; I've seen the looks change. The angle of the head, the way he looks at— It's not the first time I've seen it. He's lost something. You've lost something, too. You'll never be able to look at the boys the same way. There'll be something else mixed up in it.

PETER Why are you doing this? Who else would have been willing to come all the way up here?

LEVERETT No one, Peter.

PETER Then why are you making this up? If you're going to lose your job, that's your business. Are you trying to get me fired, too?

LEVERETT Of course not.

PETER Are you setting me up, so you can/ tell Augustine—

LEVERETT [*At* "/"] Oh, you found me out. Discovered my devilish plot to ruin your teaching career by renting an eighteen-hundred-dollar suite, putting on a wig, buying your plane fare, and confessing that I wrote an erotic poem? And you thought a hundred bucks for the wig was nuts. I'm not going to tell anyone what happened.

PETER Nothing happened.

LEVERETT Nothing.

PETER No. So why don't/ you get your—

LEVERETT [*At "/"*] Tom Stimpson.

[*Pause.*]

Tom Stimpson. The talented captain of your basketball team, headed for Holy Cross next year. I don't know how you managed it, but you had sex with Tom Stimpson. Despite your denial, despite Lauren the lovely fiancée from Connecticut. That's why I wrote the poem.

PETER What?

LEVERETT You took the thing that could not be and made it real. I thought I could, too, and look where I ended up. You're my tragic muse.

PETER Jesus.

LEVERETT I've lost my job, Peter. My career of more than thirty years. I may have lost my mind. I'd just feel a little less crazy if you gave me the details.

PETER I don't know how making/ up some story—

LEVERETT [*At "/"*] Because the wig is not enough. The gown is not enough. The poem. I'm never going to use the equipment, Peter. If I hadn't written the poem, there'd be a possibility to lie to myself about that, but I wrote the poem and I've closed that door and I'm never going to know what it would have been unless you tell me.

PETER So you were lying.

LEVERETT What do you mean?

PETER You said you think affection is enough.

LEVERETT I used to think so. Before you and Tom Stimpson.

PETER You can't provide your own fantasy life, so you need me to give you one.

LEVERETT It isn't fantasy for you, Peter.

PETER No, and it never was my fantasy, so let's stop pretending—

LEVERETT I never took the chance you did when I was young. Your age. My God, I lived under vows, I was so afraid. I'm an old man now, Peter, and I simply need a little piece of what you know to convince me I'm not out of my mind. Otherwise, I don't know how I can go back and face everything I to have to face. Just give me that little piece of what you know.

[*Pause.*]

PETER I'm sorry, Spence. It never happened.

LEVERETT Please don't.

PETER You're right that you saw something. Tom Stimpson wrote an essay for class. He asked me not to tell anyone about it. He wrote that he thought he might not be one hundred percent heterosexual. I wrote back. I thanked him for his honesty. I told him he could continue to be honest with me. The next day, he came in to class early, with a confession. He said he was in love with me.

LEVERETT Yes?

PETER I told him that was flattering. I told him I was engaged, that he was a fine boy, and that I wouldn't say a word to anyone. I told him I was his teacher, so I had a responsibility to do what was best for him even if I felt the same way— Which, I explained, I didn't. Couldn't.

[*Pause.*]

That's it, Spence. That's the whole story. It ends there.

[*Pause.*]

I'm sorry. You thought there was more.

LEVERETT The higher the hopes, the faster they fall.

PETER He's probably not even gay. It's just affection. Admiration, maybe. Kids get confused. I think it's easy to get confused about the ballistics.

LEVERETT I'm not confused. I haven't acted rationally, but I haven't lied about myself.

PETER You think I'm lying?

LEVERETT Where I place my hopes is up to me, I suppose. Flying up here on Easter Sunday was very gracious of you.

PETER I came to help and I'm doing everything I can. We'll get you packed; we'll do the paintings. You should change for the drive. Why don't you get changed?

[*Pause.*]

You want something and you thought I had it. I don't. I can drive you back, but/ there's—

LEVERETT [*At* "/"] Take my car.

PETER Spence.

LEVERETT I'm not going.

PETER I'm not going to leave you here. You need to get back.

LEVERETT I won't do anything foolish. I'm not going to kill myself.

PETER I flew up here to get you.

LEVERETT We're both disappointed then, aren't we?

PETER You don't have to talk to Augustine today. I'll tell him you're not ready. We can split the driving.

LEVERETT What would we find to talk about, the two of us? No, it'll do you good to drive back alone.

PETER And leave you here?

LEVERETT I used to love long, lonely drives. But driving up here was more than I could handle. All that time alone with my thoughts when I don't like my thoughts.

[*Pause.*]

So, enjoy the drive back, you and your thoughts! Here.

[*He tosses* PETER *the keys.*]

Give them to the concierge; he'll have someone get the car for you. You remember the concierge, don't you, Peter? Blond hair, blue eyes, the little mustache?

[*Pause. Then* PETER *starts to go.*]

I just hope you don't run into any snow.

PETER Snow?

LEVERETT We're pretty far north. You never know what could happen in the snow. You might get stuck.

PETER It's April.

LEVERETT I wouldn't want you snowed under on the side of the road somewhere. Wouldn't that be terrible? Sitting in your car with the snow coming down all around you.

[*Pause.*]

I told you: I have a theory. I saw the looks. I saw how they changed. The day after the snowstorm, the day after you and your boys lost the tournament.

PETER How do you know about this?

LEVERETT You're the one who knows all about it, not me. If you tell me, then I'll know, too. And maybe I'll be able to go back and go through everything I have to go through. You lost the tournament, Peter. I know what losing can do. That was the night.

[*Pause.*]

I'm not asking for much, am I? Just tell me what happened in the snow, or start that long drive back alone.

[*Pause.*]

Peter.

PETER It was more than they said it would be. There was almost a foot when the bus let us off at the Center. We'd been cheering for ourselves all the way back to Xavier. Anybody would have thought we'd won. I said I could drive kids back to the dorms. Most of them walked, but Kenny Lombard, O'Donnelly, and Tom said they'd take a lift. We were close to Tom's dorm, but I— I created this mental map of the campus that made it seem like I should drop him last.

LEVERETT He was in the front?

PETER The back. Passenger's side. I dropped O'Donnelly and Lombard first—

LEVERETT And there you were. You and Tom.

PETER He got out when Kenny did and moved into the front seat. It was only a hundred feet to get to Lyons. He could have stayed where he was. He could have walked.

LEVERETT But he sat next to you. The boy who wrote the essay.

PETER I pulled up in front of Lyons and the car slid off the road and stalled. He laughed. He'd had the game of his life. He didn't deserve to be on the losing team with a game like that. That's what I told him—sitting there, just the two of us. The snow was piling up on the car, burying us. The engine was stalled, so I turned off the lights. The wipers were off and snow started to cover the windows. You couldn't see out, you couldn't see in. It was like a little enclave, a little perfect— I remember thinking, "If anybody had to find me now, had to search the world, they'd never think to find me here, in the car, with Tom Stimpson, under the snow."

[LEVERETT *stands behind* PETER *and puts his hands on* PETER*'s shoulders.*]

If we hadn't lost. If he hadn't played like that and it hadn't been snowing. The season was over. He's going to Holy Cross.

LEVERETT Go on, Peter. I'm an ally. Just that.

PETER We ran out of conversation. He. He put the back of his hand on mine. I didn't understand that. His palm was up. The heater was off but it felt like a hundred degrees. We were wearing jackets, we had boots, scarves. Funny how a cock is the easiest thing to get to.

[*Pause.*]

We kissed. We used our hands. It was dry in the car, so I took his hand off me and licked his palm. He did the same. I was. We were both covered in sweat when we were done. He put his head on my shoulder and fell asleep a little.

[*Pause.*]

When he woke up, he zipped his jacket to cover himself. "I'll see you, Mr. Simmons," he said. Mr. Simmons. He opened the door and some snow fell off the roof into his jacket and it must have gone down the back of his neck. He gave a little war whoop and laughed and he closed the door.

[*Pause.*]

I couldn't move. I couldn't start the car, I couldn't get out.

LEVERETT Stuck.

PETER I couldn't breathe deep enough to make my chest move up and down. If I moved, if I started the car, I'd have to start the rest of my life. Brother Gus would fire me.

Lauren would call off the engagement. As soon as I turned the key in the ignition, all that was going to start, so I sat there in the place nobody else knew. The next day I waited for someone to come and— Nobody did. Nobody knew. And every day that went by— I started to think I got away with it. Tom never said anything. We never talked about it.

LEVERETT But you looked at each other differently.

PETER I think he wanted to keep it quiet, too. What we did was safe. I mean—

LEVERETT I know.

PETER I think you're the only one who knew.

LEVERETT Nobody knew because you never thought to send him a poem.

PETER No. I— No. Is that what you wanted to know?

LEVERETT Yes. Thank you, Peter.

PETER Is that all? Can we go now?

LEVERETT No.

PETER What do you want? I told you what happened.

LEVERETT Theseus went into the labyrinth to kill the Minotaur. He took all those twists and turns and would have been stuck in the middle, but he had a trail of yarn to guide himself out. We think we're in a little enclave, but it's the middle of the maze. How silly we didn't think to bring any yarn with us.

PETER Spence, are you going to tell Brother Gus?

LEVERETT I'm your ally. I won't tell a soul. But you can't go back.

PETER To school.

LEVERETT You can't teach anymore. You'll never look at the boys the same way.

PETER This is why you asked for me.

LEVERETT You were stuck. I wanted to know. I needed to know. But I could see that you were stuck.

PETER What am I supposed to do now? This isn't any better.

LEVERETT Exactly.

PETER We can't stay here.

LEVERETT The middle of the maze, if that's what you get to— There's no treasure. There's not even a Minotaur.

PETER There's nothing. So what are we supposed to do?

LEVERETT Mr. Simmons, it beats the shit out of me. But whatever it is, we both know we have an ally.

PETER We do. Are you ready?

LEVERETT Yes.

[LEVERETT *spreads his arms in a welcoming gesture* PETER *walks to him slowly and unties the belt of his dressing gown. He takes the gown off* LEVERETT*'s shoulders and tries to take the wig.*]

Wait, though. I mean, a hundred dollars!

PETER Spence.

LEVERETT Fine.

[LEVERETT *takes off the wig.*]

Theseus went home without the Minotaur's treasure.

PETER I'm not sure the wig qualifies. And Theseus could give up the treasure because he had other things to look forward to. What about us?

LEVERETT He didn't go there for the treasure, Peter. He went to save the young from being sacrificed. Of course, he was smarter. He went to Crete.

PETER He was also a myth.

LEVERETT Well, of course he was. None of the great ones are real. The rest of us drive fourteen hours to the north alone.

PETER Are we ready to go?

LEVERETT I think so. I'm sorry, Peter.

PETER It's not your fault. It's— Thank you, Spence.

LEVERETT Je vous en prie, Peter. Let's go.

[*Blackout.*]

• • •

Strays

Kim Katzberg

In Collaboration with
Nora Woolley and
Raquel Cion

Kim Katzberg

Kim Katzberg has been creating genre-bending performance work since 2010. The *New York Times* has described her work as "Audacious. . . . Rich with emotional truth. . . . Katzberg has a gift for writing her own material." *Strays* won the 2016 New York Innovative Theatre Award for Outstanding Original Short Script. Katzberg is currently writing her fourth play.

... production history ...

Produced at the Brick Theater, Brooklyn, New York, May 5–14, 2016. Directed by Raquel Cion.

TERRY 1, AMBER ARENA, DYNAMIC, COP Kim Katzberg

TERRY 2, PAPA, AMBER ARENA Nora Woolley

scene 1

Note: TERRY and TERRY 2 are the same character played by two different actors.

[TERRY *is zoned-out, with frosted, rocker hair and long fake nails, and wears a slinky leopard-print jumpsuit. Her eyebrows are taped up and back, leaving her eyes just slightly open.* TERRY *talks and moves as if sedated on opiates.*]

STRIP CLUB EMCEE VOICE-OVER And now, gentlemen, to the stage . . . New York Dungeon's most explicit erotic dancer, Terry!

[TERRY *enters drinking vodka straight from the bottle. She is extremely drunk.* TERRY *attempts to strip, tease, and get the audience off but does it clumsily. At first it's fun. Then the scene takes a dark turn and* TERRY *scares herself. She hits an emotional bottom in front of the crowd and runs offstage.*]

[*Blackout.*]

scene 1.5

[*Video: "2 Years Later" slides across the screen. Shot of Help Wanted Ad: "Help people from the comfort of your own home. Be their last hope!" Then a montage of* TERRY *in a cluttered, dingy office cubicle talking with three different callers at the Suicide Prevention Hotline. Video cuts from one conversation snippet to the next.*]

TERRY [*On the phone.*] Suicide Prevention Hotline, how's it going? Oh, you're on a roof? Don't jump. Hold on. I've got another call. Can I call ya back in a little bit?

. . . I hear what you're saying but you can change. I've changed. Change is possible. I used to dress like a total tramp, and now I dress like a sophisticated woman.

. . . It's all about service. That's what my sponsor told me, right before she killed herself.

[*Answering the phone.*]

Suicide Prevention Hotline, Ter speaking . . . no, no, don't hang up, maybe I can help you . . . tell me about it . . . oh, you lost your cat? His name is Tommie Tippie Toes?

Well, what's he look like? Is he in the continental U.S.? I'm sorry but I can't help you. I'm not a pet detective I'm a suicide operator.

Suicide Prevention Hotline and the Terry Effect Detective Agency, Terr speaking . . . don't be so harsh with me, man. I'm being of service, I help people . . . $600 back rent? I'll have it for you by the end of the month. Oh, it is the end of the month? Hey, did I miss Father's Day?

[*Hangs up the phone.*]

Stu, will you hand me that cat book? Yeah, that one. Bring it over.

[*Jump cut to* TERRY *looking at a huge '80s cat book. The phone rings. She answers it.*]

Kikamu. Kikamu.

[*Looking for her cat. She picks up Kikamu.*]

Do you think I could do this, Kikamu? I got all these problems and she wants me to find her cat. Wait a minute, maybe one could help the other.

[*Video stops. Lights up on* TERRY *at an Adult Children of Alcoholics Meeting.*]

scene 2

TERRY God, grant me the serenity, to accept the people I cannot change, the courage to change the one I can, and the wisdom to know that one is me. Keep coming back, it works if you work it, so work it, you're worth it.

[*Claps.*]

And live it. Oh, Bye, Jose. Fellowship? That sounds so cool, you all just sit around at a diner and talk and everything? I don't have a lot of money right now. Oh, thanks for treating me that would be really nice. I think I just need a little meditation and I need to spend a little time with myself.

[TERRY *2 enters.*]

TERRY 2 Keep coming back, it works if you work it, so work it, you're worth it.

[TERRY *and* TERRY 2 *clap together.*]

TERRY And live it.

[*They sit. Their first two lines are said at the same time.*]

TERRY Do you think my share was okay?

TERRY 2 I thought your share was great. I really liked what you said about pet shame. It made me think about when Dad used to kill our pets.

TERRY Accidentally.

TERRY 2 Accidentally. I have all this shame about all of our pets. Starting with Journal the turtle, drowned in the tub.

TERRY Remember that bat we rescued and we nursed him back to health and repaired his broken wing . . .

TERRY 2 And then he got caught in the vacuum cleaner. And remember we had that big cat—

TERRY The big fat one.

TERRY 2 Fatty . . . fat cat. And we had that little dog—

TERRY Mailbox. Mailbox was sooooo cute.

TERRY 2 I can still smell him on my hands. But then he broke his neck. I have so much shame.

TERRY I have so much shame about it. Easy does it.

TERRY 2 One day at a time.

TERRY Easy do it.

TERRY 2 We're gonna feel so good overcoming our shame and we'll find this cat, Tommie Tippie Toes!

TERRY Tommie Tippie Toes! And pay our rent, and then we'll be able to go out with people after the meeting. Bye, Jose . . .

TERRY 2 Bye, Jose . . .

TERRY Self-esteem comes from estimable actions and there's nothing more estimable than finding a cat . . . and paying your rent. But maybe I can't do it! My job is just answering the phone alone in my apartment, how am I ever going to go out and solve this crime?

TERRY 2 No, no, no, you can do it. All it takes is a little research.

TERRY I did do some research, I do have this book.

TERRY 2 See, you're already off to a great start!

[*Video: graphics come up on the screen.* TERRY *sings and moves along to a song written and recorded by her as she peruses a huge '80s cat book.*]

scene 2.5

[TERRY *and* TERRY 2 *dance and sing along with the video.*]

TERRY and **TERRY 2** CATS. CAAAAATS. CATS. CAAAAAATS. (PURRRR.)

THEY'VE GOT LOW BODIES. CATS. CAAH. C-C-C-CAAH, CAAH THEY'VE GOT LOW BODIES

PERSIAN, BLUE PERSIAN, FLAT-FACED ONES, CALICO. WOAH, WOAH, I'M NOT TALKIN' 'BOUT THE MUSICAL,

I'M TALKIN' 'BOUT THE REAL LIVE ANIMALS CAAH, C-C-C-CAAH

THEY CLIMB TREES

THEY CAN MAKE FRIENDS WITH DOGS . . . SOMETIMES IT'S NOT UNHEARD OF

CAT FART . . . PHOO . . . CA FAR, PHOO SIZZLING CATS ON THE CITY STREETS

SIZZLING CATS ON THE SIZZLING STREETS . . . WITH THE MOONLIGHT SHINING DOWN ON THEIR COATS

THEIR NAILS . . . YEAH . . . WHEN THEY CLIP CLOP-CLOP-CLOP ON THE KITCHEN FLOOR

YEAH! CA! OH YEAH, CATS C-C-C-CAH . . . YEAH

[TERRY *and* TERRY 2 *exit into the audience. Lights down. Video:* TERRY *calls* FANNY *back.*]

TERRY Hi, Fanny. I did some research. It's gonna cost ya . . . $600. When I get more clues I'll call ya.

[TERRY *hangs up the phone.*]

Hey, Stu, we gotta set up an interview with this Fanny lady. Stop eatin' peanuts with your feet up!

scene 3

TERRY [*Eating candy.*] Keep the focus on yourself. It's an inside job. Easy do it. Easy do it.

[TERRY *calls her father on a red-lips phone. Lights up on* PAPA. *He wears a Confederate flag trucker hat, drinks a tall boy, and reclines in a La-Z-Boy.*]

PAPA Hello?

TERRY Hi, Papa, happy Father's Day.

PAPA Oh, we were just talkin' about ya.

TERRY Oh, really? How's Gank, she still on that Jenny Craig?

PAPA [*To Gankie.*] Gankie, you're fine. She's fine. Terry Ann's on the phone.

[*Back to* TERRY.]

How are ya up there in New York?

TERRY I'm good, everything's good.

PAPA Haven't seen ya in a real long time, when you coming to visit?

TERRY I'm not sure.

PAPA Ahhh, you're not sure. You're gonna wait and see how things develop.

TERRY Well, no . . .

PAPA [*To Gankie.*] Hey, Miss America, you're alright. I told you, you're alright.

[*To* TERRY.]

It's all that microwaving food, Terry Ann. She's microwaving everything that goes in her mouth. Do you need some more money?

[*To Gankie.*]

Hey, Gank, she needs more money, again. I told you she couldn't do it.

TERRY I'm on to something big, I don't need your cash.

PAPA Something big? Oh, back to stripping I'll bet. Showing your titties for cash. No wonder you're not making the big bucks. They never grew much after fifteen. Unlike Gankie, who keeps growing and growing and growing. When ya coming to visit?

TERRY The reason I haven't come down is because there's just too much drinking that goes on.

PAPA What d'ya say? I couldn't hear ya.

TERRY I said the reason I haven't come down is because there's just too much drinking that goes on and it's hard for me to be around that.

PAPA What d'ya say? I couldn't hear ya.

TERRY I said the reason I haven't come down is because there's just too much drinking that goes on—

PAPA Your brother and Uncle Steve took me out to brunch this afternoon, it was real nice.

[*To Gankie.*]

Right Gank? It was real nice.

[*Back to* TERRY.]

I had some Bloody Marys, do I sound drunk?

TERRY I don't know.

PAPA No. I don't.

[PAPA *hangs up.*]

TERRY I gotta get to work.

scene 3.5

[*Video:* TERRY *interviews* FANNY. FANNY *is a crazy Southern cat lady with short spiky hair. She wears a powder blue Western outfit. The video is from* TERRY*'s perspective. While the* FANNY *interview video is playing,* TERRY *is live onstage in her apartment, eating candy and doing cat research.*]

FANNY [*Opening her apartment door.*] Oh, hi! You must be Terry. I'm Fanny. Excuse the mess. I've been up all night ever since Tommie Tippie Toes went missin'. Here's the kitchen, I'll just give you a quick tour.

[FANNY*'s kitchen is plastered with cat posters and dotted with cat figurines.*]

So, I have the Suicide Prevention Hotline on speed dial and that's why I accidently called. Thanks so much for taking the case. Can I get you some sweet tea or some hush puppies? No? Alright.

[*Looking in cabinets, underneath the sink, in the fridge, etc.*]

Well, I've just been lookin' everywhere for the little guy and I can't seem to find him. And I don't know if he ran away or or or or . . . what.

[*Zoom into two cat figurines on a little shelf above the sink.*]

I've been frantic to be honest. Ya know, Tommie Tippie Toes and I go way back, we've had a ten-year relationship. Basically, I found him in a pillowcase on the side of the road and I had a cube of cheese in my pocketbook and I gave it to him and he just sank his little pearly white fang into the cube, and we've been inseparable ever since.

[*Looking under the cat bed in the living room.*]

Anyway, I've just been lookin' everywhere for the little bugger and I reckon he's gotta be somewhere. Here's his bed. Oh God.

[*Looking under the couch.*]

I've looked from the tips of the roof to the depths of the cellar and I can't seem to find the little jester. I mean, I don't know where else to look.

[*She goes in the bedroom, looks under her comforter, and sees her old dead cat.*]

Oh! That's my old cat Earl, he's dea—

[*Jump cut to* FANNY *sitting on her bed.*]

Does Tommie Tippie Toes have any enemies? Well . . . I have this neighbor. She lives kitty corner. Her name is Amber Arena. I think she climbed through my fire escape while I was at work and took him. Amber Arena. Amber Arena.

[*Throwing a physical tantrum on the bed.*]

I'm gonna get you, girl!

Terry, you gotta find a way to look into her apartment and see if Tommie Tippie Toes is there.

[*Cut to* AMBER ARENA *leaving their apartment complex.* AMBER *is a femme fatale wearing a Delta Airlines stewardess uniform. Cut to* AMBER *on the subway train. Video zooms in on her eyes.*]

scene 4

[TERRY *shuts the cat book and starts trying on ridiculous disguises in the mirror while the next video plays. Video:* Law & Order *music.* TERRY *is dressed up in a Fed Ex worker disguise. She rings* AMBER ARENA*'s doorbell.*]

TERRY [*Tapping on the door with her long nails.*] Fed Ex.

[*Split video screen. On the left is* TERRY *outside the apartment door. On the right is* AMBER *inside the apartment looking through the peephole.* AMBER *stays still, doesn't make a peep, and doesn't answer the door.*]

Damnit.

[TERRY *leaves.*]

[TERRY *settles on a Girl Scout uniform and hides, spying on* AMBER *from behind a tree. This is happening live as a video of* AMBER *walking down the street, from the point of view of* TERRY *following her, plays.* TERRY 2 *enters and follows* AMBER *as well.* TERRY *and* TERRY 2 *hide behind a cardboard bush, then a mailbox.* TERRY *secretly exits backstage while* TERRY 2 *continues to follow* AMBER. TERRY *enters via the back of the audience. Video cuts to* TERRY*'s ex-stripper co-worker,* DYNAMIC. *She stops* TERRY *in her tracks.*]

DYNAMIC Hey, Terry, hey, what's up? I thought you were outta the business. You doin' role play now? We really miss you at the club. Whenever a girl gets the willies to go out onstage, we're like, you gonna have a Terry moment or what—

[TERRY *pushes her out of the way.*]

Ow!

[TERRY *follows* AMBER *to a bar.* AMBER *goes in.*]

scene 4.5

[TERRY *takes out her phone and dials her sponsor's number.* AMBER *on phone video:* AMBER *is hiding out in the bar bathroom talking on her cell phone. She is distressed.*]

TERRY I know. I'm sorry. No. No. You don't need to come to New York. I'm a professional, I will get the job done.

scene 5

TERRY [*Talking on the phone.*] Jose, let me start by saying: I have this job where I'm undercover and I'm going to be deep in character . . . and I gotta go into a bar. No, it's for work, it's purely for work! In no way, shape, or form am I gonna drink.

[*Listens to Jose.*]

I'm gonna get on that, I'm working on my fourth step. I'm gonna take a searching and fellatial moral inventory of myself. I know it's taking me a really long time.

Yes, I'm going back into a bar, but it's not gonna be like that St. Patrick's Day when I went on a three-week bender and woke up later in a Dumpster with an out-of-work little person dressed as a leprechaun. This is different. I'm scared, yes, but I'm gonna take it one moment at a time. I'm strong enough now I can do this. I'll bookend it with you when I get out.

Okay, bye.

[TERRY *enters the bar in spy mode. Seductive, old-time country music plays.* AMBER *sets down her drink (Long Island Iced Tea) on the adjacent bar stool as she fishes in her purse for Benadryl Allergy Relief tablets.* TERRY *picks up the drink to sit down and they catch each other's eyes. They both look away quickly as* TERRY *tries to act casual with a drink in hand. Then it hits* TERRY *that she has a drink in her hand. She tries to give it back to the bartender but starts to become seduced by the drink.* TERRY *pokes her finger into the cocktail, swirls and splashes the liquid on her neck as if it's perfume. Meanwhile,* AMBER *takes out a pet-hair lint roller from her purse and rolls it over her clothes. Just as* TERRY *is about to drink,* AMBER *sneezes and the Long Island Iced Tea spills on* TERRY. TERRY *runs out of the bar.*]

scene 5.5

[*Video:* TERRY *rushes down the street toward her apartment as she talks to Jose on the phone.*]

TERRY I went in there 'cause I had to do it for work, it's for the 600 dollars. But, uh, I white-knuckled it, I didn't have a drink, I'm not doing that again and thanks for letting me bookend it with you. Alright, thanks, Jose. Bye, Jose. Bye.

[TERRY *makes it into her apartment and catches her breath. Once we see her inside her apartment she is* TERRY 2.]

AMBER Why have you been following me?

[TERRY *is startled.*]

Why have you been following me?

[*Cut back to* TERRY.]

TERRY [*Voice-over, out loud.*] Think fast, Terry, think fast. I'm in love with you, I guess.

[TERRY *approaches* AMBER *and kisses her. Cut to* TERRY 2 *kissing* AMBER *and back to* TERRY *kissing* AMBER. *An original psychedelic animation plays of two Barbies melting together while* TERRY *is giving* AMBER *a lap dance.*]

scene 6

[TERRY *and* AMBER *are in bed, having a post-coital cigarette. They wear each other's clothes.*]

AMBER Wow, that was really intense, I feel really close to you. You're so hungry . . . I don't know what's going on with you but it's like you were hunting me in bed.

TERRY This is the first time I've had sex since I quit stripping.

AMBER This is a nice apartment, how much does it set you back?

TERRY 600 dollars.

AMBER Where do you get that kind of cash?

TERRY Oh, I do things here and there. I was kind of afraid of losing the apartment. I'm on a big project now, I'm sort of reinventing myself.

AMBER Tell me about it.

TERRY I'm doing this thing that I've never really done before. I don't really feel qualified.

AMBER Well, I can think of a few things you're qualified to do.

[*They share a laugh.*]

TERRY What are your dreams?

AMBER Dreams? A girl like you doesn't want to get mixed up with a girl like me. I probably shouldn't tell you, but I'm involved with some really really really bad people. You see there was this thing with this cat.

TERRY Cat?

AMBER Cat. It's so much bigger than this one cat. You're just touching on a world of darkness with me. I didn't realize that I was getting into this dark nether world of confusion and cats and danger. Bad things happen when you do things your body rejects. It's too late for me but not for you. Wint-O-Green Life Saver?

TERRY No thanks.

[AMBER *puts the Life Saver in her mouth. She sucks on it.*]

AMBER I probably shouldn't even be talk—

scene 6.5

[AMBER *starts choking, frothing at the mouth and dies. Sound of a cop car siren.*]

[*Cop-car video:* TERRY *is in the back of a cop car.*]

TERRY You don't understand! I think she was poisoned or something!

COP Uh-huh.

TERRY I think it was this Life Saver.

COP Mmhm.

TERRY I think there's some kind of thing going on here. Like a ring. I thought I was just finding a cat, but it turns out there's something even larger, like some kind of conspiracy is what Amber said, and then somebody silenced her. The cat got out of the bag. Who knows, it could go all the way up to the government.

COP Uh-huh. Mmm. Interesting. You know, your tits look bigger than the last time I saw 'em. You don't remember me, do you?

TERRY No.

COP Well, I remember you from your strippin' days. I saw you just a few times. Yeah, you were over there at the Cowgirls and Leather over there on Third Street. I saw you twelve or eighteen times there. You had that number with the stuffed cat. Then you moved over to The Anvil.

TERRY I don't do that anymore.

COP Then you were over at Chix on Dix, where you simulated sex on that flying harness sex swing. Then you were over at Vaginas R' Us.

TERRY I told you, I don't do that anymore. Those days are over. I'm a private investigator.

COP Yeah, yeah. Why don't you climb up to the front seat and investigate my balls.

TERRY I'm not doing that!

COP Suit yourself.

scene 7

PAPA [*To the prison guard, Malcolm.*] We like the same kind, Malcolm. Enjoy it, but don't drink it all in one night. I gave you a little something extra for your wife. Just put one in her drink every night and you will notice a world of difference. Yep, business is booming, well, thank you for asking, Malcolm. What can I say? The Internet is my friend. Malcolm, thanks again for making this workable. She's always needing me for something.

[PAPA *is seated.* TERRY *enters. She is surprised to see him.* TERRY *and* PAPA *face each other in the visiting room with a see-through divider that uses a telephone system to talk.*]

Well, well, well.

TERRY Hi, Papa, what are you doing here?

PAPA I bet you're surprised to see me, aren't ya, Terry Ann.

TERRY I am, yeah. What are ya doing here?

PAPA You're lucky I happen to be on business up here in New York City.

TERRY It's such a coincidence, Papa. I didn't even think you were employed.

PAPA A father has a sixth sense about his daughter.

TERRY Can you feel me deeply like that? Because I feel shut down when it comes to you and me.

PAPA Ya, we're gonna change that now. The fact is, Terry Ann, you've got yourself into quite a little mess on your own, haven't ya. Now, Terry Ann . . .

TERRY But I'm doing so much better than I was a couple years ago. I have a new job, it doesn't pay me quite enough, but it's a job I feel proud of and I'm sober and I'm starting to be able to trust myself.

PAPA Trust yourself? You're in the slammer, girl.

TERRY But it's not for a drug charge or solicitation. I'm innocent. I didn't do anything.

PAPA They've got you here for attempted murder.

TERRY Progress, not perfection.

PAPA You've gotta give up this fantasy, Terry Ann. I've been telling you that since you were a little girl. You have terrible instincts. This whole journey you've been on, this whole "I'm finding myself, I know who I am, I can live on my own" is a crock a' shit.

TERRY You know, sometimes I feel you run me down.

PAPA It's been a number of years without any tangible progress or concrete game plan. Now, here's the thing you need to know, Terry Ann. As I see it, you're in a real pickle, and ya got one way out, which is your dear old dad, so you're welcome.

TERRY Papa?

PAPA What?

TERRY Life is a process. I'm a work in progress, and I'm progressing. You look at everything like it's black and white, winner or loser. There's gray area, too. Can you see that at all? Have you ever thought about seeing a therapist? It could really help you.

PAPA I'll never forget when you were a little girl. And you were a Girl Scout. And you sold the most Girl Scout cookies. Remember that? Remember how you sold the most Girl Scout cookies, Terry Ann? Because you were lifting up your schoolgirl skirt showin' your panties to the neighbor men. Not much has changed, Terry Ann. You're pretending to be someone you ain't. You've gotten yourself involved with some really really really bad people.

TERRY But my sponsor says . . .

PAPA Your sponsor? That therapy mumbo jumbo is a scam. One drink won't hurt ya. Look where not drinking has gotten you.

TERRY It's not a scam.

PAPA All you need is to come home and clip the hair off my back like a good daughter. And that's my condition for bailing you out of here.

TERRY Never! I'm not coming home. I'll stay right here if I have to.

PAPA Oh yeah? You like having your nails painted in the feces of your cell mate? Does she make you lick her boots?

TERRY My other me says being a parent means loving with no strings attached. If you're gonna bail me out, bail me out. Period.

PAPA Rot in here, for all I care. Stay here in your netherworld of darkness and confusion.

[PAPA *hangs up the phone and gets up from his seat.*]

TERRY [*Knocking on the plate-glass window.*] Dad, Papa, Papa . . . please . . . Papa, I'm sorry. I'm sorry, Papa!

PAPA [*To Malcolm.*] I'm ready, Malcolm. She treats me with no respect, you see that? Well, she's sayin' she's sorry—never heard those words before.

[PAPA *sits back down to face* TERRY.]

TERRY I love you.

PAPA I know you do.

TERRY Just please help me. Get me outta here. I'll . . . do anything.

PAPA That's the Terry I remember. Meet me tonight. 105 Fifth Avenue. You're gonna clean yourself up, you're gonna come back home with me, and you're gonna help me out with Gankie, or after you get out, I'll revoke your bail. You hear me, Terry Ann?

TERRY Fine, I'll do it. Just get me outta here.

PAPA You better treat me with a little bit more respect, little miss. And do something about that breath. I can smell you through the plate-glass window.

[*He pops a Life Saver.*]

TERRY Dad . . . what is that?

PAPA What is what?

TERRY Is that a Wint-O-Green Life Saver?

PAPA Yes, it's a Wint-O-Green Life Saver. Now don't get distracted, Terry Ann. I'll see ya tonight.

scene 8

VOICE-MAIL V.O. [FANNY*'s answering machine. Beep.*] Hey, Fanny, it's Terr. I just want you to know I'm really working this case. There's this chick, Amber, and I think she was mur—

[*Beep. Beep.*]

Hey, Fanny, it's Terr again. Things have gotten really intense. I have a new lead and I think my Da—

[*Beep. Beep.*]

Hey, Fanny, it's me. I'd really love to talk to you about the case. But it better be soon 'cause I don't have a lot of minutes lef—

[*Beep.*]

[TERRY *is back in her apartment packing.*]

TERRY 2 Where are you going? Why are you packing?

TERRY I'm moving back home.

TERRY 2 Why would you even consider that?

TERRY I have to do this. You don't understand. . . . Where did I go? Where have I been? When I was in jail I disappeared.

TERRY 2 I'm having trouble hearing you, I'm having trouble seeing you.

TERRY Well, it's because I was with Papa and I feel numb.

TERRY 2 You can't move back home. You're making the problem worse.

TERRY I can't listen to you anymore, you just get me in trouble. Dad's right, I can't listen to myself, I have to listen to him.

TERRY 2 Well, he already bailed you out, so you're free. . . .

TERRY Yeah, and he'll revoke it if I don't do what he wants.

TERRY 2 Well, I don't know, but why would you go back into the belly of the beast? You don't even like him, he makes you feel terrible.

TERRY Stop saying that. He's all I have. If I'm gonna have to go home with him, I'm gonna get something stronger.

[*She grabs some pills.*]

It's the only way I can silence you.

TERRY 2 [*She grabs* TERRY *and looks her dead in the eyes.*] You gotta get your head in the game. What are you thinking? Don't be naive. Look at yourself. Yeah, things are a little dry and off, but there's potential.

TERRY I'm nothing!

[TERRY *turns the radio on really loud so she can't hear herself.* TERRY 2 *switches tactics.*]

TERRY 2 It's good to stay on top of how you take care of yourself. If I could give you some advice, I would spend a little more time highlighting the front of your hair.

TERRY You think the front? Oh, 'cause you can see the dark.

TERRY 2 Well, I like that you can see some of the dark, but if you notice my hair, there's less of it. There's a shape that comes with spiky-ness that allows the highlights to really rise.

[*Singing.*]

To the road that I must travel!
Like the sunshine rising to the universe up above!

TERRY 2 I feel like if you gave me a chance, I could make your hair look great.

TERRY Really?

TERRY 2 Yeah, because right now what's happening with your hair is, it's confused. One part of it is manipulated by the elements, and the other part of it has left the room and doesn't care.

What I'm proposing is more like this: fully doing its own thing and doesn't care what people think, and in the room and making a statement. You know I'm right. You don't have to be a victim.

TERRY Yeah . . .

TERRY 2 Terry, you okay?

TERRY I am. And I was just having a thought about Dad.

TERRY 2 What about Dad . . .

TERRY The Wint-O-Green Life Saver. He was eating one. You know what I think that means? Somehow, he's behind all of this. And we have to stop him.

TERRY 2 That's the Terry I'm talking about!

scene 8.5

[*Crime board video: The theme from* Rocky *plays as* TERRY *studies her make-shift crime board. Pictures of all the possible suspects, such as* AMBER, DYNAMIC, *Jose, Malcolm, etc., are glued to the board. String and thumbtacks connect events and characters. Cut to* TERRY *walking in slow motion down the city streets with determined purpose to meet* PAPA *at the address he gave her when he bailed her out of jail.*]

scene 9

[PAPA *is at his friend, an evil scientist's house. He is watching* Hogan's Heroes *and cat-scratching sounds are heard coming from another room.* PAPA *approaches the door to the other room with a spray bottle in his hand when the doorbell rings.*]

PAPA [*Asking with paranoia.*] Who is it?

TERRY It's Terr, Terry Ann.

[PAPA *opens the door.*]

Hey, Papa!

PAPA I knew you wouldn't disappoint, Terry Ann. You did the right thing, come on in.

[PAPA *pats* TERRY *on the ass.*]

TERRY What is this place?

PAPA Oh, I'm staying with a friend.

TERRY How do you know this friend?

PAPA It's just somebody I met at the lab.

TERRY Who?

PAPA Oh, you don't need to know about that. Just a scientist I've been doing business with.

TERRY I thought you were a janitor.

PAPA Well, I branched out. Why do you care?

TERRY Anyway, thanks for bailing me out. You really saved my bacon.

PAPA You don't have to thank me, Terry Ann, I'm just glad you came around. You know what I was just watchin'? An old episode of *Hogan's Heroes*.

TERRY *Hogan's Heroes?* The guys with the big coats and the snow. Remember, Gankie, she didn't know what country they were in.

PAPA . . . what country they were in.

[*They share a laugh.*]

TERRY Remember when you were a Hogan Hero for Halloween?

PAPA I remember. And you thought that I was a Hulk Hogan.

[*They laugh.*]

You never did have the smarts to tell what was what, Terry Ann. You never could figure it out. Nothin's changed. Ooh, hey! Remember how they had that secret tunnel under their barracks in the German prison camp?

TERRY Oh right, Papa, like you had that secret room under our house. What ever happened to that lady that lived in there? The one who was chained to the radiator?

PAPA I told you, we're never gonna talk about her.

TERRY Let me get ya a drink.

PAPA I'd love one. Whatd'ya bring for me, Terry Ann?

TERRY I got you some gin, your favorite.

[*She fixes him a drink.*]

Here ya go.

PAPA There's nothin' better. To making the right choice, Terry Ann. It took ya goddamn long enough.

TERRY You were right, Papa. New York is hard. It really wore me out. I can't do it anymore.

PAPA It's one hell of a town. You're not up to it.

TERRY It's too much . . . the grind.

[*She drinks water.*]

So tell me more about this scientist.

PAPA Sure, sure. Jail really toughened you up. I saw a side of you I never saw before. You're ready for a big-girl conversation. Get me another drink and let's have a little chat.

[*He puts the cat DNA in her drink when she's not looking. She puts the sedatives in his drink when he's not looking.*]

I could get used to this, Terry Ann. It reminds me of when you were little and you used to make me drinks. Maybe we'll have to revisit that when we get home. I got a business opportunity I might let you get involved in. Why don't you give your old papa a little massage.

[*She massages his shoulders.*]

Yeah, that feels great. Yeah, now that's the stuff.

TERRY Ya wanna lay down for a little bit?

PAPA Yeah, maybe I'll put my feet up. That's the stuff, Terry Ann.

[TERRY *helps him as he is becoming increasingly drunk and sedated.*]

TERRY Lemme just take off your glasses so you can let yourself relax.

PAPA Terry Ann . . . Terry Ann.

TERRY Papa . . .

PAPA What are you doin' snoopin' around there, Terry Ann? Why do I feel so groggy? What did you do to me?

TERRY I know you're connected to this cat crime. I've been doing my research and I think you killed Amber, so I mixed you a little Percocet and Valium cocktail. You know you said that my adventures in New York would lead to a netherworld of darkness and confusion, but they're giving me the tools to defeat you.

PAPA Well, I did something to you too, I gave you an extra dose of cat DNA.

TERRY An extra dose of what? Cat DNA?

PAPA I sent Amber to get this to you. She wasn't supposed to take it, stupid girl, she's allergic to cats. I know she made quite an impact on you. You know you two, it wasn't supposed to go down like that. The scientist who owns this place? You don't own a swanky place like this on a researcher's salary. He's involved in the black cat black market trade.

TERRY What's that?

PAPA Oh, it's a big deal. The research facility I've worked at the last thirty years is on the cutting edge. They're trying to make women more docile. Sexier. Subservient. Their plan is to combine cat DNA with a woman's DNA. They need lots of different cat DNA, so that's where I come in. I've been going all over the country procuring cats.

TERRY You monster. You stole Fanny's cat!

PAPA It's not just me. Lots of people steal cats. We've just organized it. Sorry, getting a little dizzy. Did I mention I've been injecting you with cat DNA since you hit adolescence?

TERRY What?

PAPA You were getting too independent.

TERRY It all makes sense now. I always felt like there was something different about me, you always tried to make me something I'm not, but it turns out it's because you've been injecting me with feline amino acids. What the hell is the extra dose gonna do to me?

PAPA Honestly, I have no idea. I'm a janitor, not a scientist.

TERRY Oh my God. What's in this other room, Papa?

PAPA Close that door, Terry Ann! Don't go in there!

TERRY Papa, it's not good. Why is there a cat with five heads?

PAPA You sit down there. You sit down there, Terry Ann.

TERRY You're not gonna tell me what to do.

PAPA Yes, I am, Terry Ann. You're like a cat. A stray cat. No one cares about you. And you take it and take it and never fight back. 'Cause you don't care about you either.

[*He starts choking her. There is an epic battle, a whole movement sequence.*]

TERRY I care now!

PAPA You sit down on that chair, Terry Ann.

TERRY No more! No more! No . . . meoowwww!

[*She turns into a werecat and attacks him, and calls cats from all over with her cat powers and they all devour him.*]

• • •

The Ladder in the Room

Lisa Soland

Lisa Soland

Lisa Soland's plays *Waiting*, *Cabo San Lucas*, *Truth Be Told*, *The Man in the Gray Suit & Other Plays*, and *The Name Game* have been published by Samuel French Inc. With over forty publications in all, her work can also be found in "best of" anthologies by French, Smith & Kraus, Applause Books, and Dramatic Publishing. Her newest plays include full-lengths *The Ladder Plays*, *The Hand on the Plough*, *The Sniper's Nest*, and the one-man play *Sgt. Alvin York, WWI Hero*, which is scheduled to tour throughout the 100th anniversary of WWI. Ms. Soland also writes children's books, including popular titles *The Christmas Tree Angel*, *The Unmade Moose*, *Thump*, and *Somebunny to Love*. She has produced and/or directed over eighty productions and play readings, fifty-five of which have been original, and teaches playwriting throughout the country. Visit www.LisaSoland.com.

...production history...

The Ladder in the Room was first produced in a collection of short plays by Lisa Soland, entitled *The Ladder Plays*, at the Clayton Performing Arts Center at Pellissippi State College on March 23, 2012, produced by Charles R. Miller, directed by Lisa Soland, and starring Jeni Lamm as Miss Johnson and Jennifer Brown as Nurse.

The play was then produced at Muskingum University Theatre in New Concord, Ohio, in the same collection, and opened on November 29, 2012.

The Ladder in the Room was produced again in another collection, entitled 10-Minute Play Festival—An Evening of Short Plays by Lisa Soland, by Ohio University-Chollicothe in Athens, Ohio, in April 2015, and was directed by Steven McBride.

The Ladder Plays then opened at the Hermosa Beach Playhouse on October 7, 2016, in Hermosa Beach, California, produced by Gerry Athas-Vazquez and directed by Julie Nunis.

characters

NURSE Any age.

MISS JOHNSON In her "ladder" years.

time

Evening.

place

The private room in an elderly care center.

props

Bible, tray with food, two glasses, small clock, pearl necklace, bottle of pills, eyeglasses, robe, slippers, wheelchair.

setting

A hospital bed is center stage with a pillow, sheets, and blanket. Placed straddling the bed is a hospital-type table/tray on which sits Miss Johnson's Bible. There is another larger table upstage right, which contains a hair-brush, a glass of water, and an empty glass, along with a toothbrush and paste. The lights are low but for a lit area around the bed and slightly about the room. In a darkened corner, downstage left, is the ladder.

[*At rise:* MISS JOHNSON *is lying in the bed, with* NURSE *sitting to her right, feeding her.*]

NURSE How 'bout just one more bite and I won't say another word.

[MISS JOHNSON *opens her mouth just enough for* NURSE *to spoon in one last bite.*]

It's not much but it's more than we thought.

MISS JOHNSON More than you thought.

NURSE [*Surprised that she's spoken.*] Well, hello there to you too!

MISS JOHNSON There's a reason I no longer have an appetite. There's a reason for everything.

NURSE Thank you for joining us this evening.

MISS JOHNSON People who make something of their lives believe that everything happens for a reason. Even people. We happen for a reason. Our lives mean something. I read that in the Bible.

NURSE That's in the Bible?

MISS JOHNSON "He knitted you in the womb." Doesn't that sound like to you that there's a reason?

NURSE [*Rises and places dishes on the table upstage left.*] I suppose you're right.

MISS JOHNSON [*Invites* NURSE *to sit back down beside her.*] When I was a little girl, abortion was illegal, so when my father found out my mother was pregnant, again, he forced her to drink a quart of castor oil. My word, they used castor oil for everything back then. He'd heard from his buddies down at the station that drinking castor oil would do the trick. My mother already had her hands full. He knew that, because she complained to him all the time about how her hands were always so very full. They had eight children already. They didn't need a ninth.

NURSE You're from a family of nine?

MISS JOHNSON Twelve. I'm not done with the story.

NURSE All right then, Miss Chatty.

MISS JOHNSON He had her drink the castor oil thinking that God didn't have a plan for that little baby inside of her. But he did. He did indeed. That little baby grew up big and strong, and lived a good life.

[*Beat.*]

I was a teacher, you know.

NURSE Yes, I heard that. I heard that all of your students adored you.

MISS JOHNSON Adore me? Phooey! They did something more important than adore me! They made something of themselves, and contributed something to this world, and you know how hard that is.

NURSE I sure do.

MISS JOHNSON We all need to try to leave things better than we find them. When you walk through the woods, pick up the garbage. When you walk down the sidewalk, smile to those headin' your way, even when they're not smilin' back. Sometimes it's the little things. Like the way you brush my hair. I tried to teach my students that. Some say I did . . . but I can't be caught braggin' now. I must be found blameless when the Lord comes for me.

NURSE Well, no one's coming for you anytime soon. You're in excellent health.

[*Rises, gets hairbrush, and begins to brush* MISS JOHNSON*'s hair attentively.*]

Besides, your daughter called and said she's stoppin' by to see you in the morning.

MISS JOHNSON She called?

NURSE You were napping.

MISS JOHNSON Well, let's see if she's worth her word this time.

NURSE You're the one who's forgetful.

MISS JOHNSON I'm the one who's forgotten.

NURSE Well, that's what she said. She said she was coming to see you tomorrow. Tomorrow morning.

[*Light comes up on the ladder, downstage left.* MISS JOHNSON *takes* NURSE *by the arm and they stop what they're doing.*]

MISS JOHNSON Did you feel that?

NURSE What?

MISS JOHNSON That change in the room, just now.

NURSE No, ma'am. Can't say that I did.

MISS JOHNSON The lights or something. Something changed.

NURSE [*Looks around the room.*] Nothing I can tell.

MISS JOHNSON Well, all right then.

[*They continue with their nightly ritual.*]

My daughter sets out to do something for others, but it never works out that way. Then she disguises it and says she was busy. Blames it on everything but her own misguided priorities. Self-focused. She's focused too much on herself and her own little life. It's a disease. Wish they'd come up with a prescription for that.

NURSE If they did, most everyone would be on it now, wouldn't they?

[*Puts hairbrush on table and brings* MISS JOHNSON *two glasses—one empty and one with water—along with her toothbrush topped with paste.*]

MISS JOHNSON [*Smiling.*] I suppose you're right.

[*She begins to brush her teeth.*]

NURSE There wasn't anything for me beneath our Christmas tree last year. Three kids and not one of them thought of me.

MISS JOHNSON I've never heard of such a thing.

NURSE I would have caught hell if I didn't get them every little thing on their lists. I know they don't have much, but what's wrong with making something?

MISS JOHNSON [*With toothbrush in mouth.*] Absolutely!

NURSE Writing me a poem. Anything.

MISS JOHNSON Well, sure.

NURSE But not one present under that fake tree they talked me into buying so my house wouldn't burn down. Couldn't pay the electric bill, but by God, I've got myself a non-flammable Christmas tree. I done plug it into an outlet with no juice. Ain't that the way.

MISS JOHNSON I hate to hear that.

NURSE What are you going to do?

[*She places the tooth-brushing items on the table, upstage right.*]

MISS JOHNSON I have something for you.

NURSE Now, I didn't share that personal tidbit in order to squeeze some sort of sympathy out of you. I was simply—

MISS JOHNSON Come here.

NURSE Miss Johnson—

MISS JOHNSON Come here now.

[MISS JOHNSON *removes pearl necklace from around her neck.*]

Try this on your collarbone.

NURSE [*She steps back.*] Those are your pearls. Your husband gave you those.

MISS JOHNSON I have no more need for them.

NURSE I can't accept them. I'm just your nurse.

MISS JOHNSON You've been much more to me than just a nurse now. You know that.

[*Places them into* NURSE*'s hands.*]

Put them on.

[NURSE *puts on the necklace as told. Smiling at* NURSE.]

Have yourself a look.

NURSE [*Crosses to the mirror, downstage right, and looks.*] Oh, my gracious. They're absolutely gorgeous. I have no words.

MISS JOHNSON None needed.

NURSE I bet you miss him, Miss Johnson. You never say so but don't you? Something terrible.

MISS JOHNSON The Lord was good to give us so much time together, and then have me go for such a little time without him.

NURSE [*Looks back in the mirror.*] Oh my. You sure you're ready to give these up?

MISS JOHNSON I'm sure.

NURSE They're too nice . . .

MISS JOHNSON Too nice for "someone knitted in the womb"?

NURSE [*Accepting the gift.*] Well, I'm grateful, Miss Johnson. Thank you.

MISS JOHNSON You tuck them away now when you leave or they'll think you coerced them out of me.

NURSE I'm going to wear these tonight when my man takes me out on the town.

MISS JOHNSON You're going out tonight and here I am holding you up?!

NURSE No bother.

MISS JOHNSON Where?

NURSE Nelly's.

MISS JOHNSON What's that?

NURSE A bar.

MISS JOHNSON Sounds like the name of a horse. When you walk in does everyone whinny?

NURSE You are in prime form tonight, Miss Johnson. I'm sorry I have to leave at all.

MISS JOHNSON What are you going to a bar for with a man who says he's interested in you?

NURSE That's where my Sam likes to go.

MISS JOHNSON [*Indignant.*] "My Sam."

[*Invites* NURSE *to sit down and listen.*]

When a man takes a woman out, he takes her to where she wants to go, not to where he wants to go. Got that?

NURSE Got that. But that ain't where we're going.

MISS JOHNSON Keep it in mind then, for next time.

NURSE I will.

[*Takes from* MISS JOHNSON *her eyeglasses.*]

MISS JOHNSON What time is it?

NURSE [*Crosses to put eyeglasses on table, upstage right.*] Why do you ask?

MISS JOHNSON You best be on your way. I got myself some things to do.

NURSE Miss Johnson, you ain't got nothing to do tonight but rest up for your visit tomorrow.

MISS JOHNSON I just had a very nice visit with you tonight. That's enough for me.

NURSE Now you stay put! You're lucky they found your pretty self last week, sleeping in the broom closet next to the cafeteria. What were you thinking?!

MISS JOHNSON A little bedtime snack.

[*She winks at* NURSE.]

NURSE Don't be pullin' my leg with that crap. I know sure as I'm standing here, you can't walk. If you're gonna offer up a reason for them finding you curled up in a ball beneath a pile of ol' dirty rags, you better offer up the truth, 'cause I ain't got time for nothing but. You got me into trouble, I'll have you know.

MISS JOHNSON Oh, dear.

NURSE "How else would she had gotten there?" they asked. Convinced I put you in that wheelchair and done left you there.

MISS JOHNSON I'm sorry to hear that.

NURSE They blamed me!

MISS JOHNSON [*Quietly, in secret.*] Sally, my husband was calling to me.

NURSE What?

MISS JOHNSON My Frank. He was standing over there in the corner, right there, wanting me to follow him.

NURSE You be giving me the chills now—

MISS JOHNSON He's been calling to me for days and I can't just ignore him.

NURSE I got goose bumps all the way down my spine.

MISS JOHNSON After sixty-eight years of marriage, a woman learns to listen. And obey.

NURSE You done stay in that bed, Miss Johnson, or you're gonna get yourself and me into a heap of trouble and maybe this time no one'll find you. Your husband is in heaven. And you're still here. For a reason, like you said. Let's not go mixing things up now, you hear?

MISS JOHNSON I'll do my best, that's all I can promise.

NURSE Your "best," my eye. Now let's have those slippers.

[*She removes* MISS JOHNSON*'s slippers.*]

MISS JOHNSON The Lord and I have a deal. He opens the doors and I walk through 'em.

NURSE [*She then begins to remove* MISS JOHNSON*'s robe.*] That's why you done so well for yourself, I suppose—all those doors openin' up right before your eyes. For me, they be doing nothing but slammin' shut. My rent's due and I ain't got it. I've done had it with all this "budgeting" nonsense.

[*She folds the robe and hangs it on the wheelchair stage left of bed.*]

You can't budget what you don't got.

MISS JOHNSON Do you call on the Lord?

NURSE I call on Him to mind His own business.

MISS JOHNSON Sally!

NURSE All respect to you, ma'am, but ever since my daddy died, I quit believin' in a God that refused to supply a young girl with the simple things she needed to survive in this crazy mixed-up world. He left me in the hands of takers.

MISS JOHNSON And you've been in those hands ever since.

NURSE Yes, ma'am.

MISS JOHNSON And now you believe that's all there is, don't you?

NURSE Yes, ma'am. That's right.

MISS JOHNSON I understand.

NURSE How can you believe in such a God?

MISS JOHNSON Faith.

NURSE Well . . . I need to get me some of that faith. Mine done all run out, it done run all out of my empty pockets.

[*The light above the ladder grows more intense.*]

MISS JOHNSON Do you see that, Sally? The light?

NURSE Stop that now. You're frightening me.

MISS JOHNSON You don't notice any change in the room?

NURSE Changes don't happen in a room unless a person makes them happen. And only you and me is in here, ma'am. Let's lie back down now.

[*She lowers the back of the hospital bed a bit.*]

See? I be makin' a change here, lying you back down. That's how it works. And now I be tucking you in, the way you like. Another change that I'm here doing so it's getting done.

[*She moves from stage left around the bed to stage right, tucking the sheets in tightly.*]

Nothing happens in this world unless a person do it. No magic to it.

MISS JOHNSON Sometimes I lie in bed at night, and I focus softly on the ceiling there. Like this, relaxed. But instead of focusing on the plaster and the paint, I pretend like there's something in the air just below the paint, floating. And I focus my eyes on that thing suspended in the air and suddenly . . . there it is.

NURSE What?

MISS JOHNSON Energy.

NURSE What?!

MISS JOHNSON Energy. I can see it, moving. God's hand moving through the world. No one sees it 'cause they don't believe it's there.

NURSE No one sees it 'cause they're looking at the plaster.

MISS JOHNSON That's right. That's exactly right.

NURSE Now you stay put tonight. You hear?

MISS JOHNSON The Lord and I still have that deal. Any door He opens for me, I'm still going to walk right on through.

NURSE [*She moves the wheelchair against the wall, stage left, out of the way.*] Not many more doors you walking through, Miss Johnson, 'cause . . . you can't walk. How you got to that broom closet is beyond my comprehension. Those legs done quit on you months ago.

MISS JOHNSON I can do all things through the Lord who strengthens me.

NURSE Yeah, but not walk. You and me need to get on the same page here now. The Bible wasn't talking about no walking at this point in your life, Miss. Johnson. It was talking about other stuff maybe . . . talking maybe. . . . For God's sake you be talking up a storm tonight. But not walking. No more walking for you.

MISS JOHNSON Get rid of this food now and be off with you.

NURSE [*Crosses to the table, upstage right.*] My, ain't we bossy!

MISS JOHNSON It's time for me to rest.

NURSE Ah! Now we're on the same page! Tomorrow, the hairdresser is comin' around nine and I'll help you with your makeup so you can look all dolled up when your daughter comes.

MISS JOHNSON My daughter.

[*She touches the necklace hanging around* NURSE*'s neck.*]

Maybe I better write you a note for this necklace, saying that I gave it to you, officially. My daughter might think—

NURSE I don't fight no one for nothing. She wants it, she can have it.

MISS JOHNSON Hand me that piece of paper there.

NURSE What a bother.

[*She hands it to* MISS JOHNSON.]

MISS JOHNSON "I, Thelma Johnson, here declare . . ."

NURSE [*Appreciating the pearls on the necklace, she looks closer.*] Fancy.

MISS JOHNSON ". . . that I legally and willingly gave this pearl necklace to Sally Hodge as a gift . . ."

NURSE What are these gemstones in between the pearls?

MISS JOHNSON Oh, I don't know—something or other.

[*Continues to write.*]

"And hope that she enjoys it right up to her dying day."

NURSE Well, I sure will indeed. I sure will indeed.

MISS JOHNSON Slip that into your wallet. And don't be too surprised if you have to use it.

NURSE [*Taking the note, she slips it into her pocket.*] How could you think your own daughter . . . ?

MISS JOHNSON Self-focused people get greedy. And those pearls are the real deal.

NURSE Just like you.

[*They share a smile.*]

But if these pearls were plastic, I'd appreciate them just the same. It's the thought that matters.

MISS JOHNSON But "thoughts" don't pay the bills. Next week, when all the fuss is over . . .

NURSE Fuss?!

MISS JOHNSON . . . take them to the jeweler—the Jewish man on the corner of Eighth and Vine.

NURSE Listen to you go on.

MISS JOHNSON He'll help you. Then you might open for yourself a mutual fund . . .

NURSE Mutual fund?!

MISS JOHNSON . . . and you won't have to worry any more.

NURSE [*Crosses to upstage-right table and gets pill.*] The only thing I'm worrying about right now is you.

MISS JOHNSON Promise me.

NURSE [*Crosses to her bedside.*] All right, I promise. Open up.

MISS JOHNSON What you got there?

NURSE How come when I ask you to open that mouth of yours, you shut it?!

MISS JOHNSON What is that?

NURSE Something to help calm your nerves.

MISS JOHNSON [*Shocked.*] We agreed.

NURSE I'm thinkin' you need this now, with all this talking about energy and things.

MISS JOHNSON You don't believe me, do you?

NURSE No, I do not.

MISS JOHNSON It's like the ladder.

NURSE What ladder?

MISS JOHNSON The ladder. There's always a ladder in the room. Like an opened doorway into another world, inviting us to move forward.

NURSE What in the world are you going on about now?

MISS JOHNSON Just because you can't see things, doesn't mean they're not there.

NURSE Miss Johnson, you are resting this evening. Resting. Not hanging out in the broom closet, not looking at energy, not finding yourself a friendly ghost to converse with. Resting. This will help you to rest.

MISS JOHNSON I prefer to be alert.

NURSE Open up now.

MISS JOHNSON Then hand me that glass of water there.

NURSE I'm just doing my job.

[NURSE *turns away to get glass of water.*]

MISS JOHNSON [*Putting pill under the mattress.*] And I'm just doing mine.

NURSE [*Hands* MISS JOHNSON *glass of water and* MISS JOHNSON *mimes placing pill into her mouth and then she drinks.*]

Thank you.

[*Puts water back on table.*]

MISS JOHNSON You have some blessings coming your way. I know it. Hold out now, for a good man—

NURSE [*She removes necklace.*] My Sam's a good man.

MISS JOHNSON Wear this necklace and remember that you're worth more than you know. "He knitted you in the womb." You have a purpose. To make a difference, like you've done here with me. Don't waste one day, not one day thinking otherwise.

NURSE Enough of this talk now. I'm turning out the light.

MISS JOHNSON Promise me.

NURSE I promise you. Done.

[*She puts necklace in her pocket.*]

MISS JOHNSON [*She hands Bible to* NURSE.] Remember me.

NURSE [*Taking the Bible.*] You're hard to forget.

[*She kisses* MISS JOHNSON *on the head.*]

Good night, Thelma.

[*Places Bible on the table.*]

MISS JOHNSON Good night, Sally.

[NURSE *crosses stage left.*]

I love you. Remember that.

NURSE I love you too. And thanks for the very kind gift.

[*She places her hand on her pocket, where the necklace is.*]

MISS JOHNSON 'Night.

[NURSE *turns out lights and exits. With hands folded,* MISS JOHNSON *says her prayers.*]

Our Father, who art in heaven. Hallowed be thy name. Thy kingdom come, thy will be done on earth as it is in heaven. Give us this day . . .

[*The light in the room begins to grow, but most significantly, over the ladder.*]

Oh! He's come. Frank, is that you?

[*The light grows in intensity and pours down from above the ladder and we now see it clearly.* THELMA *gets out of bed and walks, without a problem, to the base of the ladder.*]

Frank?

[*Trying to look up the ladder into the blinding light. She smiles brightly, as complete peace overtakes her.*]

Oh, my darling, I missed you so very much.

[*She begins to climb the steps. Lights out.*]

• • •

The Hoodie Play

Liz Amadio

Liz Amadio

Liz Amadio has a rich history in theater as a dancer, poet, actor, playwright, director, and producer, with credits spanning New York, regionally, and abroad. Amadio has an MFA from the Actors Studio Drama School (New School) and is a member of the Dramatists Guild, the League of Professional Theatre Women, and the National League of American Pen Women.

... production history ...

The Hoodie Play had its world premiere as an Equity-Approved Showcase. It was produced by Cosmic Orchid as its inaugural production. It had a rotating venue with performances at ART-NY's Bruce Mitchell Room, the Westbeth Community Room, and the Great Room at South Oxford Space. The show ran from October 2 to 25, 2015, with ten performances.

characters

CHRISSY/SKI RACER Zoe Anastassiou
DARREN/BLACK TEEN Don Jenkins*
JUSTIN/AUTISTIC BOY Alex Sapozhnik
SHAKTI/HIGH PRIESTESS Margaret Stockton*

*These actors are appearing courtesy of Actors' Equity Association.

Director: Liz Amadio
Production Assistant: Daniel Martin McHenry
Stage Manager: Alana Tyrrell

In the moments after being shot, Darren reflects upon his life, his spiritual path, and his connection to a diverse collective consciousness.

time

Now.

place

All across America.

characters

Each character has a defining hoodie color and prop/activity.

CHRISSY Ski Racer; Yellow Hoodie; SKI POLES (*WHOOSH.*)
DARREN A Black Teen; Red Hoodie; DRUM
JUSTIN An Autistic Boy; Green Hoodie; LEGOS
SHAKTI A High Priestess; Purple Hoodie; BELLS/CHANTS

[*The stage is bare except for the property in each quadrant, each bathed in spots: DSL—DRUM/red; USL—LEGOS/green; USR—SKI POLES/yellow; and DSR—2 BELLS/violet. The upstage wall has five different color hoodies hanging from it. From left to right—purple, blue, rainbow, green, and red. "I Zimbra" by Talking Heads (or something like it) begins to play.* SHAKTI, CHRISSY, JUSTIN, *and* DARREN *enter the stage. They meander but make no contact; investigate the objects and hoodies, as if they're not sure which is theirs. Eventually, they each put on a hoodie and face the upstage wall. Just before the song ends, they turn. As the song ends, the sound of a gunshot causes them to contract, then rush to their respective spots. Initially unaware of the others, as if isolated in separate locations, they gradually acknowledge and eventually interact with one another.* JUSTIN *is the first to sense the others' presence.*]

[*Sounds are as follows: DRUMS; LEGOS clang, like a cymbal; BELLS, two of different tones followed by a chant; WHOOSH—SKI POLES move front to back whilst all contribute to the WHOOSH sound. Characters randomly engage in their activity throughout.*]

JUSTIN My hoodie makes me feel safe.

CHRISSY My hoodie makes me feel safe.

SHAKTI My hoodie makes me feel safe.

DARREN My hoodie makes me—

SHAKTI My hoodie commands presence.

CHRISSY My hoodie makes me feel warm.

DARREN My hoodie makes me—

JUSTIN My hoodie makes me feel protected.

[*Silent moment. DRUM.*]

DARREN For as long as I can remember, I loved jazz. I remember the first time I heard Coltrane. Man, the hairs stood up on my little body. I must have been about eight. We were at a family party and my uncle, the cool uncle who lived in Harlem, he brought the tunes. He didn't bring Coltrane—it was Gil—Gil Scott-Heron. This one song he did sounded really different—"Is that Jazz?" It asked a question that went way over my head—about the nature of things—

ALL The nature of things.

JUSTIN The nature of things.

CHRISSY The nature of things.

SHAKTI The nature of things—

DARREN Not just jazz but the nature of all things. It also named a retrospective of all the jazz greats. I got the lyrics and started listening to everyone he mentions in that song. Basie, Ellington, Bird, Billie, Miles. And then I got to 'Trane.

[*Sings.*]

"Trane struck a vein of laughter and pain—adventures the mind could explore." And that was it. I became different—

ALL Different.

SHAKTI Different.

CHRISSY Different.

JUSTIN Different—

DARREN Different from that moment on. How could I turn my posse on to Coltrane? They'd think I was nuts. And my uncle? Once he caught on to my taste, he started taking me downtown to all the old Village vinyl haunts. Bought me a turntable and helped me score a collection. Things were never the same after that.

[*Pause.*]

I could never be like everyone else ever again.

[*DRUM stop. Silent moment.*]

JUSTIN My hoodie is a temple of solitude.

CHRISSY My hoodie is a temple of grandeur.

SHAKTI My hoodie is a temple of serenity.

DARREN My hoodie is a temple of isolation.

JUSTIN My hoodie protects me from the lies.

CHRISSY My hoodie hides the lies.

SHAKTI My hoodie reveals the lies.

DARREN My hoodie is a lie.

[*Silent moment. DRUM starts lightly, gains momentum.*]

SHAKTI From a very early age, I understood that creativity is the root of all spirituality. It's not that I was withdrawn, I was involved—very involved internally. I became receptive to the influence of my intuition.

[*Rings BELLS.*]

By becoming calm and waiting patiently, I learned to seek guidance from within.

[*Rings BELLS.*]

At first, this was done during a simple task—drawing a picture, listening to the rhythm of music, eventually dancing.

[*Moves her body in place—as in a dance.*]

I was a lover of dance. I could allow my body to communicate and my mind would step aside, sensing the mystery that was unfolding in my psyche. I became open to allowing my dreams to guide me. I was quite young, I guess at an age when dreams and reality were still fluid. I couldn't always delineate one from the other. I was born with the ability to trust—

ALL Trust.

DARREN Trust.

JUSTIN Trust.

CHRISSY Trust—

SHAKTI To trust my inner voice, even though I couldn't articulate it. When I did communicate, it was always through the lens of the arts. Somehow, art gave me a sense of a larger reality. Through imagination, I could see the potential in the universe. I was totally open to what could be. I did, however, appear detached from the outside. Very detached.

[*DRUM punctuates "detached." Stops.*]

This disturbed the adults. They began to take me to the experts. After a series of shrink evaluations, someone suggested that my parents take me to a priest. The priest wanted to perform an exorcism but my mother refused. She knew I had the gift. She took me abroad to see a great spiritual advisor in Austria. Why Austria? I know it seems rather random. Why not India or . . . I don't seem to remember the reason.

[SHAKTI *trails off, as if in a trance, begins chanting and ringing BELLS. A transition, then present, resolute. The others do not acknowledge her.*]

My hoodie gives me reverence.

JUSTIN [*As if he hears the word in his head.*] What's reverence?

SHAKTI My hoodie tells everyone I am to be respected.

CHRISSY My hoodie tells everyone I am to be admired.

DARREN My hoodie tells everyone I am to be feared.

JUSTIN My hoodie tells everyone I'm weird.

CHRISSY My hoodie tells everyone I am a winner.

DARREN My hoodie tells everyone I am dangerous.

[*DRUM; BELLS; LEGOS; WHOOSH. Silent moment.*]

The first time they were scared of me, I couldn't have been more than eleven. I was walking home from the courts and there they were, on the street, an old white couple. They saw me and I could feel the—

ALL Panic.

JUSTIN Panic.

CHRISSY Panic.

SHAKTI Panic—

DARREN The panic pulsing through their veins. At first, I thought something was going on—you know, another 9/11. I looked up toward the sky because when I walk, I always look down toward the ground. Not like I hate myself or anything, just connected—

ALL Grounded.

SHAKTI Grounded.

CHRISSY Grounded.

JUSTIN Grounded—

DARREN Grounded and then I got it. It was me! It was me they were afraid of. They were cringing, cringing as I got closer. There was nothing in the sky. There were no sirens or helicopters. I was the one making them—

ALL Fear.

JUSTIN Fear.

CHRISSY Fear.

SHAKTI Fear—

DARREN Fear for their life. A sudden sick feeling hit me in the stomach. It was as if my whole life I hadn't been touched by this and all of a sudden, in that moment, the collective of all that negative energy smacks me in the face—punches me below the belt—in that moment of realization.

[*Pause.*]

Should I cross the street before I pass them?

[*Pause.*]

ALL Why should I?

JUSTIN Why should I?

CHRISSY Why should I?

SHAKTI Why should I?

ALL Why should I?

[*Silent moment.*]

JUSTIN My hoodie has a life of its own.

CHRISSY My hoodie has a life of its own.

SHAKTI My hoodie has a life of its own.

DARREN My hoodie has a life of its own.

JUSTIN My hoodie saves me.

SHAKTI My hoodie honors me.

CHRISSY My hoodie frees me.

DARREN My hoodie tyrannizes me.

[*Silent moment.*]

CHRISSY When I was a teenager, I wasn't interested in what everyone else was doing. The whole adolescent thing—escaped me. I had no time for it. It's not that I was interested in sports, either—not the kind of sports they were playing in my high school. But competition?

[*LEGOS.*]

ALL Competition.

SHAKTI Competition.

DARREN Competition.

JUSTIN Competition.

CHRISSY The idea of competition sparked something in me.

[*WHOOSH.*]

I first started skiing as a child on a family vacation. My mother was a leisure skier. It's a social sport, after all. In Europe, a huge part of the festivities involves après-ski—gathering around a tall hearth in the chalet with hot chocolate for the kids and Bombay Sapphires for the adults.

[*DRUM start.*]

I did not like ski school. Skiing is a difficult sport. It's balance. It's all balance. But it can be boring. Somewhere along the way, I learned about ski racing. I think I saw a giant slalom race once whilst looking out the enormous picture window of the chalet. That was it. I was on a quest.

[*BELLS.*]

Racing down the mountain gave me a sense of freedom I had only dreamed about. The speed and the absolute sensory shutdown was sheer exhilaration. You can't hear anything but the wind when you're racing.

[*DRUM stops. WHOOSH.*]

Everything else melts away. It's as if you get to put the whole world on "mute." It's a feeling I can't describe. Once you get good at it, that's when the real competition starts. But the wild part is, while you're in the midst of the race, you have no idea what your timing is. The whole world has their eyes on you with your time right up there on the screen—but you can't see it.

ALL Can't see it.

JUSTIN Can't see it.

DARREN Can't see it.

SHAKTI Can't see it.

CHRISSY You can't see it. You're in such an adrenaline rush, there's no way for you to really know if you're beating your best time or way behind—if you're a winner or a loser. But winning? The competition is everything. To be the best!

[*Looks around to see if anyone recognizes her.*]

My hoodie prepares me to compete!

SHAKTI My hoodie prepares me for the outside world.

DARREN My hoodie hides me from the outside world.

JUSTIN My hoodie tells me there is no outside world.

CHRISSY My hoodie mutes my world.

SHAKTI My hoodie completes my world.

JUSTIN My hoodie is my world.

DARREN My hoodie ends my world.

[*DRUM, LEGOS, WHOOSH, BELLS. Silent moment.*]

JUSTIN I remember the first time they laughed at me. I didn't really feel different. They made me feel different. I tried to have fun with them but it felt like I was missing something. I would like to be aware, more aware. Sometimes, the kids at school treat me like I'm from another planet. They say I'm different—

ALL Different.

CHRISSY Different.

SHAKTI Different.

DARREN Different—

JUSTIN But I'm not different. Because I don't understand why they have to feel what they're feeling. People say they're aware of my feelings but they're not. They think I don't want to talk to anybody, don't want to be friends with anybody, just want to sit in a corner by myself and build. But that's not it. It's hard—

ALL It's hard.

DARREN It's hard.

SHAKTI It's hard.

CHRISSY It's hard—

JUSTIN It's really hard to try to talk to people, to connect with people. People aren't very clear. You have to try to figure people out. But when I build? Everything fits into place.

[*LEGOS.*]

One into another. And the colors, you don't have to figure out. Not like people, colors are there.

[*Pause.*]

Like my hoodie—

ALL My hoodie.

SHAKTI My hoodie.

CHRISSY My hoodie.

DARREN My hoodie.

SHAKTI My hoodie defines me.

CHRISSY My hoodie defines me.

JUSTIN My hoodie defines me.

DARREN My hoodie defies me.

CHRISSY My hoodie feels good.

JUSTIN My hoodie feels like home.

CHRISSY My hoodie feels like heaven.

DARREN My hoodie feels like hell.

JUSTIN Oho, that's a curse word! You're not supposed to curse!

DARREN My hoodie is a curse.

SHAKTI My hoodie is a blessing.

CHRISSY My hoodie represents me.

JUSTIN My hoodie is me.

SHAKTI You are not what you wear.

DARREN I am what I wear.

[*WHOOSH.*]

JUSTIN But I'm wearing the same thing. How can it feel so different?

[*Pause.*]

Maybe it's the color.

[*Pause.*]

I feel color. Green is my color.

CHRISSY Green circle, blue square, one black diamond, two black diamonds. No color zones. Fearless when you're skiing.

SHAKTI I feel colors.

JUSTIN They don't make me feel messy. Most colors are clear. Other colors seem too bright, too violent.

[*Silent moment.*]

DARREN When I first found out I was black, I must have been about five. It was my sister's birthday and we were shopping for a present for her—me and my mom. I saw this doll—this life-sized doll—and I asked my mother to get it for her. I think I had $3.72 saved up in my piggy bank, all in change, stuffed in my pocket. My mother promised—

ALL Promised.

JUSTIN Promised.

CHRISSY Promised.

SHAKTI Promised—

DARREN Promised that I could get my sister a birthday present of my own—from me—not the same as the one they were giving her. She even promised to chip in the difference between what I had—the $3.72—and whatever the present cost. This doll had a price tag—$15.99. Not that I had much understanding of the value of money at that age, but it didn't seem like too much money. "This one!" I tell my mother, as I raise up the doll. "No, not that one!" Maybe it was a lot more money than she could spend. I reach into my pants pocket, change pouring out onto the ground: "When I get my allowance, I can pay you back the rest." As I struggle to pick up my money, her resolute—

ALL No.

SHAKTI No.

CHRISSY No.

JUSTIN No—

DARREN "No" echoes through the aisle as she starts pulling the doll out of my hands. Just then, a little white girl comes up to me. "I want one just like that one, Mommy!" My mother manages to pull the doll from my grip, mumbles something to the other mother, and hands the girl the doll. Before I could open my mouth: "Why does she . . . ," my mother pulls me down the aisle and around the corner, desperately—

ALL Desperately.

JUSTIN Desperately.

CHRISSY Desperately.

SHAKTI Desperately.

ALL Desperately—

DARREN Scanning the shelves along the way. Finally, she comes upon a doll that, to me, looked just like the one I had in my hand. And it was $15.99. "Isn't this the one you want to give your sister?"

[*Pause.*]

I didn't see any difference. Every time I opened my mouth with "But . . ." I got shushed. We bought the doll and rushed out of the store. She wouldn't even let me chip in my $3.72. But when we got out to the car, my mother explained to me that the first doll was a white doll and it belonged to that white girl. And the doll we bought my sister was a black doll because we were black.

[*Pause.*]

I pulled that doll out of the bag and spent the rest of the ride comparing her plastic skin to mine. Didn't exactly match but . . .

[*Pause.*]

The next day I got out my Thomas the Train collection, grabbed a black marker, and colored every one of their faces black.

[*Long silence.*]

CHRISSY [*Breaks through as if cheering them up.*] I remember the first time they cheered me.

SHAKTI I remember the first time they were in awe of me.

[*BELLS.*]

CHRISSY They were in awe of you? They were in awe of me too.

[*WHOOSH.*]

JUSTIN They were never in awe of me.

[*LEGOS.*]

SHAKTI It made me feel connected.

DARREN Connected to what?

CHRISSY Connected to people.

JUSTIN People?

DARREN They're afraid of me.

JUSTIN Why?

SHAKTI Why?

CHRISSY Why?

DARREN My hoodie makes me a target.

JUSTIN A target for what?

SHAKTI For judgment.

JUSTIN I don't like to be judged.

CHRISSY All I know is judgment.

[*Silent moment.*]

JUSTIN Do you think the world is messy?

CHRISSY This is where I can go crazy!

[*WHOOSH racing down the mountain.*]

JUSTIN As long as you don't hurt anyone.

SHAKTI There are times when I don't like to have control.

JUSTIN This is where I can be messy.

[*LEGOS.*]

DARREN This is where I can be messy.

[*DRUM wild and fierce.*]

CHRISSY Racing is a place where messy is comfortable.

[*LEGOS, BELLS, WHOOSH. Silent moment.*]

JUSTIN They hate me.

CHRISSY They're envious of me.

SHAKTI They admire me.

DARREN They want to destroy me.

JUSTIN They want my hoodie but they can't have it.

SHAKTI I don't want your hoodie!

CHRISSY I want your hoodie.

DARREN Take my hoodie.

[DARREN *goes over to* JUSTIN *and gestures to give him his hoodie.* JUSTIN *ignores him and keeps building.*]

[*WHOOSH. Silent moment.*]

SHAKTI What are you making?

JUSTIN Anything symmetrical.

DARREN Do you like to build?

JUSTIN It's my favorite.

CHRISSY What are you building?

JUSTIN A house spaceship that keeps the little alien from bad aliens. When he needs to hide, he's protected by everything. If he needs to get out, he launches up.

CHRISSY And no one can see him?

JUSTIN He's the only one with eyes and no one can see him in here.

DARREN Is that you in there?

JUSTIN That's you.

DARREN That's me.

JUSTIN Do you feel like an alien?

DARREN I am the alien.

JUSTIN I made you this creation—a house as big as this whole room. And it will keep you safe.

ALL Safe.

CHRISSY Safe.

SHAKTI Safe.

DARREN Safe.

ALL Safe.

[JUSTIN *hands* DARREN *the creation, but* DARREN *realizes there is no room for both objects in his arms. He places the drum on the floor in the center.* JUSTIN *shows* DARREN *how to launch the alien, then gives him the creation.* DARREN *tries it.* JUSTIN *pulls down his hood.*]

CHRISSY He made you a beautiful home.

DARREN Thank you.

[*WHOOSH. BELLS. LEGOS.* DARREN *engages the alien, ascending, descending, in and out of the house, as* JUSTIN *speaks.*]

JUSTIN The world is so messy and so hard to understand. But here, here I have control. Do you think I am organized, that my building is organized? It is. It has to be because my mind—it's really all over the place—messy. But if I'm messy when I'm building, it's going to break. I focus real hard to build so I know what's what, so I know what I'm doing and where I am going. I wish I could have that control with people, talking to people. I wish that people would understand me, understand that's why I do this. And why I shut down. I feel like screaming when they don't get it.

CHRISSY You think it's you that doesn't understand people but you do! You gave him exactly what he needed—security.

SHAKTI You need to understand yourself.

[*WHOOSH.* CHRISSY *starts flying down a mountain.*]

What are you racing from?

CHRISSY I'm not racing from anything.

JUSTIN What are you racing to?

CHRISSY Freedom.

SHAKTI Freedom?

DARREN Freedom?

JUSTIN Freedom?

CHRISSY Sometimes you're the best and you still don't win the race.

JUSTIN A world where you're nice and you still don't get what you want?

DARREN I don't want to live in a world like that.

SHAKTI It's not fair.

JUSTIN It's not fair.

CHRISSY You're fearless when you're skiing—you have to be! One misstep and you're flat on your face. The better you are, the more you have to be careful. The really big accidents happen with the pros—the deadly ones. Funny, isn't it? The better you are, the faster you are—the more your life is at stake. But you need to keep the fear at bay. That's all. Find your rhythm and there is no fear. Here. These are for you.

[CHRISSY *hands ski poles to* JUSTIN, *who reluctantly takes them.*]

JUSTIN [*Half-heartedly.*] Thanks.

[CHRISSY *stands behind him, guiding him to race and stays with him until he gets the knack of it. She pulls his hood down.* JUSTIN *begins to race.*]

I can move. I can move around in the world now. I have power!

[*WHOOSH. BELLS. LEGOS.*]

SHAKTI Your power is your freedom now. No need to control. No need to try so hard. You can trust yourself.

[JUSTIN *skis as* CHRISSY *speaks.*]

CHRISSY Although I had some natural ability, my biggest asset was the need to be competitive. I just have to be competitive. I wanted to continuously race. Winning—that's all I think about. Always been that way. Don't get me wrong. I think competition is healthy—to a point. You have to have a confidence level that's very high in competition, as an athlete. The passion, the drive. It's not just about athleticism. On the flip side, I will never think of myself as perfect. I am just never going to be perfect.

[*BELLS.* SHAKTI *begins to chant "Om" twice with bells between.*]

DARREN What are you praying for?

SHAKTI I'm chanting, not praying.

JUSTIN What are you chanting for?

SHAKTI Acceptance.

CHRISSY Acceptance?

DARREN I want acceptance.

JUSTIN I want to be accepted.

SHAKTI I want to ignore acceptance.

CHRISSY I want to lose my need for acceptance.

SHAKTI Lose your need for competition.

CHRISSY But it's all I know.

[*BELLS.* SHAKTI *places the bells in* CHRISSY*'s hands and moves her arms to ring them.*]

SHAKTI Your acceptance is internal. Go on.

[CHRISSY *tentatively rings the BELLS and chants. Progresses with more volume and depth.* SHAKTI *pulls* CHRISSY*'s hood down.*]

CHRISSY I feel a crazy kind of connection. Thank you.

[*LEGOS. WHOOSH. BELLS.* SHAKTI *has nothing to do. She circles the drum, coveting it but afraid to touch it.*]

SHAKTI I would like permission to be human.

DARREN Human?

JUSTIN Human?

CHRISSY Human?

SHAKTI It's as if I am always floating above the ground—part of this world but divorced from it. Everyone looks up to me, as if I weren't human, as if I'm infallible. It's a prison, in a sense, all that connection to spirit.

[DARREN *puts down creation, goes to the center, gets the DRUM, and starts playing.*]

JUSTIN What are you playing?

DARREN A rhythm.

CHRISSY What kind of rhythm?

SHAKTI Is it a rhythm of life?

JUSTIN Is it a rhythm of death?

DARREN It's a rhythm of the earth. To be human, you need to be connected to the earth.

[*DRUM stops.* DARREN *gives the drum to* SHAKTI, *who is afraid to take it.*]

SHAKTI I don't know if I can.

JUSTIN You can.

[DARREN *holds the DRUM as* SHAKTI *reluctantly starts to DRUM. He takes her hand to help her create a rhythm, which she does.* DARREN *pulls her hood down.*]

SHAKTI Thank you.

[SHAKTI *DRUMs with more confidence,* CHRISSY *rings BELLS and chants.* JUSTIN *races with a WHOOSH.* DARREN *flies the alien around in the air, then crashes it to the ground, as it breaks in a million pieces. All freeze.*]

DARREN [*Steps downstage to address the audience.*] I admit it. My hoodie did make me feel safe. It made me feel warm and protected. I didn't need to be afraid. I didn't need to be angry, even if I couldn't always say what was on my mind. My fear was repressed.

[*Pause.*]

Once I realized people were intimidated by me, wearing my hoodie—yeah, I used it sometimes. But how did it come to this? So far from where it started.

SHAKTI Monks in medieval Europe.

CHRISSY Laborers in frozen warehouses.

JUSTIN Athletes.

DARREN Rocky Balboa.

SHAKTI Norma Kamali.

CHRISSY Tommy Hilfiger.

JUSTIN Giorgio Armani.

DARREN Ralph Lauren.

SHAKTI Gucci.

CHRISSY Versace.

JUSTIN "Goodie in a Hoodie" in New Zealand.

DARREN "Hug a Hoodie" from the Labour Party in England.

JUSTIN And Puff Daddy, P Diddy. Puffy.

DARREN Hoodies were a part of the music scene—hip! I don't know how a style got that much power; how a fashion became a death sentence. I know about stick-up guys and gangstas. But why am I a thug and not an Armani model?

[*Pause.*]

I don't exist as a person. I am my hoodie.

[*Pause.*]

But is it really the hoodie or is it just my black skin?

[*They all freeze for a moment, staring at* DARREN, *shocked by the question but unable to answer.*]

I don't exist without my hoodie.

[DARREN *walks to the center of the circle, takes off his hoodie, drops it, then drops to his knees.*]

JUSTIN [*Takes off hoodie, drops it in front of* DARREN.] I don't exist without my hoodie.

CHRISSY [*Takes off hoodie, drops it in front of* DARREN.] I don't exist without my hoodie.

SHAKTI [*Takes off hoodie, drops it in front of* DARREN.] I don't exist without my hoodie.

[*They stand silent as* DARREN *explores the hoodies, watching him to gauge his emotion. They move to form a close circle around him. He hands them the hoodies—even his own, left and right, one by one. They pass them around like hot potatoes, until each gets back to the right person and the last is handed back down to* DARREN. *One by one, they put on their hoodies without the hood up.* DARREN *is last.*]

DARREN My hoodie is a symbol of injustice.

SHAKTI [*Pulls up hood.*] My hoodie is a symbol of injustice.

CHRISSY [*Pulls up hood.*] My hoodie is a symbol of injustice.

JUSTIN [*Pulls up hood.*] My hoodie is a symbol of injustice.

DARREN [*Stands and pulls up hood.*] And so am I.

[*A SIREN is heard. Blackout.*]

[*"Is That Jazz?" by Gil Scott-Heron plays for curtain call.*]

Lyrics from "Is That Jazz?" reproduced by permission of the Estate of Gil Scott-Heron.

Permission for use of the song "Is That Jazz?" graciously provided by the estate of Gil Scott-Heron.

Permission for the use of "I Zimbra" graciously provided by Warner Chappell and UMPG, as representatives for David Byrne and Warner Records, and Brian Eno, respectively.

Although permission is granted for the lyrics of "Is That Jazz?" to be included in the script, any subsequent production must obtain rights for the use of both songs.

• • •

Big Easy Death Party

Mariah MacCarthy

Mariah MacCarthy

Mariah MacCarthy is a writer, producer, and creatrix. Her work has been performed in a number of theaters and nontraditional spaces, including Rattlestick Playwrights Theatre, Studio Theatre, Primary Stages, Culture Project, Dixon Place, multiple New York City apartments, and in venues in Paris. MacCarthy has received a number of honors, including the Doric Wilson Independent Playwright Award and the Lotos Foundation Award; and she has been inducted into the Indie Theater Hall of Fame. As a producer, MacCarthy has curated several evenings and cabarets, including Pussyfest, Sex with Robots, and F*ckfest. MacCarthy serves as the executive artistic director of Caps Lock, and she is a member of Youngblood. Visit www.mariahmaccarthy.com.

...production history...

Produced as part of Ensemble Studio Theatre's *Bruncha de los Muertos*, November 2015 New York, NY. Directed by Dara Malina.

BRAD Ethan Hova

LOUISE Jo Mei

SHANNON Ann Talman

Note: A "/" in the speech of one character indicates that the other character's next speech interrupts at that moment.

[LOUISE *and* BRAD *at a flea market in New Orleans. They are married. 30s-ish. We don't see the stands they're looking at; they're all behind the fourth wall.*]

BRAD What about metal kazoos? You need any of those, honey?

[*She gives him a thin smile, acknowledging the joke.*]

No? You all stocked up on those?

[*Beat.*]

Alligator heads! You need any gator heads? Any gator, uh . . . what are these, claws? Gator claws?

[*Beat. He looks to her for a response. Looks back to the stands.*]

Oh, wooden bow ties! I know you're definitely running low on— wooden bow ties.

LOUISE Honey.

BRAD Yeah.

LOUISE I am allowed to have a bad time on vacation. You don't have to make it better. You can stop trying.

[*Beat. It's not the first time they've had this conversation, but he's had it. He huffs off.*]

Oh my God, are you going to make me comfort you right now?!

BRAD I'm supposed to just let you shut me down constantly and not have any emotions about it. I'm supposed to just not be a person in this equation.

LOUISE If you would just stop trying/ so hard—

BRAD "Stop trying," like that doesn't go against everything/ I am, you're asking me to stop being who I am—

LOUISE But why is that so hard when that's what I need from you, I'm not some sullen teenager on a car trip who just needs some dad jokes/ to pull her out of a bad mood—

BRAD Fuck you, that's not fair.

LOUISE Uh, "fuck you"?

BRAD We're both dealing with this. This is how I'm dealing. By trying.

LOUISE I'm just saying you shouldn't tie that up so much in how I'm reacting/ to you—

BRAD You keep telling me not to tell you how to feel. Don't do it to me.

[*Beat.*]

Now we're that couple fighting in public.

LOUISE At least we're in public. You can't just be happy about that. That we graduated/ to fighting outdoors.

BRAD Forgive me if I don't see getting off the couch as a huge achievement.

LOUISE For me it is! For me right now it is! I could use a little encouragement!

BRAD I give you encouragement! All I give you is encouragement!

LOUISE I'm here. I came here. I'm on vacation. I'm out of the house having a miserable time. I am allowed to have a miserable time. I'm allowed. I'm allowed.

[*Shift. Frenchmen Street on a Friday night. The streets are swollen with drunk people. Maybe we see them or maybe we just feel them. They all have cocktails and beers in huge to-go cups with straws. A raucous jazz band plays in the street.* BRAD *and* LOUISE *watch. He's drunk and all over her. She's barely touched her drink.*]

BRAD [*Yelling over the crowd.*] This is so great!

LOUISE Yeah.

BRAD I miss being drunk with you!

LOUISE I'm not really drunk.

BRAD What?

LOUISE Never mind.

BRAD It's hard to hear you out here!

LOUISE I said never mind.

BRAD [*Re: the band.*] They're so great, right?

LOUISE Yeah, they're good.

[*They watch the band. He holds on to her, dancing and bopping along to the music; she just watches.*]

[*Shift. Later that night. She's still sober. He's still not. They're staggering through a quieter area.*]

BRAD I love the way this town decorates for Halloween.

LOUISE I mean, it's no different than suburban twats in our neighborhood decorating for Christmas, you just think it's "cute" 'cause the houses are all ramshackle and have, like, balconies. . . .

BRAD Nah, look. Lookit this. People get so creative. You see this one? All the skeletons with all the name tags?

LOUISE There are too many big spiders. Why so many big spiders?

BRAD Lookit this one.

LOUISE What is that?

[*A beat as they both realize what it is: a dead baby of some sort. We don't see it. She rushes away. He pursues her.*]

BRAD Honey.

LOUISE Some people have no fucking tact, what is wrong/with people—

BRAD Honey, I'm sure they just thought it was funny—

LOUISE I DO NOT GIVE A FUCK WHAT THEY THOUGHT. IT IS NOT FUNNY. IT IS NOT OKAY.

BRAD I mean, for all we know, maybe they have a—dead baby. Maybe that's how they deal with it. Gallows humor/ and all that.

LOUISE Oh my God, can you stop with the devil's advocate shit?! Why can you never just be on my side?! I am fucking upset, I don't need you to be their fucking defense attorney! Why aren't you fucking upset! Why are you never on my side!

[*She runs off.*]

BRAD [*Calling after her.*] I am literally always on your side! There's only one side!

[*Beat.*]

Babe!

[*He goes after her.*]

[*Shift. Day.* LOUISE *wanders alone up to a singing woman,* SHANNON, *who is singing a lovely song, preferably in French and preferably accompanied by a banjo or accordion and tap dancing. She might be accompanying herself or she might have backup. The point is, the song is really, really lovely.* SHANNON *might be any age.* LOUISE *stands and watches for a long moment. Suddenly she is bawling and bawling. Like, embarrassingly. The singing woman finishes her song, then approaches* LOUISE *and tries to comfort her without knowing how much she should touch the stranger.*]

SHANNON Oh God, I'm so sorry.

LOUISE Don't be sorry.

SHANNON Do you want a hug? Do you want a . . . CD?

LOUISE It's okay, you can just keep playing.

SHANNON Here, take a CD.

LOUISE I can't just take a CD from you.

SHANNON It's a gift.

LOUISE [*Digging out her wallet.*] No, no, I believe in paying artists.

SHANNON You're so nice. . . .

LOUISE [*Hands* SHANNON *all the cash from her wallet.*] It's a gift.

[SHANNON *slowly takes it.*]

You should keep playing.

SHANNON You sure you're okay?

LOUISE I just don't want you to miss out on—audience,/ or tips. . . .

SHANNON You're the only one around.

LOUISE No, you never know. Last night my husband and I were walking around and we heard this woman with this insane voice, like down the street, but as soon as we stopped to listen to her she got in a fight with her guitar player and stopped singing. I mean, we totally would've stood there and watched her, tipped her, but she just stopped. You should keep singing. You don't know who's listening, you should keep singing.

[*She's crying again. Beat.*]

I had a miscarriage three months ago and this vacation is my first time leaving the house since it happened. Like, I got fired, so I just stopped leaving the house. My husband literally dragged me out of the house into the car to the airport. And the irony is that if I'd had her, I would've gotten three months paid maternity leave. Or if she'd been born and then died—I dunno if I would've gotten the maternity leave, but I'd at *least* have gotten like two days paid bereavement leave. But you don't get shit for miscarriage. Or, like, sick days. But I used up all my sick days.

[*Beat.*]

Sorry. You don't need to hear all this.

SHANNON I don't mind.

LOUISE I'm sorry.

SHANNON This is a good place to be when you've just had a death.

LOUISE I think it would've been a good place when I was like twenty-one. 'Cause then I would've just gotten drunk and fucked a bunch of people whenever bad stuff happened. I don't even want to get drunk anymore. Bourbon Street feels like Times Square for frat boys.

SHANNON This city is so alive. That's why we are all so obsessed with death. You have to take both.

LOUISE I kind of find all the skeletons oppressive.

SHANNON Skeletons are good. Skeletons remind us who we are. We're all animated meat on bones, running around on a flying ball of dirt, isn't that cool? You know what Sunday is, right? Dia de los muertos?

LOUISE Yeah. Yeah, I know what Sunday is.

SHANNON So you should celebrate. Your baby will be closer to you. You will feel her presence. This will be a good thing. A cause for joy. This is a day where death is a little bit different.

LOUISE . . . How did you know she was a girl?

SHANNON You said. Didn't you say?

LOUISE No, I didn't.

SHANNON [*Smiles and shrugs.*] I'm sorry you're going through this.

Losing a child is not something that we have words for. But this is the right place to be.

[*She hands* LOUISE *a flyer.*]

I'll be at this party on Sunday. My friends have it every year. After Katrina I lost my husband, my brother, my dog. I only lived because I wasn't here. And that was the first year they did this party and I felt them with me. I felt them all day. Like they were holding me in their arms. Everyone brings photos of their dead and we sing and we drink and we eat sugar skulls and we paint a mural on the wall and we celebrate them and we all feel a little closer to them. You could bring an ultrasound picture. Or you don't have to bring a picture. But you could come. I'd like you to come.

[*Beat.* LOUISE *looks at the flyer. She hugs* SHANNON.]

LOUISE Thank you.

SHANNON Of course.

LOUISE You should keep singing. I'm gonna go. But you should keep singing.

SHANNON Will I see you there?

LOUISE Maybe!

SHANNON Sunday!

LOUISE Maybe! Keep singing!

SHANNON Okay!

[*Shift. But maybe* SHANNON *stays onstage. This scene has music of some sort underneath it. Maybe Sturgill Simpson's "The Promise"? Maybe it gets progressively louder as the scene goes on?* LOUISE *and* BRAD*'s hotel room or wherever they're staying.*]

BRAD Where were you?

LOUISE On my walk.

BRAD I was worried about you.

LOUISE I said I was going for a walk.

BRAD I thought "walk" meant half an hour. I didn't know you meant three hours. I was scared to leave because you didn't pick up your phone, so I thought maybe your phone had died or been stolen or fallen in the Mississippi and I didn't want you to come back here and not know where I was. I've just been sitting here for three hours.

LOUISE . . . I left my phone here.

[*Beat.*]

I just. Wanted to unplug.

BRAD You just can't worry me like that. . . .

LOUISE Okay, I'm here, I'm okay, don't worry, okay?

[*Beat.*]

I actually had a really nice walk. I was. Feeling pretty good on my way in here.

BRAD And now I've ruined that by having the nerve to be worried/about you.

LOUISE I didn't say that—

BRAD You know I don't ever mean to be an asshole, right? You know that, right?

LOUISE Just comes to both of us a little more naturally these days?

[*Beat.*]

I can't live without you, okay?

BRAD Why would you ever have to?

LOUISE I met this woman on my walk who lost her husband and the whole way home I was thinking, "I would collapse if that ever happened, I think I would/ stop existing"—

BRAD Baby, I'm right here.

LOUISE I can't live without you. So we're gonna have to figure this out, how to be two people who both lost a thing, because I can't live without you.

BRAD I can't either.

[*Beat.*]

I wanna try again/ with you—

LOUISE Honey—

BRAD I wanna knock you up again, I wanna make you a mom—

LOUISE I can't talk about that yet.

BRAD I'm hanging on to that, it's the only thing that's letting me be okay—

LOUISE You're gonna make me a mom. Eventually. That doesn't mean I can think about it right now. Okay?

[*Beat. He notices the flyer in her hand.*]

BRAD Whatcha got there?

LOUISE [*Smiles.*] I got invited to a party. Like a college freshman or something.

[*She shows him the flyer.*]

BRAD What is this?

LOUISE We should go.

BRAD Really?

LOUISE Yeah! Yeah, I wanna go!

BRAD Why?

LOUISE [*Laughing.*] I don't know! I don't know, I just do!

BRAD [*Laughing.*] Why are you laughing?

LOUISE I don't know!

BRAD Okay! Okay, cool! You laughing! That's a thing that happens now! Awesome!

[*Beat.*]

LOUISE Could you come here?

BRAD Are you okay?

LOUISE I mean, no, but—

BRAD I didn't mean—

LOUISE I know.

[*She puts her arms around him. They sway to the music.* SHANNON *addresses the audience.*]

SHANNON Hello! Thank you all so much for being here. Thank you to everyone who's contributed photos to the altar, it's really beautiful to look and see how many people we've loved. How many people have loved us. This altar is such a staggering reflection of Life. Life. So—everyone here, I just wanted us all to take a moment for our loved ones, those we've loved and lost, just bow your head and close your eyes and quietly, without speaking out loud, give this person a little eulogy, inside your own mind, just take a moment to reflect on that person with love, and with joy.

[*We all do this.*]

Please join me in raising a glass.

[*She raises a glass. We all raise our glasses.*]

To the dead. And all they have given us. And all they continue to give us. To the dead. We love you. We thank you. We feel your presence today. Thank you. Thank you. You gave us so much. To the dead.

[*Blackout*]

• • •

Rations

Mark Bowen

Mark Bowen

Mark Bowen is a member of New Voices Playwrights Theatre in Southern California, where *Rations* was first performed. His first full-length play, *Weeks of Sloth*, opened at Community Actors Theatre in San Diego in June 2016. He teaches history and theater in the Los Angeles Unified School District.

...production history...

Rations was first produced in June 2016 at the Summer Voices Festival at Stage Door Repertory Theatre in Anaheim, California, directed by Bob May.

MR. LOWENSTEIN Robert Purcell

BILLY Mark Grabador

JACK Carlos David Lopez

EDDIE Mason Meskell

characters

MR. LOWENSTEIN The Proprietor; 60s–70s

BILLY A Young Customer; 16–18

JACK A Sailor; 20s

EDDIE Another Sailor; 20s

scene

Interior of a small gas station; Small Town USA.

time

May, 1944.

[*At rise, we are right in the middle of an exchange with an irate customer.* BILLY *is at the counter, in* MR. LOWENSTEIN*'s face.*]

MR. LOWENSTEIN I can't do that.

BILLY You're not listening to me!

MR. LOWENSTEIN No, Billy, you're not listening to me.

BILLY When my old man finds out—

MR. LOWENSTEIN Don't bring him into this . . .

BILLY I'm just saying . . .

MR. LOWENSTEIN Don't threaten me.

BILLY I'm not, I'm only telling you—

MR. LOWENSTEIN Billy, let's just—

BILLY Turn on the pump.

MR. LOWENSTEIN I can't do that, Billy.

BILLY The hell you can't!

MR. LOWENSTEIN No, Billy, I can't. You know how much we all get to use every week.

BILLY Oh, don't give me that crap!

MR. LOWENSTEIN Billy, if there isn't something else I can help you with—

BILLY You know damn well what you can help me with!

MR. LOWENSTEIN I don't make the rules.

BILLY Then follow them! I've got the coupons right here.

MR. LOWENSTEIN I can't accept those.

BILLY You mean you won't accept them.

MR. LOWENSTEIN No, I mean that the OPA requires—

BILLY And I've got their damn coupons!

MR. LOWENSTEIN I know where you got those, Billy. And even if I didn't, that's why they require that I be the one to tear those out of the book so they can—

BILLY [*Exploding.*] Turn on the goddamn pump!

MR. LOWENSTEIN Billy!

BILLY I'm not messing around with you anymore, Big Nose!

MR. LOWENSTEIN Alright, that's enough, I'm going to have to ask you to—

BILLY I'm not leaving until I get what I came here for!

MR. LOWENSTEIN Billy, you need to calm down or leave my store . . . don't make me call the police.

[BILLY *pauses for a moment, takes a deep breath, then gets out his wallet.*]

BILLY Alright, look. How much is it gonna take?

MR. LOWENSTEIN That's not how it works, either . . .

BILLY Hey, what the hell do you know about how the system works? If you ever worked with my old man—

MR. LOWENSTEIN [*Overlapping.*] I've already asked you not to bring him into this.

BILLY [*Continuous, overlapping.*] —you'd know that he's one of the few who are footing most of the bill for this whole sham of a war that—

MR. LOWENSTEIN Billy!

BILLY Look, just hear me out! Thirty seconds!

MR. LOWENSTEIN [*Resigned, but amused.*] Go on . . .

BILLY Good! Now, let me ask you. Do you have any idea how long ago the Reds would have been licked if they weren't still being propped up by a bunch of radicals in Washington?

MR. LOWENSTEIN No, Billy, I wouldn't have any idea.

BILLY That's right, you wouldn't! And considering how we're the ones whose dough they're confiscating to pay for it all, you're not exactly in any position to judge.

MR. LOWENSTEIN I'd say your thirty seconds are up now, Billy.

BILLY Look! All I'm saying . . . You don't rise to that level without knowing a thing or two about "how the system works" . . . now everything has got a price, you people should know that.

MR. LOWENSTEIN [*Sighs and turns to go.*] I think I'll go and finish that crossword puzzle now. . . .

BILLY What was it, thirty pieces of silver?

MR. LOWENSTEIN Don't forget the other little item you came in here for.

[*He goes into the office.* BILLY *picks the bag of what he purchased up off the counter and, in a rage, throws it at the office door and storms out, bumping into a sailor,* JACK, *on his way out the door.*]

JACK Excuse me.

BILLY Yeah.

JACK Say, you wouldn't happen to—

BILLY [*Exiting.*] Screw you!

JACK Hey.

[JACK *looks around the shop for a moment and then another sailor,* EDDIE, *emerges from the bathroom.*]

EDDIE Hey. Did you . . . ?

JACK No, I was out talking to the other folks. Couldn't get anybody to—
[*Sees that his friend has placed a finger to his lips, shushing him.*]
What?

EDDIE The old man . . .

JACK Yeah, what about him?

EDDIE Oh, just when I came in here to use the john, there was this kid trying to . . . you know.

JACK What, you mean that jackass that just left?

EDDIE Look, he . . . he was just being a real hard-ass about those coupons.

JACK Oh . . . well, I think he was trying to—

EDDIE Well, just . . . I don't think he needs to know too much about what we're doing.

MR. LOWENSTEIN [*Coming out of the office.*] Hello, sailors!

JACK Good afternoon, sir.

MR. LOWENSTEIN Can I help you?

JACK Yeah. [*Takes out two rationing coupons and set them on the counter.*] Pump number two. . . .

MR. LOWENSTEIN Alrighty, then . . .

JACK Something wrong?

MR. LOWENSTEIN You boys do know the law requires that I be the one that tears these out of the book?

JACK Umm . . .

EDDIE Well, yeah, see—

MR. LOWENSTEIN Black market out there for some folks that are selling these to others who want to use more than their allotted amount. OPA is cracking down on that now.

JACK Yeah, well . . .

EDDIE Look, here's the thing—

MR. LOWENSTEIN Of course, those books are pretty flimsy, and the coupons have been known to just fall out if you're not careful. . . . I'm sure that's what must have happened.

JACK Uh . . .

EDDIE Yeah. Yeah, that's what happened.

MR. LOWENSTEIN Number two?

EDDIE Two.

MR. LOWENSTEIN Alright, you're all set.

JACK Thank you.

[*To* EDDIE.]

Hey, why don't you—

EDDIE Yeah, I'll go fill up, you get the other stuff.

JACK Okay . . . anything special you think she might like?

EDDIE What?

JACK For Ida.

EDDIE Look, forget it.

JACK Eddie, all we've got to do is—

[EDDIE *turns back, gives him a hard "shut up" look, and a subtle gesture to the stranger who shouldn't be hearing this.*]

EDDIE Don't forget the smokes.

JACK I won't.

EDDIE [*Exiting.*] Alright.

[JACK *goes around the store, getting the cigarettes and selecting some other items.*]

MR. LOWENSTEIN So . . . how much longer you boys got?

JACK What's that?

MR. LOWENSTEIN Gotta be back to your ship by when?

JACK Oh yeah . . . yeah, we ship out of Norfolk at the end of the week.

MR. LOWENSTEIN Norfolk? What's that, only like a two-day drive from here?

JACK Something like that. . . . You'd have to ask Eddie, he's calculated everything.

MR. LOWENSTEIN I'd say that's about right. . . . I don't see why he shouldn't be able to see that girl of his!

JACK What? No, we—

[*Chuckles.*]

MR. LOWENSTEIN Oh, these ears hear it all. . . .

[JACK *has approached the counter.*]

That be all for you?

JACK Yeah.

MR. LOWENSTEIN Sure your friend doesn't need anything else?

[*He has picked up the bag* BILLY *threw and presents it to him.*]

Here . . . no charge, already paid for. Courtesy of the young man that just left.

JACK What are you . . . ?

[*Looks in the bag, and then gets embarrassed.*]

Hey, this is his wife we're talking about here!

MR. LOWENSTEIN Alright, just trying to help. After all, ole what's his name won't be needing them. . . .

JACK You mean that kid who came storming out of here?

MR. LOWENSTEIN Oh yes . . . she's a good ten miles up the road, and he's not gonna make it under the OPA's limits.

JACK His girl?

MR. LOWENSTEIN [*Shrugs.*] One of them, I suppose. Gotta be hard to keep them straight.

JACK Sounds like him and Eddie are in the same boat.

MR. LOWENSTEIN Somehow, I find that rather hard to believe.

JACK No, I just meant . . .

MR. LOWENSTEIN Yes, I know. . . . I just find it a little hard to believe that, with your status, they didn't give you enough.

JACK Well, we had other family to see. It's been one heck of a trip across country.

MR. LOWENSTEIN Oh . . . well, that's a darn shame.

JACK Of course, me, I did get a chance to see my wife, Pearl.

MR. LOWENSTEIN Married?

JACK Yeah.

MR. LOWENSTEIN She wasn't so far out of your way, huh?

JACK Well, actually her too. We kinda flipped for it . . . and I must say I'm feeling pretty lousy about winning right about now.

MR. LOWENSTEIN Aw, son, look, you shouldn't—

JACK I mean, I should have insisted, but then I kept telling myself, I mean I figured . . .

MR. LOWENSTEIN What?

JACK Nothing, never mind.

MR. LOWENSTEIN [*Smiles.*] Figured you could always buy a few more of those coupons on the black market?

JACK Uh, look, sir . . . you see, this is something that—

MR. LOWENSTEIN Son, I ain't the Office of War Management.

JACK [*Pauses, then returns the smile.*] Thank you.

[*Sound of the horn honking offstage.*]

EDDIE [*Offstage.*] Come on, let's go!

JACK Alright, I'll be there in a minute! How much for the gas and everything?

MR. LOWENSTEIN Four thirty-five.

[JACK *starts emptying out his pockets on the counter, and* MR. LOWENSTEIN *sees a postcard he's taken out.*]

MR. LOWENSTEIN Say, is that . . . ?

JACK What?

MR. LOWENSTEIN That postcard . . . I've seen it before.

JACK It's from France.

MR. LOWENSTEIN Yes, yes, I know. From the time of the Great War.

JACK Yes.

MR. LOWENSTEIN My son, when he first arrived in France, one of the first things he did . . .

[*He goes to the bulletin board on the wall behind the counter and takes down another postcard.*]

JACK That's not the same one.

MR. LOWENSTEIN Yes, yes, I know. It's the closest thing we could find when we went there afterwards trying to put the pieces back together.

JACK You've been to France?

MR. LOWENSTEIN Oh yes. Twice. Then it was just to . . .

[*Chuckles.*]

But trust me, it had been a lot prettier twenty years earlier.

JACK You were looking for a duplicate?

MR. LOWENSTEIN I don't know how my wife could have lost the first one. The postmark indicated he must have sent it within a couple days of his arrival, but the mail moved pretty slowly across the Atlantic. It arrived here two days after he went missing.

JACK That must have been so difficult.

MR. LOWENSTEIN Sometimes I think maybe it was deliberate. I knew, of course, I could never ask her, but somehow I just . . . couldn't get it out of my head, the image of her just . . . burning it.

JACK You don't really think she . . . ?

MR. LOWENSTEIN No, I'm not saying that it was right, I just . . . I think at first she didn't want to hold on to it. Not until it was for sure. Didn't want to accept that it really would be the last thing we'd ever . . .

JACK I'm so sorry.

MR. LOWENSTEIN Don't be. Just . . . one thing I was going to ask you. How much would you sell me that for?

JACK Oh no, you see—

MR. LOWENSTEIN Twenty dollars?

JACK Oh, sir, I just couldn't do that. You see, my wife, Pearl, gave me this. It's something her father sent to her mother.

MR. LOWENSTEIN May I . . . ?

JACK Oh, sure.

[*Shows him the postcard.*]

MR. LOWENSTEIN [*Reading the back of the card.*] He got to meet General Pershing in person?

JACK Somehow I doubt it . . . if you knew my father in law, you'd understand.

MR. LOWENSTEIN Oh, I think I do.

JACK Sure.

MR. LOWENSTEIN Fifty dollars?

JACK Look, I know how you must feel about this, but Pearl gave me this. The whole General Pershing lie . . . it had been a family joke with them for years. But then with me? Well, since he came back unharmed, she just figured . . . told me to keep it on me at all times. Said it would bring me good luck.

MR. LOWENSTEIN I know what you mean. It's just . . .

[*Pause.*]

A hundred dollars! I'm sure that could really help you and your friend to find some way to—

JACK No!

[*Pause.*]

I'm sorry, I just can't. I hope you can understand.

MR. LOWENSTEIN Of course.

[*He goes to put his own postcard back on the bulletin board while* JACK *counts out the exact change. As he finishes,* EDDIE *bursts in.*]

EDDIE Are you coming, or did you wanna walk the rest of the way?

JACK Almost done. Gonna go use the head before we get back on the road.

EDDIE Well, hurry up, okay?

JACK Fine.

EDDIE And you're driving the next shift!

JACK What?

EDDIE You're driving. . . . It's been me since the diner.

JACK Oh, come on, that was only two hours ago!

EDDIE So?

JACK So I was gonna sleep a couple more hours. . . .

EDDIE Yeah, well I'm tired too.

[*Takes out a coin.*]

And I call heads!

[*Flips it.*]

There, like I said, you're driving.

JACK [*As he goes off into the bathroom.*] Asshole.

MR. LOWENSTEIN You two decide a lot with a coin toss now, don't you?

EDDIE No, not really. But when you do, it's kinda nice when . . .

[*He shows off both sides of the two-headed coin and smiles.*]

Wait, what did he tell you about . . . ?

MR. LOWENSTEIN Relax, he just told me about your wives and how—

EDDIE Look, whatever he might have said—

MR. LOWENSTEIN Hey!

[*Pause.*]

That's all I know.

EDDIE Thank you.

MR. LOWENSTEIN Hey, wait a minute . . . I thought your friend said you lost that last toss. . . .

EDDIE What?

MR. LOWENSTEIN I thought you were the one that wasn't gonna get a chance to see your wife.

EDDIE Yeah, so . . . ?

MR. LOWENSTEIN So then how do you lose a coin toss when you've got one of those?

EDDIE Who says I lost?

[*Long pause.*]

Look, I've known Jack all my life. We both know this might very well be the last time the wives get to . . . you know? I'd been telling him how I felt about Julie growing up not knowing her father. Said if there was one thing me and Ida should use this time for, it was to try to give her a brother or sister.

MR. LOWENSTEIN I see.

EDDIE So he knew how important it was to me. But I knew how important it was to him. So I put my foot down . . . and I called heads!

MR. LOWENSTEIN [*Smiles.*] That really is one heck of a story.

EDDIE Just don't tell Jack.

MR. LOWENSTEIN Your secret's safe with me.

EDDIE Thank you.

JACK [*Emerging from the bathroom.*] Ready?

EDDIE I think you know, I've been ready.

[*To* MR. LOWENSTEIN.]

You take care of yourself now, you hear?

[*To* JACK, *indicating the stuff on the counter.*]

You gonna help me with this?

JACK Yeah, sure.

[*Gathering up the stuff with* EDDIE.]

So long, sir.

[MR. LOWENSTEIN *just nods and doesn't say anything until they've turned to walk away, and then:*]

MR. LOWENSTEIN Well, boys, I'm gonna go on back into my office now. I'll just leave those coupons there on the counter. . . . I sure hope the wind doesn't blow 'em away.

[*They just stand there, frozen, as he goes into the office, then exchange a furtive glance at each other, then a smile.*]

JACK I'll meet you outside in a minute.

[EDDIE *nods, then takes the stuff that* JACK *had been carrying and goes out ahead of him.* JACK *walks over to the counter, takes a quick look around, then picks up the coupons. He turns to go and then stops; he stares off into space, deep in thought. He takes the postcard out of his pocket and stares at it for a minute, until the horn is heard honking again offstage.*]

EDDIE [*Offstage.*] Come on, let's go for crying out loud!

[JACK *walks over to the bulletin board and pins the postcard onto it, next to the other one, then starts to go. He walks halfway out, then turns to take one last look, considering, then smiles and turns to finally leave as the lights fade.*]

• • •

Man. Kind.

Don X. Nguyen

Don X. Nguyen

Don X. Nguyen's full-length plays include *Hello, From the Children of Planet Earth*, *The Supreme Leader*, *Red Flamboyant*, *Sound*, *The Commencement of Will Tan*, and *Man from Saigon*. He is a member of Ma-Yi Writers Lab, the Public Theater's Emerging Writers Group, and the Civilians R&D Group. For more information, please visit www.thenuge.com.

...production history...

The play was produced by the Working Theater Director's Project "To Serve and Protect" on March 22, 2016, at the Wild Project, 195 E. 3rd St, New York, NY 10009. Directed by Nathaniel Claridad.

CREDO Bradley Anderson

DALFEDE Lucy DeVito

characters

CREDO Male, any age, a caveman.

DALFEDE Female, any age, a cavewoman.

setting

On a plateau during the dawn of man.

scene 1

[*Lights rise on a plateau.* CREDO, *a caveman, enters. He looks around. The coast is clear. He pulls two flint rocks and some tinder out of his rucksack. He strikes the flint against the tinder until it begins smoking. He blows and blows until it becomes fire.*]

CREDO Finally! Sweet.

[*He pulls out a joint, lights it, and takes a hit.*]

I've been waiting for this moment all my life!

[*A rustling of bushes.*]

Shit. Shit!

[CREDO *throws the joint into the fire and stomps it out.*]

Ow, ow, ow!

[*It hurts because he's barefoot.* DALFEDE, *a young cavewoman, enters, crying.*]

DALFEDE Oh.

CREDO 'Sup.

DALFEDE What are you doing here?

CREDO Nothing. Just chillin'.

DALFEDE This is my spot.

CREDO I don't think so. I come up here all the time.

DALFEDE Well, I come up here all the time too.

CREDO I don't see how that's possible if I'm here all the time.

[*She looks at the aftermath of the fire.*]

DALFEDE I see you've discovered fire.

CREDO Yeah, I totally did! Today we can officially declare that man has discovered fire.

DALFEDE That's great. I discovered it yesterday.

CREDO You . . . what? No.

DALFEDE Yeah, I totally did.

CREDO You did not! The only way to make fire is with these two flint rocks, which have been in my possession since . . .

DALFEDE Since yesterday?

CREDO Ummm . . . .yeah. How did—

DALFEDE Because I left them behind those bushes yesterday so no one would find them.

CREDO Well, apparently you didn't hide them well enough because I managed to find them.

DALFEDE So you admit to finding them, which means you admit they're mine, which means you admit I discovered fire a day before you did!

CREDO I . . . Uh . . . DAMNIT!

DALFEDE Bam! How ya like dem indigenous apples?

CREDO Why don't you go back to your cave or something?

DALFEDE I . . . I can't ever go back to my cave. That's why I'm here.

[DALFEDE *begins crying.*]

CREDO Oh, shit . . . no, no, no, no, no, don't do that. Are you . . . leaking salty water drops?

[*She is.*]

Shit. Okay, okay, I can do this. I can do this.

[*He takes some deep breaths as the crying continues.*]

What . . . what's . . . wrong?

DALFEDE It's Lothar the Terrible. He's terrorizing the entire clan, raping and pillaging. He set fire to our caves. I have no cave to return to.

CREDO Oh. I see. Well, that's too bad. Sucks to be you.

DALFEDE What? You're not going to offer to help?

CREDO Nope.

DALFEDE No? Really?

CREDO Yeah, really.

DALFEDE What's wrong with you? You're supposed to help me.

CREDO No, I'm not.

DALFEDE Yes, you are.

CREDO Who says I am? Besides you.

DALFEDE Well, it's . . . no one says, but it's just implied.

CREDO No, it's not. If it's not literally written in stone, then I don't have to do anything.

DALFEDE Are you fucking kidding me?

CREDO I am not, because I haven't fully developed a sense of humor yet.

DALFEDE How can you believe that? How can anyone believe they're not put on this earth to help one another?

CREDO Yeah, see, that whole helping each other thing . . . that's not gonna work here. We're not supposed to help each other. It's survival of the fittest. In fact, if I helped you, I would be going against the laws of nature, and who am I to defy nature? It's actually quite dangerous to help each other because then we risk becoming emotionally beholden to each other, and I don't know about you, but that just sounds *terrible* to me.

DALFEDE To be emotionally beholden?

CREDO Yes. That would be worse than drowning in tar pits or being trampled by a stampede of woolly mammoths. Next to the tar pits.

DALFEDE . . .

CREDO Listen, it's just that . . . I don't think we're going to be on this planet much longer because, you know, there's gonna be another big sky rock crashing down on us very soon.

DALFEDE Oh yes, and don't forget all the animals that are three times as big as us.

CREDO Yes, exactly! We're like, near the bottom of the food chain. It would be miraculous if we survived much longer. So for the limited amount of time that we are in existence, I would like to just smoke my happy sticks and live out my short inconsequential life all by myself. Beholden to no one.

DALFEDE You chickenshit.

CREDO Well, that's not very nice.

DALFEDE You don't deserve *nice* because you're not willing to be *nice*. And you're wrong, dead wrong about being on this planet for a short amount of time.

CREDO Oh, I am, am I?

DALFEDE Yes. We are going to be on this planet for a very, *very* long time.

CREDO And how do you know this?

DALFEDE I had a dream.

CREDO You had a dream?

DALFEDE Yes.

CREDO You had a *dream*?

DALFEDE Yes!

CREDO I see. And what exactly is a dream?

DALFEDE Life living in my head.

CREDO I thought those were thoughts?

DALFEDE Life living in my head when I'm asleep.

CREDO I see. I don't think I have those. At least not yet. Anyway, continue, cavewoman.

DALFEDE You don't have to call me cavewoman. My name is—

CREDO No, no. We don't need to know each other's names. Just tell me about this "dream" you had.

DALFEDE It was a frightening dream.

CREDO Oh, you mean nightmares. See, I've had tons of those. Mostly about drowning in tar pits and . . . go on.

DALFEDE I see people with pitchforks and polio and world wars and Hitler and concentration camps and the atom bomb and sirens and guns and Selma and the *Challenger* explosion and AIDS and 9/11 and policemen and tanks and the Internet and Occupy Wall Street and guns and guns and policemen and protests and more protests and endless protests.

CREDO Yeah, see, none of that makes any sense to me. Like, I literally don't know what you're talking about.

DALFEDE I don't know how to make you understand my dreams. But I know they're real. I mean, they will be real. Someday. And the thing is, even though these were all bad dreams, there were good dreams as well.

CREDO What were the good ones?

DALFEDE I couldn't see them clearly. But I could feel them. Here.

[*She places her hand over her heart.*]

CREDO Yeah, I don't feel anything in that area. I feel things here.

[*He places his hands over his crotch.*]

DALFEDE You are capable of dreaming good things here.

[*She points to his head.*]

And feeling good things there.

[*She points to his crotch.*]

CREDO It's a long way from here

[*His head.*]

to there

[*His crotch.*].

DALFEDE So meet yourself in the middle. Here.

[*She points to his heart.*]

CREDO [*Laughs.*] That is so *dumb*! Why do you want me to help you? I have no ambitions in life.

DALFEDE Well, your non-ambition is actually an ambition if you think about it.

[*He thinks about it.*]

CREDO Damnit! Stop using your brain! Cavewomen are not supposed to do that!

DALFEDE If you help me, I'll show you where you can find more flint. Just think of all the fires you can start. And all the "happy sticks" you could smoke?

CREDO That's beguiling. But no.

DALFEDE Why don't you care?!

CREDO It's not that I don't care!

DALFEDE It's so obvious that you don't care!

CREDO No, it's because—

DALFEDE It's because what?

CREDO It's because I'm afraid.

DALFEDE You're afraid? Afraid of what?

CREDO I'm afraid of my nightmares coming true.

DALFEDE Just don't go near the tar pits and—

CREDO No, it's not just the tar pits. It's a different nightmare. One I didn't tell you about.

DALFEDE So tell me about it.

CREDO You'll think I'm crazy.

DALFEDE That would imply that you care what I think.

CREDO I don't care!

DALFEDE Then what's the harm in telling me?

CREDO My nightmare is that . . . we as humans will become a group.

DALFEDE How is that—

CREDO Because we complicate things when we're in a group.

DALFEDE We already are in groups. We have clans.

CREDO Yes, even now, these clans, they're all . . . starting to need things from each other. And the more you need the more you want, which attracts chaos. And out of that chaos, we try to establish order. And order means control. And that will bring about laws. But man and laws are not made for each other. We think we are but we're not. We make laws for the benefit of service. But service will eventually become servitude and then out of our misguided attempts of preserving the idea of service, we create protection. And protection works for a while but there will be those that take it upon themselves to decide who needs protection and who doesn't. And protection that was meant for everyone will begin to serve only a few, like, those that are deemed law-abiding. But that won't work because the only law man can abide by is the law of nature. Which is why raping and pillaging and killing each other now is fine because, because that's . . . nature.

DALFEDE You have deeper thoughts than I expected.

[CREDO *holds up his happy sticks.*]

CREDO This is some good shit.

DALFEDE So if Lothar the Terrible raped and killed me right now, you would accept that? As the law of nature?

CREDO That's . . .

DALFEDE You would not feel badly for me?

CREDO That's not the point!

DALFEDE That is the point!

CREDO You're arguing with intelligence! Stop it, cavewoman!

DALFEDE Stop calling me cavewoman! I have a name! It's Dalfede.

CREDO I said I don't want to—

DALFEDE Dalfede!

CREDO I don't want to hear your n—

DALFEDE Dalfede!

CREDO Ah! Stop it!

[*He covers his ears.*]

DALFEDE Dalfede!

CREDO I can't hear you!

DALFEDE Dalfede!

CREDO I can't hear what you're saying because I'm covering my sound holes!

DALFEDE I am Dalfede!

CREDO Shut up, shut up, shut up!

DALFEDE DALFEDE!

CREDO STOP IT, DALFEDE!

DALFEDE . . .

CREDO Well, that's just great. You tell me your name and now my brain hurts with complexity.

DALFEDE What's your name? It's okay, my brain can take it.

CREDO My name is Credo.

DALFEDE [*Snorting.*] Really?

[*Off this look.*]

I mean . . .

[*She offers her hand.*]

Credo, will you help me? Protect Dalfede from Lothar the Terrible?

CREDO Fuck. Fine. You realize we might be ruining mankind by doing this.

DALFEDE Or we might not. Our nightmares might come true. Or we might die from a large falling rock from the sky. We don't yet know the things we know. So let's not know them together.

[CREDO *takes* DALFEDE*'s hand. They disappear into the bushes.*]

• • •

Security

Israel Horovitz

Israel Horovitz

Israel Horovitz has written over seventy produced plays, several of which have been translated and performed in as many as thirty languages worldwide. His play *Line* is now in its forty-seventh year of continuous performance Off-Broadway, NYC's longest-running play ever. In summer 2016, *Security* was produced at the Atlantic Theatre Company, NYC, as well as Horovitz's *Out of the Mouths of Babes* at Cherry Lane Theatre, NYC, and *Man in Snow* at Gloucester Stage, Massachusetts, followed by its transfer to La Ma Ma Theatre, NYC. Horovitz is founding artistic director of Gloucester Stage and the New York Playwrights Lab, and teaches a bilingual screenwriting workshop with writers from la Fémis, France's national film school, and Columbia University's graduate film program. He is married to Gillian Adams-Horovitz, former British national marathon champion. The Horovitz family divides its time among homes in Gloucester, Massachusetts, NYC's Greenwich Village, and London's Dulwich Village. Mr. Horovitz visits France frequently to direct French-language productions of his plays. He is the most-produced American playwright in the history of French theater.

...production history...

During the past fifteen years, Israel Horovitz has written a series of plays dealing with racism as it specifically relates to struggles in the Middle East and its effect on Americans. Among these plays are *Beirut Rocks*, *A Mother's Love*, *What Strong Fences Make*, *The New Girl*, *Breaking Philip Glass*, and *Security*. The first draft of Security was written in 2002 and had its first production under the auspices of Barefoot Theatre Company at Theatre Row, NYC. Subsequent productions were seen in regional and university theaters around the USA, as well as productions in France, Italy, and Germany. Horovitz adapted *Security* for the screen in 2008, and an award-winning film was directed by Matthew Linnell, which was seen at international film festivals, including Next Reel International Film Festival in Singapore and the Palm Springs International Film Festival. The film of *Security* won a prize from the National Board of Review in 2009. In 2016, Horovitz revised the stage version of *Security* for Playwrights for a Cause, produced by Planet Connections at the Atlantic Theatre Company, NYC.

[*A white, empty space, white folding table, white chairs. Six industrial caged-bulb lights hang down from overhead. There is a tape recorder on a table. We hear a recorded greeting, offstage, in distance.*]

VOICE OF LOUDSPEAKER [*Offstage, in the distance, far away.*] Welcome to the United States of America. Travelers holding American passports or green cards, use the lines to the right. Visitors and visa holders, use the lines to your left.

[*Stage-light up, suddenly, on* ZELLY *and* WEBSTER, *mid-sentence. Both are forty-ish.* ZELLY *is white,* WEBSTER *is black. They wear black pants, white shirts, black neckties. Both wear pager-phones on their belts. We shouldn't realize that they're security guards, until later in the scene, when they re-dress, strapping on guns/holsters, putting on uniform jackets. They are, at the moment, on a lunch break, eating sandwiches, drinking soda from cans. From time to time,* WEBSTER *reads a newspaper.*]

ZELLY See what I'm sayin'? She couldn't if she would.

WEBSTER That makes no sense. If she would, she would. If she couldn't, she couldn't.

ZELLY You still see my point, though, don't'cha?

WEBSTER I don't.

ZELLY Whatever.

[WEBSTER *shrugs, which angers* ZELLY.]

I'm saying that she would meet up with me, in a *heartbeat*, but the husband would find out and kill her, 'cause he follows her everywhere. He's got her checkin' in by cell phone, every fifteen minutes. Man's got computer chips in her fuckin' *socks*! So, even if she would, she couldn't. Now, you see what I'm sayin'?

WEBSTER [*Makes time-out signal with his hands.*] Time.

ZELLY What?

WEBSTER You're missing some major info, Z.

ZELLY What?

WEBSTER They're split up.

ZELLY What are you tellin' me?

WEBSTER They're split up. The husband's moved out—moved *away*. He's living in an M state. Montana . . . Michigan . . . Shelly's been seein' Ronnie What'sis from Accounting for maybe two, three weeks.

ZELLY Bullshit.

WEBSTER Serious.

ZELLY Bullshit.

WEBSTER I'm talkin' hugging in public, quick kisses . . .

ZELLY Bullshit.

WEBSTER . . . Hands and shit.

ZELLY You are fucking with me.

WEBSTER Not. I see them on this train, her hand's on his leg, way *here*.

[WEBSTER *touches his own thigh, just below the crotch.*]

Friendship is her hand, like, maybe *here* . . .

[*His hand on his own knee.*]

Let's say maybe knee to maybe mid-thigh. I am seein' tree-line to dick! This is not friendship.

ZELLY You're fuckin' with me, Webster.

WEBSTER On my mother's grave!

[*Suddenly.*]

Massachusetts!

[*Explains.*]

The husband.

ZELLY Why am I just now hearing this?!

WEBSTER She calls him "big guy"?

ZELLY What's this?

WEBSTER I know. I'm goin' to myself, if she's callin' this runty little dude "big guy," he's gotta' be blowin' his paycheck on Internet Viagra.

ZELLY Ronnie, the flabby little Jew from Accounting?

WEBSTER Fogliato.

ZELLY Him. Ronnie Fogliato.

WEBSTER Ronnie Fogliato.

ZELLY Him.

WEBSTER I think he's Italian.

ZELLY That's a Jew, if I ever saw one.

WEBSTER She's a Jew.

[WEBSTER *picks up copy of* New York Post, *begins to read. After a moment . . .*]

ZELLY Why are you fuckin' with me?

WEBSTER He's a Jew, man. Shelly fuckin' Goldfarb. That's a definite Jew name.

ZELLY Webster, will you get fuckin' real! She's a *redhead*!

WEBSTER Shelly *Goldfarb*!

ZELLY Bruce *Springsteen*!

WEBSTER Shelly *Goldfarb*!

ZELLY Lenny *Kravitz*!

WEBSTER Shelly *Goldfarb*!

ZELLY Whoopi *Goldberg*!

WEBSTER Fine. Whatever, Z. I'm just sayin' save your breath to cool your oatmeal, Z. I'm tellin' you, man: Shelly Goldfarb is surfin' a whole nother wave.

ZELLY Bitch is givin' me looks, no more than two days ago.

WEBSTER You know what they say: once the floodgates open . . .

ZELLY What? Once the floodgates open, what?

[WEBSTER *looks up from his newspaper, confused.*]

WEBSTER Who the fuck knows? Flooding.

ZELLY What are you givin' me, you?

WEBSTER You see this?

ZELLY What?

WEBSTER Now, they're sayin' the ISIS leader they killed is still alive. He made a video.

ZELLY I saw this on TV.

WEBSTER One day, he's dead, the next day, he's alive.

ZELLY He's alive. He's makin' videos. He ain't doing that dead.

[*Beat.*]

Fuckin' world's a mess. You see the new suicide-bomber shit on TV this morning?

WEBSTER My cable's shut off.

ZELLY What? She didn't pay your bill again?

WEBSTER Don't get me started.

ZELLY School bus full'a little kids.

[*Makes sound of bomb exploding.*]

PCOOOWWWW!

WEBSTER World's goin' nuts.

ZELLY You ain't got kids.

WEBSTER I got kids.

ZELLY Livin' with you.

WEBSTER Yuh, so?

ZELLY You put your kids on a school bus every morning, you see shit like that on TV, gets you crazy. Kid gets on his bus, the bus driver blows up. What is that shit?

WEBSTER Thank God it ain't happenin' here.

ZELLY Give it five minutes. That's what the ISIS leader's sayin' in his new video. We're next. Trump is a hundred percent right. Fuckin' Arabs gotta be stopped!

WEBSTER [*Reads aloud from his newspaper.*] "The Roman Catholic Archdiocese of Boston is likely to declare bankruptcy as a way to grapple with the lawsuits filed as part of the sex abuse crisis."

ZELLY I saw this on TV.

[*Small pause. And then . . .*]

WEBSTER You're Catholic, aren't you?

ZELLY So what?

WEBSTER You ever have any of that shit happen?

ZELLY Not in Bayonne, New Jersey. Priest ever tries that shit, he ends up in a barrel.

[*Beat.*]

Assistant scoutmaster once tried something on my cousin Raymond.

WEBSTER Catholic?

ZELLY My cousin?

WEBSTER Scoutmaster.

ZELLY Assistant scoutmaster. Who the fuck knows what he was. It was Scouts! Non-denominational. Could've been anything. Big German guy, blond, ripped—must've worked out with weights. Carl . . . Something-German.

[*And then . . .*]

He put his finger in Raymond's mouth.

WEBSTER You are making this up!

ZELLY So help me, God!

WEBSTER In his mouth.

ZELLY In his mouth.

WEBSTER How'd he do that?

ZELLY I dunno. We were on a camping trip up in the Watchung Reservation . . . in Jersey. He calls Raymond into his tent. Next thing I know, Raymond comes back, tells me.

WEBSTER What did Raymond do?

ZELLY I guess he stood there for a while with the guy's finger in his mouth. Then he bit the motherfucker.

WEBSTER That's what I was thinkin'!

ZELLY We were just kids. Raymond was scared he was gonna get into trouble.

WEBSTER That's the thing.

ZELLY World's fucked up, isn't it?

WEBSTER [*Referring to photo in his newspaper.*] You like Trump? You votin' for him?

ZELLY I dunno. I guess. He's tough.

WEBSTER How so?

ZELLY He ain't gonna take shit from them. He'll stand up to them. Why? You don't like Trump?

WEBSTER You like Hitler? He's not a racist.

ZELLY You like Hilary Clinton?

WEBSTER You like Bernie Madoff? He's not a crook.

ZELLY You like Bernie Sanders?

WEBSTER Never felt the Bern. Didn't even get warm.

ZELLY You like Obama?

WEBSTER I like his complexion. But he can't get nothin' done, can he?

ZELLY Who do you want for president?

[*Beat.* WEBSTER *turns his newspaper toward* ZELLY, *showing* ZELLY *photo of Denzel Washington in a movie ad.*]

WEBSTER Denzel Washington.

ZELLY You're fuckin' with me.

WEBSTER Denzel would be cool.

ZELLY He's an actor.

WEBSTER And Trump ain't? Denzel could pull things together, a shitload easier than Trump. Denzel goes on TV, says, "Hey, ISIS leaders, come on out and let's talk!" All the ISIS leaders hop right the fuck outta their caves, man, goin', "Yo! This shit is *cool*! I'm gonna meet Denzel Washington!" Let's face it, Z. *Everybody* wants to meet Denzel Washington!

ZELLY World's a mess, man!

WEBSTER Can't blame Denzel!

ZELLY What the fuck kinda name is Denzel?

WEBSTER Black name. It's a racial thing. When you're black, you gotta give your kid a black name, otherwise, nobody would ever know he was black. You see what I'm sayin', Zelly?

ZELLY Somebody must've dropped you on your head when you were little, man. You are *cracked*.

[*Beat.*]

WEBSTER What kind of name is Zelly?

ZELLY Nickname.

WEBSTER What's your real name.

ZELLY Zelly's short for my real name.

WEBSTER What's your real name?

ZELLY I don't use it.

WEBSTER Yuh, but what is it?

[*Beat.*]

ZELLY Zelmo.

WEBSTER You shittin' me?

ZELLY I never use it.

WEBSTER What the fuck kind of name is Zelmo?

ZELLY It's a *white* name, asshole!

WEBSTER No. Hold! I know a couple of white folk, and none of them ain't named no fuckin' Zelmo!

ZELLY It's a family name, from back in Europe.

WEBSTER You from Europe?

ZELLY You know I'm not from fuckin' Europe!

WEBSTER Where you from?

ZELLY Bayonne. You know this.

WEBSTER You got a lot of dudes livin' in Bayonne named Zelmo?

ZELLY Fuck you, Webster! You're really startin' to annoy me!

[*And then . . .*]

Where'd your mother come up with "Webster"? Off the front cover of the *dictionary*? What? She was too lazy to even open the thing and look *inside*?

WEBSTER Fuck you, Zelmo! I—

[WEBSTER*'s walkie-talkie (Motorola DTR410™ One to One Calling Radio) buzzes.* WEBSTER *pushes button on walkie-talkie in its holster at his waist. We hear—* SHELLY GOLDFARB*'s voice, thick Brooklyn accent.*]

SHELLY [*Offstage.*] Webster? You there?

WEBSTER [*Startled; to* ZELLY . . .] Her.

ZELLY How come the bitch's pagin' you, 'stead'a me?

[WEBSTER *shrugs, grabs his walkie-talkie from its belt holster, presses talk button.*]

WEBSTER I'm here, Shelly. This is Webster.

SHELLY [*Offstage.*] You guys eating still?

WEBSTER [*Checks his watch.*] 'Nother two minutes.

ZELLY [*Checking his watch.*] Three.

WEBSTER Zelly's sayin' three.

SHELLY [*Offstage.*] I got a J-7 for you guys, mother and son. How soon can you do 'em?

ZELLY Three minutes.

WEBSTER Three minutes.

SHELLY [*Offstage.*] Okay, I'll bring 'em to the blue room. One's of youse two come get 'em. McCarthy's got their yellow papers.

ZELLY Which one of us?

[WEBSTER *looks up.* ZELLY *explains.*]

Which one of us does she want to come out for 'em?

WEBSTER [*Into walkie-talkie.*] Zelly wants to know which one of us you want to come get 'em from you?

SHELLY [*Offstage.*] I don't give a shit.

[WEBSTER *and* ZELLY *exchange a look of confusion.*]

ZELLY Tell her *you're* comin'.

WEBSTER I'll come get 'em.

SHELLY [*Offstage.*] I'll have 'em in the blue room. Mother and son, last name's Naderi. McCarthy's got their yellow papers, so stop at him before me.

WEBSTER No probs.

[*And then . . .*]

Hey, Shel?

SHELLY [*Offstage.*] You call me?

WEBSTER Yuh. How's Ronnie doin'?

SHELLY [*Offstage.*] He's doin' great.

WEBSTER Say hi to the big guy for me, yo.

SHELLY [*Offstage.*] I will.

WEBSTER [*Looks at* ZELLY *for reaction.*] Cool. Catch you in a minute.

[*We hear sound of* SHELLY *signing off.*]

[ZELLY *and* WEBSTER *clean up their sandwich wrappers, begin to redress for work.*]

[ZELLY *is furious.*]

ZELLY [*As he straps on his holstered gun.*] Is there one of them you can trust?

WEBSTER [*Strapping on holstered gun, pulling on uniformed jacket.*] You want a coffee or something while I'm out there?

ZELLY My fuckin' appetite's wrecked.

WEBSTER Don't obsess, Zel. Things change.

ZELLY What really gets my ass is the "I don't give a shit" part!

WEBSTER I can see that.

[*And then . . .*]

I'm heading over.

[*And then . . .*]

I shouldn't say nothin', right?

ZELLY Tell her I'm bowlin' with her husband tonight. Tell her he moved back from Massachusetts.

WEBSTER You're kidding on this, yes?

ZELLY Yes, I'm kidding on this, moron.

WEBSTER Cool. I'm heading over.

[WEBSTER *exits.* ZELLY *takes iPhone from pocket, voice-dials a number.*]

ZELLY Call Elizabeth.

[*While waiting for his call to connect, he adjusts his shoulder holster. He speaks into iPhone.*]

It's me. What are you up to?

[*Beat.*]

Just finished.

[*Beat.*]

Tuna and pickle on whole wheat.

[*Beat.*]

I know. I know. They were out of rye.

[*And then . . .*]

Kids get off to school alright?

[*Beat.*]

Yuh, well . . . I saw this new suicide bombing on TV. . . . A *school* bus. . . . Horrible! . . . You saw?

[*Beat.*]

Why are you watching stuff like this, Elizabeth?!

[*Beat.*]

How many kids got killed? . . . You are *kidding* me!

[*Beat.*]

They're animals! . . . They catch who was wearing the bomb?

[*Beat.*]

Her? A little *girl* was wired with a freakin' bomb? You are *kidding*!

[*Beat.*]

These people are animals!

[WEBSTER *re-enters, leading* AZAR *and* AMIN, *an Iranian mother and son.* AZAR *is in her late thirties.* AMIN *is ten. Both are traditionally dressed.* AZAR*'s head is covered with scarf (chador).*]

[ZELLY *into phone.*]

I gotta go, Lizzie. Crap, it's already five o'clock. You and the kids better start supper without me, okay?

[*Beat.*]

I've got to do this thing.

[*Beat.*]

Elizabeth, this is *work*! We're on high alert. I gotta do this!

[*Looks up at* AZAR *and* AMIN.]

I really gotta go. I'll call you back.

[*Beat.*]

Me too.

[ZELLY *pockets iPhone, explains to* WEBSTER.]

Elizabeth.

[ZELLY *looks across at* AZAR *and* AMIN, *studies them carefully before speaking. Note:* ZELLY *never puts his jacket on, remains in white shirt with holstered gun visible.*]

WEBSTER Sit down, please.

[*Hands paper to* AZAR.]

These are your rights. Everything you say will be recorded.

[*Hits "on" button. Video recorder begins to record. Note: When* AZAR *or* AMIN *speak, their voices will be slightly amplified through video recorder's live microphone . . . and, if possible, we will see their image on video screen.*]

ZELLY You speak English?

AZAR [*In Farsi.*] *Bebakhshid. Man engilissi harf nemizanam. Pessaram yek-kami harf mizanaeh.* (I'm sorry. I don't speak English. My son speaks a little.)

[*To* AMIN.]

Inhara Beheshoon begoo. (Tell them what I said.)

AMIN [*In English with thick accent.*] I speak a little English. My mother not.

ZELLY Good.

[*To* WEBSTER.]

You got the papers?

WEBSTER [*Handing papers to* ZELLY.] They're from Iran.

[*To* AZAR.]

You're from Iran, yes?

AZAR [*In Farsi, to* AMIN.] *Chi miporse?* (What is he asking?)

AMIN [*In Farsi.*] *Miporse az che keshfari miaym.* (Where we are coming from.)

[*To* ZELLY.]

Iran. We home near Tehran.

ZELLY Ask your mother what you're doing here.

AMIN [*In Farsi.*] *Mikhad bedoone ma indja chi kar mikonim.* (He wants to know what we're doing here.)

AZAR [*In Farsi.*] *Behesh begoo.* (Tell him.)

AMIN My father is here.

WEBSTER Why's that?

AMIN Working work.

[*To* AZAR, *in Farsi.*]

Behesh goftam ma indja-im baraye inke Baba indja kar mikone. (I told him we're here because Daddy is working here.)

AZAR [*In Farsi.*] *Khoobe.* (Good.)

ZELLY Where's he working? Where are you going?

AMIN Buffalo, New York.

[ZELLY *and* WEBSTER *exchange a glance.*]

WEBSTER How long has your dad been in Buffalo?

[AMIN *doesn't quite understand the question.*]

ZELLY We're asking you how long your father has been in Buffalo, New York.

AMIN [*In Farsi, to his mother.*] *Chand vaghte ke Baba dar Buffalo, New York, boode?* (How long has Daddy been in Buffalo, New York?)

AZAR [*In Farsi.*] *Yek Mah*. (One month.)

AMIN One month.

WEBSTER There's a lot of weird stuff goin' down in Buffalo. Are you aware of that?

[*No response.*]

Does your father have any connection to any political groups?

[AMIN *stares at* WEBSTER *blankly, doesn't understand the questions.*]

ZELLY Al Queda or ISIS?

WEBSTER Or ISIL.

ZELLY Or ISIL.

[*No response from* AMIN *or* AZAR.]

WEBSTER Are you aware that certain people of your, uh, racial group, uh, were recently arrested in Buffalo, New York.

AZAR [*In Farsi.*] *Chi migan?* (What are they saying?)

AMIN [*In Farsi.*] *Nemidoonam*. (I don't know.)

AZAR [*In Farsi.*] *Beheshoon begoo*. (Tell them this.)

AMIN I don't speak well English. . . . I don't understand all.

[WEBSTER *looks at* ZELLY.]

ZELLY What's your father's name? His name. Your father in Buffalo.

AMIN My father Hoomane Naderi.

WEBSTER How do you spell that?

[*No reply. Hands paper and pencil to* AMIN.]

Can you write down your father's name? Your father's name.

AMIN My father's name.

[*In Farsi.*]

Mikhan man esme Baba ro benevissam. (They want me to write down Daddy's name.)

AZAR [*In Farsi.*] *Khob beneviss*. (Do it.)

[AZAR *writes name on paper. In Farsi.*]

Beheshoon begoo ke parvazema be Buffalo chand daghigheye digast, va ma mikhaym berim andja ke Baba ra bebinim. In moheme ke ma in parvaz ra az dast nadim. (Tell them that we have our flight to Buffalo soon, and we need to go there to see Daddy. It's important we won't miss this flight.)

AMIN We must find plane to buffalo to my father, very soon.

[WEBSTER *looks at* ZELLY.]

WEBSTER Does your father have friends in Buffalo?

AMIN My father very nice, has many friends.

WEBSTER Friends from home?

AMIN Sure!

AZAR [*In Farsi.*] *Chera mara indja negah midarin? Ma parvazemoon bist daghigheye digast. Agar az dastesh bedim, nemitoonim berim Buffalo emrooz, va in adbakhtiye bozorgui khahad bood. Shohareman oondja montazereman khahad bood. Oo dar daneshgah dars mideh*. (Why are you keeping us here? We have a plane to catch in twenty minutes. If we miss it, we can't get to Buffalo today, which would be a catastrophe. My husband will be waiting for us. He teaches at the university.)

ZELLY What the hell is she saying?

AMIN Airplane to my father soon. We want to leave.

ZELLY Yuh, well, you can't leave.

[*To* WEBSTER.]

Webster, we need to do them one at a time. Call the bitch and ask for a translator.

WEBSTER The kid can translate for her, Zel.

ZELLY How do you know he's translating right, Webster? It's his *mother*. Call in for a translator.

WEBSTER What language are they speaking?

ZELLY How the fuck should I know?

[*Looks at papers.*]

Iranian.

WEBSTER [*To* AMIN.] Iranian? Is that what you're speaking?

AMIN Farsi. We speak Farsi.

[WEBSTER *looks at* ZELLY, *shrugs.*]

ZELLY Call her.

[WEBSTER *calls* SHELLY *on his walkie-talkie.*]

WEBSTER [*Into walkie-talkie.*] Hey, Shelly, Webster here. We need somebody who speaks Iranian.

SHELLY [*Offstage.*] Is that a language?

WEBSTER I don't know. I think so.

AZAR [*In Farsi.*] *To indja beboon, man miram sa'ate parvazemoono bebinam. Beheshoon begoo.* (You stay with them, and I'll go check on the flight. Tell them what I'm doing.)

WEBSTER [*Into walkie-talkie.*] The kid speaks some English, but the mother's speaking total Iranian.

SHELLY [*Offstage.*] I'll hav'ta call in for this. You sure you need it?

WEBSTER Zelly's sayin' we do. He thinks we need to do them one at a time.

SHELLY [*Offstage.*] Okay. I'll call in, but I can't promise.

[*We hear sound of* SHELLY *signing off.*]

AMIN My mother asks to go to plane to Buffalo.

AZAR [*In Farsi.*] *Boarding passo behem bede*. (Give me the boarding pass.)

[AZAR *moves to* AMIN. *He carries a small backpack with his books, their boarding passes, etc. As soon as* AZAR *touches backpack,* ZELLY *misunderstands, becomes frightened.*]

ZELLY What the hell are you doing, lady? What's in there? Get the fuck back, lady!

[AZAR *doesn't understand what* ZELLY *is saying, continues to rummage through backpack, which* ZELLY *now thinks contain a bomb. He draws his gun.*]

Get back from him, lady!

WEBSTER Yo! What are you doin', Z! Chill out, man!

ZELLY It's gonna blow! The kid's wired!

WEBSTER *Jesus! Get back, lady!*

ZELLY *Both'a'yas! Hands in the air, NOW!*

AMIN [*In Farsi.*] *Maman, nakon! Boro Aghab!* (Mummy, don't! Get back!)

AZAR [*In Farsi.*] *Man boarding passo mikham!* (I want the boarding pass!)

AMIN [*In Farsi.*] *Maman, boro aghab!* (Mummy, get back!)

[AZAR *turns, sees* ZELLY*'s gun, and is outraged. She screams at* ZELLY.]

AZAR [*In Farsi.*] *Chi kar mikonin shoma?! Man faghat daram boarding passamo dar miaram! Movazeb bashid ba in!* (What are you doing, you?! I'm just getting my boarding pass! Be careful with that!)

ZELLY Hands away, lady!

[AZAR *digs deeper into the backpack. Blam!* ZELLY, *panicked, shoots* AZAR, *who falls on floor, grabs her leg. Blood gushes from wound.* ZELLY *trains gun on* AMIN.]

AMIN [*In Farsi.*] *Maman-djan! Maman!* (Mummy! Mummy!)

ZELLY Hands off the bag! Hands up!

WEBSTER [*Draws gun, trains it on* AMIN.] You got a bomb in there, boy?

AMIN [*Sobs.*] *Keh-taab een Kehtaab ameh.* (Books. Those are my books. My books.)

[WEBSTER *cautiously empties* AMIN*'s backpack. Books/papers tumble onto floor.*]

[AMIN *sobbing, in Farsi.*]

Maman-djan! Maman! (Mummy! Mummy!)

[AMIN *kneels on the floor next to* AZAR, *who writhes in pain.*]

AZAR [*In Farsi, quietly.*] *Be baba telefon kon. Behesh begoo.* (Call your father. Tell your father.)

[AMIN *looks up at* ZELLY *and* WEBSTER; *screams at them.*]

AMIN [*In Farsi.*] *Chera in karo kardin?!* (Why you do this?)

SHELLY [*Off, over* WEBSTER*'s walkie-talkie.*] Webster? You read me, Webster? Something happening in there?

WEBSTER [*To* ZELLY.] There's no bomb, Z! Oh, shit! You fucked up, man! You fucked up, big time. Gimme the gun, Z. Gimme the gun.

[ZELLY *hesitates.*]

ZELLY She went for the backpack! You saw that!

WEBSTER Gimme the gun, Z! Gimme the fucking gun!

[ZELLY *relents, hands* WEBSTER *his gun.* WEBSTER *takes* ZELLY*'s gun, places it safely on the center of the table.*]

SHELLY [*Offstage, over* WEBSTER*'s walkie-talkie.*] Webster? You read me, Webster?

VOICE ON LOUDSPEAKER [*Offstage, in distance, far away.*] Welcome to the United States of America. Travelers holding American passport or green cards, use the lines to the right. Visitors and visa holders, use the lines to your left.

SHELLY [*Offstage, over* WEBSTER*'s walkie-talkie.*] Webster? You read me, Webster?

AMIN [*Sobbing, in Farsi.*] *Maman-djan! Maman!* (Mummy! Mummy!)

SHELLY [*Offstage. Over* WEBSTER*'s walkie-talkie.*] Webster? You read me, Webster?

[ZELLY *and* WEBSTER *stare at each other, silently, as* AZAR *moans in pain.*]

AMIN [*Stands, screams at* ZELLY *in Farsi.*] *Chera in karo kardin?! Akhe chera in karo kardin?!* (Why did you do this? Why did you do this?!)

[AMIN *runs at* WEBSTER*, screaming, crying, pounding his fists into* WEBSTER*'s chest.*]

[AMIN *stands, screams at* ZELLY *in Farsi.*]

Chera in karo kardin?! Akhe chera in karo kardin?! (Why did you do this? Why did you do this?!)

[WEBSTER *pushes* AMIN *away.* AMIN *turns, grabs* ZELLY*'s gun from the table, holds the gun, two-handed, aimed at* WEBSTER*'s head.* WEBSTER *and* ZELLY *freeze, stunned.* AZAR *screams out.*]

[*Tableau. Music in—a single saxophone riff. The lights fade out.*]

• • •

Doughnut Hole

Donna Hoke

Donna Hoke

Dramatists Guild WNY regional representative and Road Less Traveled Productions playwright in residence, Donna Hoke has been produced worldwide. Plays include *The Couple Next Door* (Princess Grace semi-finalist), *Safe* (winner Todd McNerney, Naatak, and Great Gay Play and Musical Contests), and *Brilliant Works of Art* (2016 Kilroys List, multiple awards). For three consecutive years, *Artvoice* named her Buffalo's Best Writer.

... production history ...

Greenbrier Valley Theatre Festival of New Voices, Lewisburg, West Virginia, February 2015.

Knox Theatre Collective, Just Acts 2015, Calgary, Canada, February 2015.

Summer Shortcuts IV, Open Eye Theater, Margaretville, New York, August 2014.

characters

SALLY 70s, senior citizen bowler with highest average in the league.

GRACE 70s, Senior citizen bowler with her eye on the only available widower.

CHARLOTTE 70s, senior citizen who just got back from the trip of a lifetime.

setting

A bowling alley during morning league time.

time

Present.

synopsis

In a dog-eat-doughnut world, the last peanut log can lead to life-changing decisions.

[*Bowling alley, where a morning senior citizen league is in progress. Sounds of bowling. There is a table with empty doughnut boxes on it. One box has one doughnut left.* SALLY *and* GRACE *approach the table.*]

SALLY There's only one doughnut left.

GRACE One *peanut* doughnut.

SALLY They always buy too many peanut. We should let Alice know not to buy so many peanut.

GRACE It's only eleven o'clock. Where did they all go? I always have my second doughnut at eleven.

SALLY Charlotte brought her daughter and her kids.

GRACE There's always a Boston cream left. I don't like peanut.

SALLY Me either. Those kids probably have allergies.

GRACE We should tell Alice. Maybe she could get it put into the bylaws that you have to be a league member to get a doughnut. Charlotte's daughter doesn't pay dues.

SALLY But she's a lawyer. She'd probably fight it.

GRACE If she's a lawyer, she can afford her own doughnuts.

SALLY I'm so sick of hearing about that lawyer daughter. She didn't cure cancer.

GRACE If she did, she could cure Betty.

SALLY Well, she didn't. She's a personal injury lawyer who doesn't advertise. Big deal.

GRACE Charlotte's all tan from that two-week trip to the Bahamas.

SALLY But her team lost six games with that sub. I'm high average now, and the banquet's only two weeks away.

GRACE She knew you were nipping at her heels, and she went anyway.

SALLY That's the risk she took.

GRACE I heard she swam with dolphins.

SALLY In a bathing suit? They probably thought *she* was a dolphin.

GRACE Just one more reason she shouldn't eat extra doughnuts.

SALLY That's what I'm saying.

GRACE Her daughter probably had to buy her two seats on the plane.

SALLY She can afford it.

GRACE Planes used to be fun, like an adventure. Now they make you take off your shoes. You don't even get a meal. That's why I don't fly anymore.

SALLY I heard you get a snack in first class, like bananas and Doritos. Charlotte's daughter probably flies first class.

GRACE And Charlotte probably eats both of their snacks! I would, if they were giving away free Doritos.

SALLY She probably figures she's making up for the doughnuts she didn't eat while she was gone.

GRACE No way, you snooze, you lose. Betty was out sick with the chemo last week, and she didn't come waltzing in today demanding last week's doughnut.

SALLY Betty knows how it works.

[*Beat.*]

Should we split it?

GRACE It's peanut.

SALLY I know.

GRACE I wanted Boston cream. My mouth was all set for Boston cream. If I eat the peanut doughnut, it's going to be very disappointing for my mouth.

SALLY But that's all there is.

GRACE [*Slams the box closed.*] Darn that Charlotte!

SALLY There she is! And she's eating a doughnut!

GRACE Is it a Boston cream?

SALLY She's talking to Ed.

GRACE [*Whirling around.*] What?! Why is he talking to *her*?

SALLY Maybe he needs a lawyer.

GRACE Last week, I brought him coffee.

SALLY Maybe you should bring him the last doughnut.

GRACE It sure doesn't look she's offering him any of hers.

SALLY You should do it.

GRACE Oh! I could tell him I was worried he wouldn't get his second doughnut, so I brought him the last one.

SALLY And you could say that they seemed to go *reeeally* fast this week for some reason.

GRACE Do you think he'll know what I mean?

SALLY I'm not sure. He's not the brightest bulb sometimes.

GRACE At our age, one can't be choosy about wattage.

SALLY If you care about that sort of thing.

GRACE Charlotte obviously does. What does he see in that old cow?

SALLY Maybe she's giving the milk away for free.

GRACE Oh! You are so bad.

SALLY She's probably telling him all about the Bahamas.

GRACE He wouldn't be interested in someone who's always gallivanting around.

SALLY And missing bowling.

GRACE Who would cook for him?

SALLY Who needs to cook when you eat doughnuts all the time?

GRACE He just laughed! He has such a nice laugh.

SALLY Get hold of yourself. Take the doughnut and go over there.

GRACE What if he doesn't like peanut, either?

SALLY Look out, here comes the daughter.

GRACE She's introducing her! "Hi, I'm Abigail. I'm a personal injury lawyer. I don't advertise."

SALLY Big whoop.

GRACE My daughter's a preschool aide.

SALLY Stop dithering. Go!

GRACE She was going to take me to lunch yesterday but I had to wait for the cable company to call.

[SALLY *opens the box, picks up the doughnut, tries to shove it at* GRACE.]

SALLY Come on!

GRACE My DVR's on the fritz, and I need it because *Wheel of Fortune* is on at the same time as *Entertainment Tonight*.

SALLY You can't miss *Entertainment Tonight*.

GRACE That's what I'm saying.

SALLY Take the doughnut.

GRACE He just pulled a quarter from that little girl's ear!

SALLY That's one of the doughnut-stealing grandchildren. Here.

[SALLY *gives the doughnut to* GRACE, *who hesitates, then takes it.*]

Go.

GRACE He's going over to sit by her lane.

[GRACE *puts the doughnut back in the box.*]

SALLY You dithered.

GRACE I did not dither.

SALLY Yes, you did. You dithered and now you missed your chance.

GRACE He probably doesn't like peanut anyway. Nobody likes peanut. That's why they're always left.

SALLY Next week, you can bring him coffee again. Maybe Charlotte will be off on some other trip.

GRACE But it's a week before the banquet.

SALLY What does she care? She's not getting a trophy.

GRACE You snooze, you lose.

SALLY She signed up for that Catskills trip at the senior center.

GRACE See?

SALLY Maybe we should sign up.

GRACE Buses are worse than planes.

SALLY Do you want to go for coffee and a doughnut *after* bowling?

GRACE I like to be home for *Days of Our Lives*. And we'd have to pay for it.

SALLY Oh, don't look now—

[CHARLOTTE *enters.*]

CHARLOTTE Hello, girls!

GRACE Hi, Charlotte. That's a nice tan you've got there.

CHARLOTTE Abby, my daughter, took me to the Bahamas! She's a personal injury lawyer, but—

GRACE/SALLY She doesn't advertise.

GRACE She must be very successful.

CHARLOTTE Oh, it was the trip of a lifetime.

SALLY Did you really swim with dolphins?

CHARLOTTE I didn't just swim with them. I *rode* a dolphin. Can you imagine? At my age?

GRACE You rode it?!

CHARLOTTE And it kissed me! I laughed so. Underwater! I wouldn't trade that experience for anything.

SALLY Anything?

CHARLOTTE Nothing! What's new with you two?

SALLY Um . . .

GRACE Er . . .

CHARLOTTE We should go out for lunch one day when we're done here. To catch up. I'm always famished after bowling.

GRACE Sure . . . maybe.

[*A bowling ball rolls across the stage.* CHARLOTTE *turns and laughs.*]

CHARLOTTE My granddaughter. Well, we're starting, so I'd better get back. I just came over to get Ed a doughnut. Oh, good, there's one left!

[CHARLOTTE *scoops up the last doughnut.*]

And it's peanut! That's Ed's favorite. Let's do that lunch thing. I know the cutest little restaurant. I bet you've never been there. You'll love it.

[CHARLOTTE *exits.*]

GRACE Do you *believe* that?

SALLY You dithered. You dithered about the doughnut.

GRACE I did not!

SALLY Still . . .

GRACE Maybe it's for the best.

SALLY His favorite is *peanut.*

GRACE That's what I'm saying. Who likes peanut?

SALLY [*Beat.*] So what do you think about that Catskills trip?

GRACE What would we do there?

SALLY They stay at a resort. See shows. Betty went last year, and she said it was fun.

GRACE Before the cancer?

SALLY *After.*

[*Beat.*]

GRACE It's a long bus ride.

SALLY I heard they serve doughnuts on the bus.

GRACE Really?

SALLY That's what I heard.

GRACE Maybe we should think about it.

SALLY I could get more information.

GRACE If we go, I'm taking two doughnuts before Charlotte even looks at them.

SALLY That'll show her.

GRACE She's not the only who can go on trips.

SALLY We should head over there. You know how anxious they get if we're late. I'll get the brochure later.

[GRACE *and* SALLY *start walking away.*]

GRACE Betty said it was fun?

SALLY She loved it.

GRACE You're going to cinch that high average today.

SALLY You bet I am.

• • •

acknowledgments

From Bill Demastes: Thanks to John Patrick Bray for so ably assisting me with this volume. It's a much better book thanks to his tireless efforts. Thanks, also, to the folks at Applause, especially Bernadette Malavarca, whose skills in handling wayward editors are unsurpassed. Thanks, too, to June Clark for helping me through professional thick and thin. Finally, to Jean, Erin, and our old friend Z, thanks for everything, especially patience.

From John Patrick Bray: I would like to thank Bill Demastes for his guidance and his trust. Thanks, also, to the great folks at Applause Theatre & Cinema Books. Thank you to June Clark, my agent, for supporting this project. And thank you, always, to Danielle, Danny, and Sadie for everything they do—seen and unseen.

From both editors: The playwrights in this book make it what it is, and for that, they deserve all the credit.